(DR. NABNEY)

A120

UNPERSON

A Life Destroyed

UNPERSON
A Life Destroyed

DENIS LEHANE

with a Foreword by
PHILLIP KNIGHTLEY

QUARTET PUBLISHING LIMITED

First published in 2009 by
Quartet Publishing Limited
27 Goodge Street, London W1T 2LD

A catalogue record for this book
is available from the British Library

ISBN   978 0 7043 7155 2

Typeset by Antony Gray
Printed and bound in Great Britain by
T J International Ltd, Padstow, Cornwall

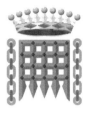

To Juliet and Christopher Monckton

Contents

Acknowledgements

Some people have helped me over the years. I have dedicated this book to Juliet and Christopher Monckton quite simply because, without their love and commitment in 1998 to getting me released from a living hell where it had been intended that I should remain under torture at Her Majesty's pleasure until I died, and then their caring for me at their home in Scotland while I recovered from what had been done to me, I should not be alive today.

Others I must thank include Phillip Knightley; Pam and Brian Glanville; Neil Middleton; Douglas Gageby; Ernest J. Cantillon; Pat Coughlan; the late Father Joe Moran; Father Gearoid Manning; Joe Trento; the late Dr William Corson; Naim Attallah of Quartet Books; Colette 4 and all the very many Samaritans who have comforted me in my despair; the members of the Simon Community who work for those sleeping rough and took me from the streets of Dublin; Richard Tompkins of the Spirazi Survivors of Torture Programme; Dr Eithne Flood, my wonderful GP in Dublin, now, alas, retired; Dr Declan O'Brien, my young and brilliant GP in Blackrock, County Cork, who always believed in my sanity and veracity and who left his wife and young family on Christmas Day 1999 to save me from heart failure; Dr David H. A. O'Connell; Danny Barr and all my other friends in my incarceration; and Elsie Campion.

Last, but not least, this book could not have been produced without the support, friendship and access to computers and other materials kindly provided by John Fitzsimons, Jim Hargis, Betty Ash and all their colleagues at the St Andrew's Resource Centre, Pearse Street, in Dublin's South Docklands. It is a wonderful operation and they are wonderful people.

When I was living in the Salvation Army Hospital, I asked for the use of a computer to write this book and was offered a Community Employment Scheme, which doubled my income. In return for the use of the computer, I agreed to mention the St. Andrew's Resource Centre at the front of the book. It is a pleasure to fulfil my side of the bargain.

D. C. L.

Dublin, January 2009

The Author

Denis Lehane was born in 1949. He is an Irish citizen. Both his parents left school in Kanturk, North Cork, at the age of twelve in 1935. Their parents, two agricultural labourers and their wives, had 30 children between them. All but three had to emigrate. That was routine in Ireland until the Celtic Tiger arrived in the 1990s. Lehane's parents went to London in 1941. His father worked as a builder. Lehane was born in Greenwich and brought up in neighbouring Deptford, a deprived inner-city docklands area of south-east London, which had a large expatriate Irish community. He attended a primary school in Deptford and a grammar school in nearby Lewisham, from which he went to Pembroke College, Oxford, where he became a Bachelor of Arts (Honours) in Modern History. In 1971 he became a journalist.

Foreword by Phillip Knightley

Denis Lehane is a prize-winning journalist and author, an MA from Oxford (political and constitutional history) who in 1982 was awarded a coveted Harkness Fellowship to study in the United States. There he attended the School of Foreign Service at Georgetown University, Washington DC, and became an intern in the political-military section of the university's Center for Strategic and International Studies.

Initially he enjoyed the experience. It was intellectually challenging and his colleagues on Fellowships were among the best and brightest from around the world. Then something strange and threatening happened to him and his life was turned upside down.

He was forced to flee the United States and was progressively reduced to an existence in a cubicle in a Dublin hostel for homeless men. He became estranged from his family and few friends. At the time of writing, he is living on a disability allowance, has not had a real job for eighteen years and is in constant pain.

How could a life full of promise have gone so disastrously wrong? If you believe Lehane, as I do, then he was destroyed by the American Central Intelligence Agency and the British Security Service, MI5, because he rejected an offer while he was at Georgetown University to join the CIA. Further, he threatened to tell the world about his attempted recruitment.

The man Lehane accuses of trying to recruit him is Dr Allen E. Goodman. Dr Goodman dismisses this as nonsense and describes Lehane as a trouble-maker, a fantasist in need of psychiatric help, a man with an alcohol problem who threatened to blow up Georgetown's graduation ceremony and who, at that time, was suspected of being the serial rapist who had terrorised Washington for several months.

Dr Goodman is a man of power and importance with a reputation for probity. Before going to Georgetown in 1980 to be Director of the Master of Science in Foreign Service (MSFS) programme, Dr Goodman had served as special assistant to the Director of the National Foreign Assessment Center and then as Presidential Briefing Co-ordinator for the Director of the CIA during the Carter administration. After Georgetown he became President and CEO of the Institute of International Education, America's largest non-profit educational and cultural exchange agency.

Yet, as with many stories involving the secret world of the international Intelligence community, nothing is entirely what it seems. Baroness Shirley Williams, the founder of the Liberal Democratic Party and respected academic, has spoken about this story to both Lehane and Goodman, but says she finds it impossible to decide which man is telling the truth.

However, there are aspects of Lehane's story that are corroborated by convincing sources. The Honourable Christopher Monckton, a one-time member of Mrs Thatcher's Downing Street policy unit, confirms much of Lehane's story and says of the rest that his accusations have substance and deserve further investigation.

The late Colonel William R. Corson, a retired Marine Corps Intelligence officer who at one stage of his career was on special assignment with the CIA, looked into the matter. Corson said later that he had inspected Lehane's CIA file, spoken with his own 'old associates' in MI5, and had been given a 'detailed assessment' of Lehane's MI5 file.

As a result of all this, Corson said he decided that Lehane's story about the CIA's attempt to recruit him was true. 'The idea of using Harkness to recruit an experienced journalist wasn't surprising. What was surprising was Lehane's outrage. Most British journalists in those days played ball with the government.'

Next, Joseph Trento, an American television journalist, spent months developing a documentary on Lehane for CNN's investigative unit. (The unit was closed down before Trento had finished the script.) He discussed Lehane's case with American and British Intelligence officers, interviewed Harkness officials and Lehane's Harkness colleagues and confronted Dr Goodman, both off and on camera.

Trento concluded: 'Lehane is a man who frightened two Intelligence services to the point they felt he had to be discredited and destroyed.' He believes that they feared that Lehane would make such a big thing out of the attempt to recruit him that he would imperil their undercover use of the Harkness programme for obtaining future spy candidates from the cream of young men and women from Commonwealth countries. Their solution was to discredit him.

'Lehane was the perfect candidate to discredit. He was a fighter. He did not stand on polite society and he took the attack on him as part of the British class system. It was a sophisticated career assassination of a very good journalist. It was in my view one of the greatest injustices I have ever witnessed as a reporter.'

There was certainly a sustained campaign of slanderous accusations against Lehane in Washington during his stay there, culminating, he says, in pressure from Goodman and officers of the Harkness Fellowships office in New York for him to seek psychiatric help voluntarily or face being committed for treatment.

This indeed eventually happened – but in Britain, not the United States. After he made a foolish but scarcely credible death threat in a letter to the CIA, the weight of American and English law descended upon Lehane and in 1997 he was put on trial at Southwark Crown Court and charged under a near defunct act passed in 1861 with having made threats to kill. The court ordered that he be held indefinitely in a secure unit for psychiatric evaluation and treatment. He was duly sent by court order to the Crofton Clinic at the Bracton Psychiatric Centre in Bexley Hospital, Kent, were he was physically forced to undergo a course of Depixol, a psychotropic drug, to 'cure' him of his 'delusion' – that the CIA had tried to recruit him and when he refused its offer had destroyed his career.

He said that the drug dulled his intelligence, made concentration difficult and – most disturbing of all – made reading almost impossible. It ate away at his memory, rendered conversation a tremendous, disquieting and profoundly uncomfortable ordeal and caused him to feel continuous unease and distress. There were physical side-effects including headache, muscle pain, stiffness of the joints and difficulty in sleeping.

Yet it turns out that not one of the four psychiatrists who decided that Lehane was deluded and needed treatment made any attempt to check whether his story might have been true. They all regarded his CIA recruitment story and its disastrous aftermath as a textbook example of delusion caused by paranoid psychosis. Apparently psychiatry has learnt nothing from the case of American author Ernest Hemingway, who in the final years of his life complained that the FBI had him under constant surveillance. This too was put down to paranoid delusions. Only after Hemingway's suicide in 1961 did it emerge that the FBI had indeed been spying on him and reporting on him for years.

Lehane was released from his psychiatric torment in Britain only when Monckton, a former colleague from the *Yorkshire Post*, took up his plight. Monckton went to visit Lehane and, appalled at his condition, wrote to the judge at Southwark Crown Court. Monckton recalls: 'I said that if he neither released Denis nor gave me good grounds for his future detention, I was minded to report him to the Attorney General for consideration for prosecution – for torture, contrary not only to the British Criminal Justice Acts, but also to international conventions.'

Monckton told Lehane that if the judge had not acted he would also have gone to the media. 'Torture at the instigation of psychiatrists is something that might be expected in Soviet Russia or Nazi Germany but in Blair's Britain at the end of the twentieth century it is a story.' But as Lehane knew only too well by now, the media were not interested in his story. It was too complex, too subtle and Lehane too difficult and demanding a character to deal with. There was also the legacy of the CIA's destruction of Lehane's credibility so that no one believed him.

For the past twenty-five years, his attempts to interest the media and publishers in his story have failed – until now. His dogged, brave refusal to accept the injustices meted out to him have finally borne fruit. His gripping account of his treatment at the hands of lawyers, psychiatrists, the secret services and the media is remarkable in that he frankly admits that his own shortcomings and character failings contributed to his troubles. Nevertheless, we should be ashamed at the way our society treated him.

PHILLIP KNIGHTLEY

1

'Attempted murder . . . '

Somebody must have made a false account against
Joseph K., for he was arrested one morning without
having done anything wrong.

Opening lines of
The Trial, FRANZ KAFKA, 1914

It was ten at night in Arlington, Virginia, a suburb of Washington. I
had just watched *Cheers* on TV and was waiting for the NBC
commercials to end so that I could catch *Hill Street Blues*. The
phone rang.

It was Detective Charles Leinau of the 19th Precinct in New York
City. He told me that the previous day a Ms Geraldine McInerney
had filed a complaint of attempted murder against me, 'with fists
and feet', at an unspecified time, place and date in New York City
in September 1983.

I had known Ms McInerney for little more than six months,
between October 1980 and April 1981. I knew that in Ireland and
the US she had made false allegations against other men before.
All the same, I was stunned. I had not been within 200 miles of
New York City at any time in September 1983. I had only been
there once, for 24 hours, since I had moved to London in April
1981, and had not seen her since then. There was no evidence of
any kind to indicate that the allegations could possibly be true. Yet
my life was about to be destroyed.

Detective Leinau told me that he 'knew' I had attempted to
murder Ms McInerney in September 1983, four months previously,
and said he would arrest me if I ever returned to New York. Ms
McInerney's story, apparently, was that I had tried to murder her
by the novel method of 'sitting on her'. Detective Leinau did not
explain why Ms McInerney had waited four months before

reporting this alleged (and rather comical) *modus operandi*. Nor did he explain why Ms McInerney could not produce any medical reports or other evidence of physical damage from the alleged attempt. Nor did he explain why I, a strong man, had failed in my attempt to kill her. No part of this bizarre allegation hung together.

Geraldine McInerney had been born in April 1943. At the age of six her father died of cancer. She believed, on the basis of a conversation she overheard between her father and her mother, which she later realised was them discussing her father's imminent death, that she had been responsible for her father's death. Her mother got her a psychiatrist. That psychiatric treatment had continued to the point when I had last seen her in April 1981. She was diagnosed as having a personality disorder.

Her mother was also seeing a psychiatrist. Her mother and this psychiatrist began an affair. Geraldine interrupted them in bed having sexual intercourse and threw a tantrum. Geraldine was married at the time. Her mother later committed suicide. Geraldine now believed she was responsible for the death of her mother as well as her father.

At the age of 19 she married a man she did not love to spite her mother. She became pregnant with twins on her wedding night. She had a third child immediately after. She determined to have no more children. On her 30th birthday, she came home to find a letter from her husband telling her he had left her. His business had gone bust. He had fled the country and would not return to his marital duties under any circumstances when tracked down.

She was celibate for two years. She got a job in Dublin reading the news on RTE television, the first woman to do so. She had a few flings but did not like promiscuity. During that period she was beaten up by two of her partners. She went to the police with both sets of allegations a number of times. They refused to believe her. However, she noted the way such allegations were handled by the police. She realised that she could inflict significant damage on men by making such allegations, even if false, because of the way the police dealt with them.

In the summer of 1977 she took leave of absence from RTE and flew to New York with $80 in her pocket. She worked waiting tables in an Irish bar. Then she was given a job in advertising, and the man who gave her the job (and the Green Card that went with it, giving her the right to work in the US) left his wife and four small children for her. As soon as her Green Card came through in September 1980, she threw him out of her apartment. She had already moved on to a better job. On Christmas Day 1980, he slashed his wrists and telephoned Geraldine. She was not there. She was in Florida with me. She had met me in October, two weeks after she had thrown him out.

When I last saw Geraldine, she 'owed' me $2,000 which she had 'borrowed' from me in dribs and drabs over the previous six months. She would routinely leave the apartment with no money in her pocket. This was her usual practice. She had brought her previous boyfriend to bankruptcy.

Why did Geraldine leave her reasonably well-paying, high-profile job in Dublin? I don't know. I knew her for no more than six months and could not cope with her. She was a dazzling personality who was also deeply disturbed and had problems I did not understand and could not solve. Before her previous boyfriend slashed his wrists, he used to telephone her seeking his clothes. She would slam the phone down on him. I once said to her: 'Why don't you give him his clothes? You are like a cat playing with a mouse.' She replied: 'What if I am? I enjoy it.'

She knew she could manipulate people. That is how she got her apartment in fashionable East 41st Street. It was advertised as an open show in the paper. When she arrived there were hundreds there. She saw a flustered young lady estate agent trying to get them all to go away and contact the office later. Geraldine put her arms around her shoulder and said: 'Oh, you poor thing, how awful for you, all these people, let's get away from them and have a cup of coffee.' A couple of cups of coffee later, she had the flat.

Geraldine made friends easily. She was very attractive and very popular but she did not believe anybody liked her. Deep down she was the small, frightened child who had mistakenly thought she had killed her Daddy. I have seen that child with tears pouring down her face. And I have listened to the woman explain in detail how to persuade New York cops that people she wanted hurt had tried to kill her when they had done no such thing.

She told mutual friends that her allegations were intended to do me harm. She laughed that I had offended somebody in Washington

DC and was already in trouble when her allegations landed there. She was delighted. When I later telephoned from England to ask her why she had made the allegations, she told me I had got what I had deserved.

All that I had done was to end a relationship that I could no longer cope with. I was not equipped to handle Geraldine McInerney, any more than her previous boyfriend had been.

I had won a Harkness Fellowship to study international relations at Georgetown University, and the course had been going well. Arlington is across the Potomac from Washington, linked to the capital by a bridge. When I took the call from Detective Leinau I had been living there for almost five months, in an apartment on a hill at the site of Fort Bennet, a Civil War redoubt. I had taken a two-year sabbatical from journalism to study for the degree of Master of Science in Foreign Service at Georgetown University. Harkness Fellowships are awarded by the Commonwealth Fund of New York, a philanthropic organisation based in Manhattan.

Georgetown University, founded by the Jesuits in 1789, is one of the oldest universities in the USA. The university colours – dark blue and grey – symbolise the unity of the Federal North (dark blue) and the Confederate South (grey) during the American Civil War of 1861 to 1865. During my time there, the university's president was Fr Timothy Healy, SJ. From my apartment in Arlington I could see the university, high on its hill across the Potomac. The School of Foreign Service had been founded in 1919 and described itself as the most prestigious seat of learning in international relations in the USA. I was scheduled to take my degree in May 1985, and had planned to pursue a long and interesting career in international relations. At the end of January I was well pleased with my life. I was where I wanted to be, doing what I wanted to do.

When I had arrived at Georgetown in August 1983, I had assumed that the International Relations Program was just what the brochure had advertised: those accepted for the programme were 'mature persons' who had had some experience of life after their primary degrees. The brochure was wrong.

It transpired that the MSFS programme was not academically high-powered. Its core content had little to do with international relations and, while it was true that some 20 per cent of the students were from countries other than the USA, all but a handful of my colleagues had gone straight to Georgetown after getting their bachelor's degrees.

Frankly, the course was not what I had expected. I was aged 33. The age difference between me and the bulk of the other students was usually no more than a decade, but at that time of life such a difference is huge. I found my colleagues very young and inexperienced in life. They found me very old.

At the start of the first semester at the School of Foreign Service, I had seen an advert in the MSFS office offering internships in the Political-Military Section at Georgetown University's Center for Strategic and International Studies. It is one of the most respected of the many think-tanks in the USA. At that time Henry Kissinger and James Schlesinger, former US Secretaries of State and Defense respectively, were based there. Their names were at the top of the CSIS letterhead.

The presence of such stars, with several other celebrated academics and former senior military men, made CSIS tough to get into. But, once in, one could be made for life. Had I known about CSIS when I was making my applications for the two-year tenure of my Harkness Fellowship back in the winter of 1982, I should have applied to spend the two years at CSIS. Had I done so, and been accepted, none of the strange events I shall describe would have happened.

The practice of students working as interns at various bodies in Washington during their studies is an excellent idea. They spend 20 hours a week attached to working operations where they can gain experience and improve their knowledge of their academic subjects. I tended to use CSIS as my base – 'somewhere to hang out', as Paul Cole put it when we first met – and had normal office hours there, the notional 20 hours per week going by the board.

The CSIS advert said applicants should telephone Paul Cole at its offices in downtown Washington. I did so. It was morning. Paul Cole, an MSFS graduate himself, said he was having lunch with some friends: would I like to join them? I agreed. We lunched with two other people. Coke Mead was another MSFS graduate. The fourth at the table was Paul Stairs, an Englishman on a Rocke-feller Scholarship at the Brookings Institute, another prestigious think-tank.

The lunch was an enjoyable meeting with high-powered

specialists in foreign affairs who shared my educational and professional background: exactly what I had sought, and would not get, at the School of Foreign Service. I could not have been more pleased. Paul got me a post at CSIS, and we became friends.

I soon became friends also with Lieutenant-Colonel Bill Taylor, the CSIS Chief Operating Officer, and Lieutenant-Colonel Mike Freney, his deputy. Cole, Taylor and Freney were three of the finest men I have had the privilege to know. In my nine months in Washington, they were my friends, good friends. It hurt when I lost them.

While I was working at CSIS, Dr Kissinger published his memoirs. The book retailed at around $30. Because I was a CSIS insider at the time, I had the privilege of buying my copy of the book and giving it to Dr Kissinger's secretary, who, a week or so later, returned it to me with the famous man's handwritten dedication:

To Denis Lehane
Kind regards and best wishes
Henry Kissinger

At that first lunchtime meeting in September 1983, Paul Cole was frank in his opinion that the MSFS programme was inadequate. As Paul and I became friends, I learned with growing dismay that he was right. Early on, Paul explained in great detail how the School of Foreign Service was used as a recruiting-ground by the CIA.

The morning after Detective Leinau's perplexing call, I went into the Center for Strategic and International Studies as usual. I told Paul Cole and Jim Townsend, two colleagues, about Leinau's call. Paul telephoned an attorney, Mario Pasqualli, whom I had met at lunch the previous September. Mario kindly told me he would deal with Ms McInerney.

I wrote a formal letter of complaint to Ed Koch, New York's mayor, against both Ms McInerney and Detective Leinau. The complaint spelt out what Leinau had said to me, including his statement that 'if you ever come back to New York I will arrest you'. I denied Ms McInerney's allegations. Mayor Koch's office sent a formal acknowledgement, but I never heard anything further.

The Director of the MSFS programme was Dr Allan E. Goodman, who had worked for the CIA. His deputy was Jerry Sheehan. Working with them was a 40-something divorcee, Ms Janet Lichty.

She was more than a secretary but much less than Goodman and Sheehan.

Paul Cole and my student colleagues at MSFS told me that Dr Goodman held the futures of his students in his hands. If he decided to fail a student, that would be a bad career move.

If there is a parallel for such arbitrary personal power in the hands of university teachers in Europe, I am not aware of it. At Oxford one's fate was determined not by one's tutors but solely by the results of one's final examinations. At Oxford there was a very different relationship between the fellows and the undergraduates and postgraduates. It is one of the very many differences between the young American state and the old establishments of Europe.

Goodman instilled real fear in many of his students. I never took him seriously until he struck at me. For most of my time at the School of Foreign Service I paid little or no attention to him, politely declining an invitation to his home and everything else he offered me. I never saw him as a threat. I never believed he had either the power or the desire to harm me.

One of the invitations I declined was to provide him with ten copies of my *curriculum vitae*. Most, if not all, of the other students gave him their CVs. Goodman wanted to help his students to gain jobs after graduation, but I was not interested in such assistance. My future after Georgetown and my two years' tenure of the Harkness Fellowship was in my own hands. Or so I believed.

Juha-Pekka Rentto, a Finnish lawyer, was one of the foreign students on the MSFS programme. He was a good friend of Trisha van Klaveren, a fellow MSFS student who was an intern assistant to Goodman. Juha-Pekka told me how once, when calling on Trisha in Goodman's office, he had accidentally come across all Goodman's files on the MSFS students. He had had a good look through them. He told me the files were astonishing in their intimate, often trivial, detail. My mail was intercepted and read from the moment I arrived at Georgetown. The letters were always several days later than they needed to be, and they were all sealed with sticky tape. When I returned to Britain in the spring of 1984, I asked one of my close friends, who must have written to me three or four times a month when I was in Georgetown, if he had ever sealed his letters with sticky tape. No, he replied. However, he complained that I had often replied very late to his letters. I told him that all his letters had reached me late, and all had been sealed with sticky tape. He was as astonished as I was that the letters had all been intercepted and then resealed.

What on earth could have justified such a policy? What did the security services hope to find in reading the mail of people like myself? In Belfast, where I had become accustomed to the *Wilderness of Mirrors* world of the intelligence community, many people had been angry at the thought that their telephones were tapped by British Intelligence. I never understood the reason for the fuss.

My view had been that if British Intelligence wanted to devote so much of the long-suffering taxpayer's resources to listening to all my personal telephone calls and cataloguing the intimate trivia of my ordinary life, I didn't give a tinker's blinkers. My only complaint about my letters in Georgetown being intercepted and read was that they reached me days later than they should have done.

When I knew Goodman, he was in his forties, about 5 ft 4, with unkempt jet-black hair and thick-lensed glasses. In his office, he used to sit on a high chair so that he could always look down on any guest. Behind his back his American students used to call him 'Big Al'.

At this and many other points throughout this narrative, I have good reason to be warmly grateful to Joe Trento, a high-flying maker of television documentaries for CNN, who later spent six months making a full-length documentary about me, only to have it cancelled at the last minute without explanation. His documentary was pulled off the CNN schedule shortly before it was due to be broadcast and he suddenly lost his job, inferentially because he had caused offence in powerful circles by having had the courage to take my story seriously. Yet his professional, painstaking and systematic investigation was to provide vital evidence that allowed others to verify what I had told them, and thereby – as this book will explain – to save my life.

I have not always been as grateful to Joe Trento as I should have been. Indeed, the reader, too, may not find me exactly *simpatico*. Take me or leave me. I am who I am – a rough diamond, if you like. I don't do social graces. So be it. My magnetic attraction of misfortunes is partly my own fault – I recognise that – because I have never been the sort to cool it, chill out, bend with the wind, drift with the tide, run with the pack or go with the flow. To Joe

Trento and to all others whom I may have hurt at one time or another by sometimes standing my ground perhaps a little too firmly, I want to say, 'Sorry.' Nevertheless, what was done to me by the public authorities in three countries should never have happened to me or to anyone, and I have written this book in the hope that those with the power and the duty to protect the innocent citizen from the unloving, uncaring savagery of today's police state will pay heed and then change the law to make absolutely sure that what was done to me can never be done to anyone else anywhere ever again.

Joe Trento had heard about my bizarre story from Dr William Corson, an independent-minded CIA veteran with a conscience (and therefore a precious rarity in the intelligence community). William Corson, who had served as CIA liaison to three presidents in the White House, had very courageously tipped off Joe Trento about my plight, and had then quietly helped him and me to verify many aspects of the tale. I am most grateful to Dr Corson too. He is now dead, and I shall always think of him with affection and profound gratitude.

Without Joe Trento and the late William Corson, very nearly everything contained in this book would seem like nonsense. Thanks to these two brave and diligent souls, much that would not otherwise have seen the light of day has been revealed.

Joe Trento told me later that Goodman was 'a liberal Kennedy Democrat' who had been educated at Harvard University and gone into the CIA as a career agent: 'one of 16,000 CIA officers,' as Paul Cole always described him to me.

Goodman had served in Vietnam in the 1960s and 1970s, where he had interrogated captured Vietcong and North Vietnamese prisoners. His status as a career CIA man was well known. He even published a book about his years in Vietnam. William Corson told me that, despite the US defeat in Indochina, Goodman had continued to find favour with the Agency.

Goodman's last posting before Georgetown, in the late 1970s, had been as the Presidential Briefing Coordinator for the CIA on President Jimmy Carter's National Security Council. He once told me that at each meeting he was always the first person to speak.

It was during this period that the regime of the Shah of Iran, an important military and political ally of the USA in the Persian

Gulf, imploded. There was nothing Goodman or Carter could have done to prevent the fall of the Shah, which was caused by internal influences in Iran. But, as is the way of American politics and its spy agencies, those closely associated with a failed policy tended to be tainted by it. Goodman had also been on the losing side over Vietnam; the far higher-ranking William Corson, for example, had vigorously opposed US policy in Vietnam both inside and outside the CIA from the mid-1960s, and was thus on the winning side.

Yet Goodman's career was not blighted, apparently because in both cases he had not been a major mover and shaker but an implementer of policy decisions made by his superiors. When the Democrat President Jimmy Carter was defeated and the Republican Ronald Reagan replaced him in January 1981, Goodman's career survived intact.

Paul Cole told me that Goodman had been offered, as his next CIA career posting, the choice of running the MSFS programme at Georgetown or serving as CIA liaison at the Strategic Arms Limitation Talks in Geneva, Switzerland. Goodman had a young family and had decided, for the sake of their education, that he preferred to remain in Washington.

It was a routine career posting which would normally have been followed by another posting within a few years. Goodman's job for the CIA at the School of Foreign Service was to identify potentially valuable assets among foreign as well as US students, so that he could recruit the best of them for the Agency.

The CIA was looking for assets who, 10–20 years ahead, would repay the investment when they occupied important positions of power in major corporations or, if they were foreigners, in the civil service and political hierarchy back in their home countries.

As the chief academic on a Masters' programme, Goodman had enormous power to help or damage a student. I learned that his power over his students was similar to that held by professors on every other American Masters' programme. Curiously, the American students were not in the least concerned, let alone outraged, that the CIA was in effect the arbiter of their future lives. On the contrary, they wanted to do well and impress Goodman because they knew he could be invaluable to them in their subsequent careers.

A significant branch of the Georgetown CIA operation was the 'Friends of the MSFS Program', a group composed of CIA assets in major business concerns, some of them household names. One of the Friends was Strobe Talbott, a graduate of the School of Foreign Service, a Rhodes Scholar at Oxford and senior editor at *Time Magazine*, who went on to become Deputy Secretary of State under President Bill Clinton.

Clinton himself, after taking his primary degree at Georgetown University's School of Foreign Service, became a protégé of William Corson's old friend J. William Fulbright, a senator from Arkansas. Clinton got an internship in Senator Fulbright's office on Capitol Hill while working on his degree. The powerful Arkansas senator got Clinton a Rhodes Scholarship to Oxford. Clinton and Talbott met at Georgetown and went to Oxford together. Strobe Talbott is the most high-profile 'Friend of the MSFS Program' but he is not untypical. These 'Friends' comprise the cream of Washington's ruling elite. Had some of them been working secretly for the CIA since their student days?

Each MSFS graduate would be placed in a suitable career. Job descriptions would be put in my folder in the MSFS offices, where jobs were posted on the notice-board. As well as recruiting assets to work within multinationals, major US and foreign banks and business concerns, the CIA openly recruited at the School of Foreign Service. The Agency had posters on the wall. The recruitment meetings were advertised openly.

The CIA did not have any sinister or pejorative connotations for American students. Americans believe that they are the major force for good in the world, the leaders of the free world, and that all peoples throughout the world look to the US for leadership and hold its security forces in high esteem. President Reagan, who was in the White House at the time, called the US 'a shining beacon on the hill'.

The American national anthem describes the US as 'the land of the free and the home of the brave'. Many Americans believe that they are loved, respected and admired throughout the world by less fortunate peoples. The CIA fits comfortably into this system of self-esteem and self-belief: it is seen as a force for good.

Every year, on the last Thursday of November, all 280 million Americans go home and celebrate Thanksgiving, an event that unites people of every faith and ethnic background. They give thanks for being Americans. The CIA is one of the bastions of

American freedom and civilisation. Few normal Americans fear it. Most are fiercely proud of it.

I am not American. I am Irish, and so is my world-view. The USA is a new nation historically. The Irish are an old nation. Goodman was an American liberal Democrat. I am an Irish conservative. I view the world as it is and not as it might be or should be. Therefore I did not throw up my hands in horror as soon as Paul Cole told me the true nature of the School of Foreign Service.

Ireland's secret service had been very effective in the War of Independence, but its *raison d'être* had ended with that war and it had ceased to exist. The British, on the other hand, have very extensive and effective secret services. I had lived and worked as a journalist alongside British Intelligence in Northern Ireland between 1972 and 1975.

British Intelligence had opened a file on me and had sent a summary of it to Goodman. The file recorded that MI5 had tried to recruit me in 1974. I had told them I was not interested, and they had left me alone. William Corson would later obtain the summary for Joe Trento, which is how I know about it.

It had never occurred to me in Belfast that the security services would make any attempt to coerce me. Besides, I had no dark secrets, no skeletons in the cupboard which could be used against me. I was clean. I was still clean in Georgetown a decade later. I was not a nuclear scientist: I was a journalist. Journalists are a dime a dozen. There was nothing about me which gave any reason to suppose that any extreme effort would be made to recruit me.

I thought – wrongly, as it turned out – that the same rules which had applied in Belfast in the early 1970s would apply in Washington in the early 1980s, and my wish to retain my independence and integrity as a journalist would be respected.

I could do the academic work for the Foreign Service programme with my eyes shut. I soon settled into a happy and comfortable life centred on CSIS and my friends there. In my first semester, from September to December 1983, my grades for the four MSFS courses I took were A, A, B+ and B. Had I bothered to do any work, I could have got better grades, but I saw no need to bother. The courses were boring.

Instead, I found intellectual stimulation at the CSIS. Within weeks of getting an internship there, I became a trusted insider, doing work of the highest quality at the highest level. Over a private Christmas drink in 1983, while the Chief Operating Officer, Bill Taylor, was away on business, his deputy Mike Freney told me that he and Bill had been impressed with my work in the four months I had worked at CSIS. He apologised for the low pay but said that he and Bill wanted to create a special full-time staff post with an appropriate salary package for me at the end of my Harkness Fellowship. I was touched and flattered. Whether I would have taken up the offer, I do not know. But the CSIS had become my American family. I was happy there.

The New York Police Department sent Ms McInerney's false allegations to Goodman shortly after they were made, with the rider that, although there was no evidence on which to arrest and charge me, Detective Leinau believed that Ms McInerney had told the truth and that I had attempted to murder her in September 1983. Goodman kept the police report on file, but took no action.

At the end of February 1984, the Director of the Harkness Fellowships programme in New York, Howland Sargent, suddenly died. Sargent was a retired CIA man who, according to Joe Trento, had been deeply involved in the CIA propaganda tool Radio Free Europe, of which I know absolutely nothing. My old friend Neil Middleton once said to me that I must have been the only person in the world who did not know, when I applied for a Harkness Fellowship in 1982, that the program might sometimes serve as a source of recruits for the CIA. I had thought of the Harkness Fellowships as a purely academic scheme run by a wealthy American philanthropic body.

The Commonwealth Fund's major beneficiaries were medical charities. In 1983–4 the Fund was worth some $500 million, of which $1 million annually was allocated to the Harkness Fellowships. I had met Howland Sargent just once, at the end of August 1983 in New York.

The Fund occupied an impressive mansion on Central Park at 1 East 75th Street. In August 1983, en route to Washington, I went there to attend a formal reception for the Harkness Class of 1983. It was a pleasant and civilised buffet dinner with the minimum of speeches. Afterwards we all went out to a bar on Fifth Avenue and sat outside on the pavement drinking expensive American beer. The next morning I flew to Washington.

I was sorry to hear of Howland Sargent's death. The telegram said that he was to be buried on Saturday, 3 March and that a service was to be held in an Anglican church in lower Manhattan close to Wall Street. I phoned the New York office and was told that the burial would be a purely family-and-close-friends affair but that the family would be delighted if as many Harkness Fellows as possible were to attend the service.

I got the train from Washington early on that Saturday morning and attended the church service. Afterwards Margaret Mahoney, the President of the Commonwealth Fund, invited me back to the Sargent apartment for the reception. There I spoke to Howland Sargent's widow and family, expressed my regrets and condolences, and had a drink with other 1983 Harkness Fellows whom I had met back in August and who had also attended the service. I was introduced to Mrs Priscilla T. van der Workeen, who had been Deputy Director of the Harkness Fellowships until a few months earlier. I also met her husband Van, Mrs Deirdre Leonard and Gail Potter, who worked in the New York office.

At one point Ms Mahoney, in the company of Ms Potter, asked me how I found the MSFS programme. I told them frankly that it was disappointing. They replied that such programmes often turned out to be less than what the brochure offered. Ms Mahoney told me that there was no need for me to spend a second year on the MSFS programme. She said that if I sent her a brief note seeking a transfer she would grant the request by return of post and I could find somewhere else to study in my second year.

The entire exchange cannot have lasted more than a minute. It was a piece of small talk. As I was leaving the reception, Ms Mahoney invited me to have lunch with her when she was visiting Washington later in the month.

I left the reception at about 1.30 p.m., with most of the non-family guests. I decided to spend some hours in New York before returning to Washington. However, the later train was overcrowded, so I decided to spend the night in New York. I called up Mrs van der Workeen at her Manhattan home and asked if I could stay that night and return to Washington in the morning. She said I could. I arrived at the apartment on the West Side by Central Park at around 10 p.m.

I had a glass of whiskey and a chat with them both and then

went to bed in the guest room. The following morning I had break-fast, thanked them and took the train back to Washington. Nothing out of the ordinary had happened.

In the first week of March I went to Goodman's office on the Georgetown campus and told him I was not going to be returning for the second year of the MSFS programme. Goodman took it much as I expected. He expressed regret at my decision but nothing more than that. There was no reason why he should do anything else. I was just one of many students on his programme; there was a drop-out rate on that programme, just as there was on all such academic programmes, and it is not uncommon for students to transfer elsewhere in mid-course.

On my return from the Sargent funeral I had asked CSIS whether I could spend the second of my Harkness years there doing some research into international relations. The response was wholly positive. Thus, in a few days, I had attended Howland Sargent's funeral service and arranged to leave Goodman's MSFS programme and spend my second Harkness year at CSIS. I was more than content. I had no reason to believe that there would be any problems. How wrong I was.

At the end of the week the mid-semester two-week break began. I had arranged to visit my family in Britain, and also to interview military and other experts in London for a book that CSIS was producing. Paul Cole had asked me to research and write a chapter, and CSIS was paying my round-trip airfare to London.

Under the rules of the Harkness Fellowships scheme all trips outside the USA had to be notified in advance. In February I had duly notified the late Howland Sargent, who had acknowledged the notification.

Later, I realised that the knowledge that I should be out of the USA for twelve days in March had died with Howland Sargent as far as the Harkness Fellowships was concerned. This was a macabre irony: Margaret Mahoney would have been spared a lot of trouble if she had known I had not been in the USA for twelve crucial days in March.

I flew to London on 7 March and stayed with my sister, who lived with her husband, a London lawyer, and their three children in Welling, Kent. During the week beginning Monday, 12 March I met the following in pursuit of my CSIS researches:

1   Gordon Wetherill, British Foreign and Commonwealth Office Press Department
2   David Gowan, Foreign and Commonwealth Office official
3   Peter Sullivan, Foreign and Commonwealth Office (Western Europe) official
4   J. Dawson, DS12 office, Ministry of Defence
5   A. Elford, DS12 office, Ministry of Defence
6   Commander Phillips, D13 office, Ministry of Defence (Navy)
7   Group Captain Leffard, A.D. NATO (Maritime) Ministry of Defence
8   Commander Wellesley, Director Maritime Plans, Ministry of Defence
9   Keith Speed MP, former Minister for Defence (Navy) under Margaret Thatcher
10 Professor Peter Naylor, Naval History, Royal Naval College, Greenwich
11 Commander Anthony Preston, Naval Editor, *Jane's Monthly*.

I also took the opportunity to make a courtesy visit to Dr D. A. Parsons, my father's doctor and mine, because I was worried by my father's medical problems. The previous year Dr Parsons had certified to the Harkness Fellowships that I was in good health and had suffered no serious health problem for the previous five years. It had been my custom to give him a bottle of sherry each Christmas. As I had not been in Britain for Christmas 1983, I gave him a bottle of sherry at his surgery on 17 March 1984.

Two days later my brother-in-law drove me to a London Underground station on his way to work. I took the Tube to Heathrow Airport. The previous night he and my sister had taken me out to dinner. We had made plans for them all to visit me in the USA in the summer. They had never visited the States before. When I said goodbye to them all that morning, there were no clouds on the horizon. There soon would be.

I flew to Washington and, on the morning of Wednesday, 21 March, I went into CSIS. The first person I saw was Paul Cole. I went into his office and gave him a bottle of Glenfiddich malt whisky. He was delighted. On my desk in the office I shared with Jim Townsend I found the 100 CSIS business cards that I had ordered for my trip. It was not usual for student interns to be issued with cards, but I had had the status of a research associate almost from the moment I started work there. Jim told me the cards had arrived the day after I left.

I attended a class at CSIS that afternoon. Bill Taylor, the Chief Operating Officer of CSIS, led a discussion on 'National Security Decision-Making and Debate'. I was on terms of the closest friendship with Bill and had been to his home, in a Maryland suburb of Washington, for Sunday lunch, which would commence with pitchers full of Bloody Marys and progress to Pennsylvania Hoagies, enormous sandwiches in soft long rolls of white bread, washed down with plenty of beer.

Bill Taylor was in his fifties. He had had a distinguished career in the US army, and had been a senior officer at the US Military Academy at West Point, New York. Paul Cole assisted him in leading that day's class. Paul and I were closer in age. I liked and admired him enormously. He was the closest friend I made in the nine months I was there. Washington has only one industry – the US Government – and it is a fun town. There were *always* parties to go to at weekends.

I remember that class on 21 March at the CSIS offices, before the horror commenced, as though it were only yesterday. It was the last time I was entirely happy. The class took up some three and a half hours. The students were divided into four groups representing respectively the Soviet Government, the US Government, the Chinese Government and the United Nations. It was a war game. We were supposed to act as we thought the heads of those four entities would react to a breaking international crisis.

Bill Taylor began by informing us all that at 4 a.m. that morning US Intelligence sources had confirmed that the Soviet Union had invaded northern Iran. The four groups were sent off to separate rooms and given 45 minutes to formulate their strategy, as though at a notional conference. On our return to the conference room, we each gave our response. Then we were issued with more-up-to-date information and allowed a shorter period to consult privately before returning. It was interesting and intellectually challenging. I took an active and enthusiastic part in the class. Over a drink afterwards, Paul Cole told me that Bill Taylor had been impressed by my input. That drink was the last one that Paul and I would share before the thunderbolt struck.

2

Nineteen Eighty-Four

The Party told you to reject the evidence of your eyes and ears. It was their final, most essential command. His heart sank as he thought of the enormous power arrayed against him, the ease with which any Party intellectual would overthrow him in debate, the subtle arguments which he would not be able to understand, much less answer. And yet he was in the right! They were wrong and he was right. The obvious, the silly and the true had got to be defended. Truisms are true, hold on to that! The solid world exists, its laws do not change. Stones are hard, water is wet, objects unsupported fall towards the Earth's centre.

from *Nineteen Eighty-Four,* GEORGE ORWELL

The following morning, Wednesday, 21 March 1984, I went into CSIS as usual. When I arrived, I got a message that Mike Freney wanted to see me. He was tense and nervous. He shook my hand and thanked me for a postcard I had sent him from London. Then he said that owing to a drop in funding he had to dismiss me.

I was astonished. I had been working at CSIS for seven months. I knew how the place worked. I was only getting $100 a week. Any drop in funding that meant that such a paltry sum had to be shaved off the budget would have meant that the Center was bankrupt.

The explanation was absurd. I knew it. Mike knew it. He was clearly uncomfortable. He added: 'I understand that you are under pressure on the MSFS programme.' This also astonished me. I told him I was not aware of any pressure.

I went to see Paul Cole. He was stunned. He had had no notice of my dismissal and could not understand it. He stormed into Bill

Taylor's office to demand an explanation. He was told to mind his own business: Mike knew what he was doing. The security guard took my office keys and I went home.

The following morning, 22 March, I went into the MSFS offices on the Georgetown campus for the first time since my return from London. In my file I found a series of frantic telephone messages from the Harkness Fellowships office. The messages had started a week previously and had continued until that very morning, often two or three times a day. All of them said the same: call the office urgently.

I telephoned at once and spoke to Gail Potter. There was a huge difference in her attitude towards me. Gone was the relaxed and friendly person I had met at the Sargent funeral. Icily cold and formal, she told me to attend the Cosmos Club in Washington at noon the following day. The new Acting Director of the Fellowships, Professor Albert H. Garretson, would be expecting me. Something was up. But what?

What had happened is this. On 14 or 15 March, Allan Goodman had telephoned Margaret Mahoney at the Commonwealth Fund's office in New York. He had told her that Ms McInerney had filed a complaint of attempted murder against me with the New York Police Department in September 1983; that he believed me guilty; that I had violently raped several students in the Georgetown area early in 1984 (the rapes were in fact committed by a young black American, not by a not-so-young white Irishman); that the Washington police were on the point of charging me with the rapes; that I had suffered a massive mental breakdown at the turn of the year (somehow neither Dr Parsons nor any of the eleven senior British officials and Ministers I had just interviewed had noticed); that I was 'out of control' and drinking heavily; that I had assaulted Elizabeth Ewing and Trisha van Klaveren, two fellow MSFS students; that I had told him I intended to attack them again; and that I was a leading Provisional IRA terrorist.

None of these allegations was true, as Ms Mahoney would discover a few weeks later. She was concerned to protect the Commonwealth Fund's reputation: the arrest and trial of a Harkness Fellow on charges of multiple rape and attempted murder would have been a public-relations disaster for the Commonwealth Fund.

To be fair, it would not have been easy for Ms Mahoney to

imagine that no less a personage than the Assistant Dean of a major US university's prestigious school of international relations would have made such allegations if they had not been true.

Ms Mahoney had no wish that I should remain in the USA as a Harkness Fellow for another year and more, raping and attacking women.

I was already out of the USA when Goodman made his allegations, but Ms Mahoney did not know this. Had she done so, all she need have done was cancel my US student visa, as she would do the following month when I was back in London. But Howland Sargent had died and his long-time Deputy Director, Mrs van der Workeen, had resigned. No one else had known of my trip to London.

Ms Mahoney found herself having to take immediate charge of the crisis necessitated by Goodman's allegations.

William Corson later told me that when, by the early summer of 1984, the CIA finally worked out what Goodman had done, it summarily dismissed him without pension rights and expunged all record of his ever having been a career CIA officer.

Erasing Goodman from the CIA's books was not as easy as all that. After all, he had been Jimmy Carter's Presidential Briefing Coordinator on the National Security Council. William Corson said the CIA had explained that away by saying Goodman had been hired on a fixed-term, freelance contract.

Why did Goodman make his baseless allegations against me? Why was it worth his while to go to such extravagant lengths to discredit a mere journalist?

Corson told me that a fundamental – and, for me, catastrophic – error of judgement on Goodman's part lay behind the whole affair. Not long after my arrival at Georgetown, in the early autumn of 1983, Goodman had told his CIA superiors that I had met him and told him I should be willing to spy for the Agency under the cover of my career as a journalist once I had completed my MSFS degree.

No such meeting ever took place. Had we had such a meeting, and had Goodman broached the subject of my working for the CIA, I should have politely rejected the idea. There would have been no chance of my agreeing. That is not what journalists are for.

Corson said that not long after Goodman had met me he had formed a high opinion of me. Thereupon he had told his superiors I was a willing recruit. Accordingly, my news that I should not be returning for a second year on the MSFS programme had been a bombshell to Goodman. I had thought Goodman had taken the news in his stride, but in fact he had panicked, fearing he would have to disclose that he had lied to his superiors the previous autumn.

In October 1986, Dr Parsons gave an interview to CNN in which he stated that I had had no history of mental illness before going to the USA in 1983, that he had seen no symptoms of any mental illness in me when I visited him in March 1984, and that he had seen nothing in me, or in my account of what had happened, to indicate that I suffered from a mental illness.

The basis for the allegation of mental illness was this. On 4 January 1984 my then girlfriend had driven me to Georgetown University Hospital, where I had spent three nights. I had become dependent on a doctor-prescribed medication and I had decided, given that the start of the second semester was two weeks away, to ask the doctors to take me off it. They had agreed. After three days they had changed their minds, so I checked out and returned to my apartment. There was no secret about this. I had informed Mike Freney at CSIS.

Phillip Knightley, who has kindly contributed the Foreword to this book, is a celebrated journalist who has written many critically acclaimed books on the CIA. He is probably the foremost expert on spy agencies writing today. Phillip has looked at what Goodman did to me in some detail. His conclusion is:

> The CIA's destruction of Lehane's credibility was brilliantly done and could have come straight out of a secret service's training manual.
>
> Never invent the charge against the subject. It can be too easily exposed as false. Instead, take the subject's genuine faults, no matter how insignificant, and then exaggerate them. If the subject likes a drink, spread the word that he is a drunk with an alcohol problem. If he has had difficult love affairs, give him the reputation of a batterer of women. If he has had several jobs, put it about that he cannot get on with his colleagues. If he has had a consultation with a psychiatrist, for no matter what reason, spread it about that he has had a nervous breakdown.
>
> In this way, anyone checking the allegations against the subject

will discover sufficient substance to be left with a lingering doubt that they might indeed be true. Then, no matter how strongly the subject may protest, he will never entirely be believed. This is what happened to Lehane.

When I took a taxi from my apartment in Arlington, Virginia, to meet Professor Garretson on 23 March, I knew something bad had happened. But that was all I knew. I did not know until I met Professor Garretson that any such allegations had been made.

Joe Trento has described the Cosmos Club in the heart of down-town Washington as an 'old-man's club'. When I arrived there at 11.55 a.m. that is exactly what I found waiting for me – a large, shaggy old man in his seventies with grey hair that needed cutting. He wore a rumpled grey suit, white shirt and club tie. At that time this veteran Intelligence officer was Professor of Law at New York University.

I was to learn at once that what the professor believed was the law and what I understood by it were opposites. We went straight to the table in the fusty dining-room. There was no small talk. The professor informed me that I could have one glass of wine or one of beer only. We gave our orders to the waiter and the professor began his interrogation as though he were delivering a bad script from a hack detective series: 'Tell me what you have done.'

'I don't know what you are talking about.'

'Yes, you do. I know all about it, so tell me what you have done.'

'What are you talking about?'

'You've been suffering from a nervous breakdown for three months. I know all about it. At Howland Sargent's funeral everybody could see it. Mrs Sargent said to me: "Oh, look at that poor boy. He's just like a zombie!" Everybody could see. All your friends were very worried about you. Now tell me what you've done.'

'That was three weeks ago. If I was obviously suffering from a nervous breakdown, why has it taken so long for you to tell me? Why didn't "all my friends" that day tell me then and help me to get treatment?'

'Never mind about that. I want you to tell me what you've done. We know what you've done. I want you to tell me.'

'I don't know what you are talking about. If you know already, why do you need me to tell you?'

And so it went on and on for three hours as we ate our lunch, the dining-room filled up with other old men in their club ties, and Professor Garretson chomped away on his food while he grilled me with the same question over and over again: 'What have you done? We know what you have done. So tell me what you have done.'

In those three hours I conceived a profound antipathy for this man that remains undiminished. As I write, the very taste of him is in my mouth and it revolts me. Later I would learn that he believed Goodman's allegations that I had attempted to murder Ms McInerney in New York in September 1983 and had raped a number of women in the vicinity of the Georgetown campus in early 1984. That was what he wanted me to 'confess'.

The professor's grilling violated both principles of natural justice: that none should be the judge in his own cause, and that both sides should be fairly heard. The US Bill of Rights provides that even the most evil of criminals who has committed the most heinous of crimes has a right to be informed of the charges against him, to be informed of the evidence on which the charges are founded and to a fair trial.

Harkness House had received unsubstantiated and, as it happened, false allegations against me from Goodman. Because he had seemed an impeccable source, they had forgotten the Bill of Rights and had made no attempt to verify whether any of the allegations were true. One call to the Washington police would have told them that I was not and had never been a suspect in any of the cases of rape (my age and skin colour rather compellingly ruled me out) and that there were thus no plans to arrest me at all, let alone that my arrest was imminent, as Goodman had told them. Instead they found me guilty *in absentia*, though I had not even been charged, and sent Garretson, supposedly a Professor of Law, who ought to have known better, to pronounce sentence on me.

At length, after three hours I never want to repeat ever again, the lunch long over and the coffee cups empty, Professor Garretson delivered that sentence: 'Your transfer out of the MSFS programme is cancelled. You are to go and see Dean Goodman and ask him to get you a psychiatrist and Dean Goodman is to supervise your psychiatric therapy.'

I replied, 'What is the diagnosis?'

He answered, 'You know what it is already.'

I said, 'No, I don't. I have no idea what you have been talking about.'

He said again, word for word, 'Your transfer out of the MSFS programme is cancelled. You are to go and see Dean Goodman and ask him to get you a psychiatrist and Dean Goodman is to supervise your psychiatric therapy.'

With that, we parted. I had shaken his hand when I had met him. I did not shake it a second time.

A decade later, when I was interrogated by two boy-detectives of Scotland Yard's Organised Crime Squad, I felt no discomfort or fear. They were arrogant and obnoxious but essentially inexperienced and immature young men. They did not trouble me. Professor Garretson was of a different order. He was frightening. I parted from him at about 3.15 that Friday afternoon. He had said absolutely nothing to me about what lay behind this sea-change in the attitude of Harkness House towards me.

I was now very frightened indeed, and that deep fear would remain with me until I flew to London almost four weeks later. Professor Garretson's final words made it clear that Goodman was somehow involved, since he and Harkness House had been speaking about me. Goodman's involvement also made sense of what Mike Freney had said to me when he had fired me the previous day: 'I understand you are under pressure on the MSFS programme.' I wasn't, but who would have told him such a lie? Somebody had. The footprints were those of Goodman, both at CSIS and Harkness House. But why?

I went straight from the Cosmos Club to CSIS. I had not been banned from the office, just fired. I went to Paul Cole's office. He was in. I told him what had happened. He was as stunned as I was. I went over the previous three months. I had attended all sorts of formal and informal gatherings at or centred on CSIS. One had been a private party at the home of a German associate at CSIS. The guest of honour was a leading West German politician. I asked Paul if my behaviour at this party was in any sense indicative of my suffering from a nervous breakdown. I had had great craic with the German political leader. Paul told me the politician had singled me out for favourable mention in the small talk when Paul had driven him back to his hotel.

'And,' Paul recalled, 'you spilt ice-cream all over your shirt in front of him, which he thought was very amusing.'

I went through event after event, party after party, and to all of my questions Paul replied that I had shown no symptoms of a nervous breakdown. At length, I said to him, 'Did you think I was suffering from a nervous breakdown at Wednesday afternoon's class?'

Paul answered, 'No.'

I asked, 'Do you think Bill Taylor or any of the students could have thought I was suffering from a nervous breakdown?'

'No.'

'How many of the people present that day do you think would be prepared to swear to that on oath?'

Paul replied, 'None.'

I knew what he meant. I was in deep trouble and nobody was going to lift a finger to help me. Washington is that sort of town. Mario Pasqualli, Paul Cole's attorney friend, for example, who had kindly offered to act for me against the NYPD in connection with Ms McInerney's allegations of attempted murder, politely declined to help me either with Goodman or with Harkness House.

That evening, when I returned to my apartment, I had exactly 24 days left in the USA as a Harkness Fellow. I was baffled. None of this would make sense to me until I met William Corson in February 1987, and that was almost three years away.

That night I did a lot of thinking. I had spoken on the telephone to Mrs van der Workeen in New York. She had confirmed my own recollection of the Sargent funeral. She had been astonished to hear what Professor Garretson had said to me about everybody there being so sorry for me because I was 'obviously mentally ill'.

'But Margaret Mahoney was *all over you!*' she exclaimed.

It was good to find one sane voice in a sea of insanity. We discussed the Harkness Fellowships, so that I could work out what my rights were. It seemed I had no power to challenge the decision to cancel my transfer out of Goodman's programme. But there was no way they could force me into psychiatric treatment, under Goodman's supervision or anybody else's.

At that time, my only interest was to find out what had happened. At no point did it occur to me to leave the USA and abandon my Harkness Fellowship tenure there. Common sense said that, while Goodman was bad, the Commonwealth Fund was not necessarily so; that, if I could find out what was behind the change in attitude towards me at Harkness House, I could deal with it.

I was fighting a war on two fronts against two different enemies. On the one hand, I had to deal with Harkness House. Their priority was to get me out of the USA. Professor Garretson's orders had been, in their eyes, simply a short-term measure to get me under control before I 'raped' any more women.

On the other hand, Goodman did see the professor's orders as a long-term solution to his problem. Thus I was subjected to concerted pressure from Harkness House and Goodman to do two contradictory things. Harkness House exerted all its power to get me to leave the USA for good, while Goodman used all the power he had as a CIA officer to keep me in the USA, but under his control.

Harkness House wanted me to resign the tenure of my fellowship and leave the USA. They told me in writing that, if I did that, I should be given a one-way airline ticket to London. I refused. They refused to give me any reasons for their change in attitude towards me.

The key term here is '*the tenure* of the Harkness Fellowship'. The Fellowship, like the Rhodes Scholarship, is for life. The one or two years' study in the US is 'the tenure'. 'Fellowship' is a word like 'community' or 'club'. One belongs to a community or a club usually for life unless one resigns or is expelled. One is always a Harkness Fellow. I later had to get a lawyer to force the Commonwealth Fund to stop listing me as a Fellow in their annual Directory. They did not want me officially to leave the Fellowship. That in itself confirms the distinction between the Fellowship and the tenure of that Fellowship.

Ms Mahoney and Professor Garretson wanted me to resign that *tenure* of the Harkness. Harkness House wanted to keep me on the books as a Fellow so that it looked for all the world as though nothing had happened. What they did not want to do was formally to cancel *the tenure* – i.e. the period which the member of the Fellowship spends living and studying in the USA. It had never happened before. If they cancelled it, they might be obliged to provide a public explanation which, in theory, could be challenged in the courts: unlikely, but a possibility they had to take seriously. They wanted a clean and quick surgical removal that gave no indication to anybody outside that anything untoward had happened.

Goodman's campaign of action neatly divides into two. Until

Friday, 6 April, he bent every fibre of his power to get me under his actual physical control via psychiatrists. From Monday, 9 April, he admitted defeat on that. From then on, he tried to bribe me.

When Professor Garretson had left me at the Cosmos Club, it had never occurred to him that I should not do as he had told me. He found out early the following week that I had not obeyed him. We spoke on the telephone. For the one and only time, he was lost for words. I told him clearly that I had discovered he had the right to cancel my transfer but no right to force me into psychiatric treatment I did not need under a man I had no time for.

'But I thought you agreed,' he stumbled.

'I agreed no such thing. I asked you repeatedly what was the diagnosis and you refused to give me one. What is this all about?'

I never used abuse or obscenity towards Professor Garretson, but I left him in no doubt that such terms would not have been inappropriate had I used them.

Mrs van der Workeen was extraordinarily kind in these awful weeks. I had many telephone conversations with her as I tried to find out what was happening and somehow undo what had been done. At one point she gave me Margaret Mahoney's home telephone number. I called it that evening. Ms Mahoney refused to talk to me. Harkness House had no wish to talk to me, to explain, to assist or inform. By the end of March, Goodman knew that I had no intention of asking him to get me a psychiatrist and asking him to oversee that psychiatrist's psychiatric treatment of me. So he did two things. First he launched into a black propaganda campaign among those who knew me in Georgetown and Washington from his office at the School of Foreign Service. He told two young ladies whom I knew that they should move out of their apartments and go into hiding because I had told him that I intended to attack them. They did so. At the same time, he forbade all other students to associate with me in any way. For weeks he spread his false allegations about me to each and every person who knew me.

Joe Trento would later interview for CNN many of the people in Washington to whom Goodman had spoken. He would write:

I learned, by interviewing US Harkness Fellowships officials, that claims about Lehane being drunk at a funeral, or acting in a bizarre manner, all coming from Dr Goodman, were simply not true. I spoke to people who knew Lehane in Georgetown and they told me that Dr Goodman made the same claims about Lehane there.

I should in due course learn that not only Geraldine McInerney but also another former girlfriend, Fiona Macdonald Hull, had laid false allegations of attempted murder against me.

In his interview with Joe Trento, William Corson describes Ms McInerney as having been the mistress of Vincent Browne, an Irish journalist, at the same time as she was going out with me. He mentions Ms MacDonald Hull, whom I had known between 1972 and 1973, as another 'bad relationship'.

Fiona Macdonald Hull comes from a very unhappy home background. I wanted to marry her, but I ended up recognising that, if we had married, we should have been divorced by the time I was 30 and I should only see my two children at weekends. I say two because she had decided how many she wanted.

I shared my life with Fiona for precisely a year. As a journalist in the sensational show-business lower end of the market, she had great success. From the *News of the World* she moved to *The Sun* and was a star columnist there until she suddenly disappeared from view in the mid-1990s. The internet shows that she subsequently wrote a biography of P. J. Proby, a 1960s' pop star. She had a son out of wedlock in August 1980, whom she named after her father, and 'gave the elbow' to the father, a *Daily Mirror* reporter, a week after the birth.

Fiona and her sister Susan had both gone to Liverpool University, Susan to study medicine, Fiona law. They had shared a flat. Because of emotional problems, Fiona took four years to get her degree and she switched from Law to History.

Susan was blonde and classically beautiful. In her first year, she had had some photographs taken by a modelling agency but had never followed it up. In her final year, she discovered that the agency had blown up one of the pictures it had taken of her to about four feet by six feet and hung it over their reception desk. When she enquired, fascinated, the response had been: 'Where have you been for two years? We tried to find you everywhere. We wanted to offer you a contract.'

Fiona was not like her sister. She did not have classic beauty but she was striking to look at and very attractive. She had a fun personality and her voice was very sensual and sexy. I thought Fiona was much more attractive than her sister but Fiona regarded herself as the ugly duckling in comparison.

While still at school, at the age of 17, Fiona had spent a year in Spain as part of some scheme to learn Spanish. She lived with a well-to-do Spanish family and became engaged to the young man of the house. This engagement involved her taking instruction in Catholicism. The engagement did not last. The relevance, in my view, is that Fiona was obsessed with getting married, as was her sister.

Fiona and I met in August 1972. We were among eight graduate trainees in journalism recruited by the Thomson Organisation, which then owned the two *Timeses* and a stable of regional newspapers. I had been allocated to the *Belfast Telegraph*, Fiona to the *Reading Evening Post*. We were on a four-month course in Cardiff. Two weeks after we met we started going out. Two weeks later she moved into the flat I was sharing with two other trainees.

Her moving in was not a planned thing. The lodgings she had been found by the people running the course turned out to be a disaster. The landlady was in a dispute with her son-in-law about money. One day he turned up and took possession of Fiona's bed. She had to stay somewhere and so she moved in with me. We slept in a single bed but we were both quite slim and it worked. Fiona's tantrums apart, we were very happy. I managed them in those months. I found them amusing often.

One night, she was determined we go out to the cinema. We went out most evenings, but that evening I was physically shattered and needed a night in. To the delight of our two flatmates, Fiona insisted we go out. I politely told her I was not up for it. In ever increasing levels of annoyance at not getting what she wanted, she insisted, then demanded we go out. She absolutely had to go to the cinema, she said. All right, I said, go to the cinema, go ahead, nobody was stopping her. She was shocked at the idea but, realising I was not moving, she left.

On her return a few hours later, she was depressed. I had seen it as a light-hearted incident of no significance. She was hurt. She had wanted to go to the cinema. I was her boyfriend so I should have taken her to the cinema because that is what she had wanted to do. The idea that I would refuse to do that stunned her. On a smaller level, it was what would happen between Susan and her boyfriend. Both girls expected to get their own way with the men who loved them and could not understand when told there were reasons why the men would not or could not do it.

I met Lady Elisabeth and the Colonel one weekend when they drove down to Cardiff to visit Fiona. I was embarrassed to have to pretend that I was sleeping on the sofa in the flat. Her parents knew it wasn't true. It came up because her mother wanted to know which of us was the gallant young man. She was being mischievous.

When the course ended, we came to an agreement. I would spend two years in Belfast and then return to England to work for the *Sunday Times*, which as the brochure for trainee journalists said, was the purpose of the scheme we were on, and she would also get a job there. Then we should get married. In the meantime, we should work at our respective papers, with each visiting the other one weekend a month and spending holidays together.

Fiona and I spent New Year 1973 in a hotel in Reading. In that era it was routine for young graduates in their early to mid 20s to get married. The man was still regarded as the primary bread-winner. Women with degrees and careers would frequently give up work and have babies not long after such marriages. The idea of putting off children to their mid to late 30s for career women had not come yet. Also, the idea that a woman's career was equal in value to a man's just did not exist, so that a man subordinating his career to that of his wife was rare.

Yet during 1973 it became clear that Fiona wanted to wear the trousers, career-wise. We were both trainee journalists on the Thomson Scheme. However, Belfast was one of the top news stories in the world at that time. Reading was just a Home Counties backwater.

Initially, Fiona said she was willing to move to Belfast. She would have had to ask for a transfer from her newspaper to the *Belfast Telegraph*. However, she insisted that I arrange everything. I could not do this: the rules required that she should apply for the transfer herself. When I told her this, she dropped the idea.

In career terms, Belfast provided me with an enormous opportunity, one which I took with both hands, writing *Political Murder in Northern Ireland* with Martin Dillon. The book was published in October 1973.

My mother told me that she felt Fiona was jealous of my success. She found this strange: she would have expected Fiona to have been proud of me.

By the summer of 1973, relations had become difficult. The Fiona I had met and fallen in love with in Cardiff had morphed into somebody else. She repeatedly told me that, while she had been faithful to me in Reading, lots of attractive men were lining up to take my place. Unless I moved to Reading, she would take up with one or more of these men. She told me that if I wanted her I had to leave Belfast. She wanted to get married now. I told her repeatedly that I would not be subject to such ultimata. If she wanted to take up with one of these men, she should do so and I should not stand in her way.

On a Sunday night in August, after supper in a restaurant in Leicester Square, she started to complain bitterly to me. The complaining lasted from Leicester Square all the way to Charing Cross left luggage, where I collected my bags. It ended outside the gents' lavatory, where I stopped her and told her that I had had enough. I had told her over and over again that I should not accede to her demands that I should give up my career in Belfast and subordinate myself to her life and career. I had told her that I should end the relationship if she did not stop. She had not stopped. The relationship was over.

Fiona was shocked. We parted. She went to Reading. I went back to my mother's flat and told her what had happened. She confided that at one point over the weekend, when I was elsewhere, she and Fiona had been talking. Fiona had told her that one of the things she liked about me was how easy I was to manipulate. My mother said to me: 'I knew then that she was in trouble.'

Over the next seven weeks Fiona telephoned me most nights asking me to leave Belfast and return to Britain to marry her. I told her that I should not do this. At the end of September she issued me with a final ultimatum and I turned it down. This shocked her.

Political Murder in Northern Ireland was published at the end of October to great success. Early in November I got a telephone call from Fiona one evening. She said she was calling from a hospital bed in Reading. She had almost died. She had had a fallopian tube removed. It had been an ectopic pregnancy and I had been the father. I said I was sorry to hear the news and glad that she was getting better.

I knew that my required response was to fly to her bedside and be there holding her hand when she awoke next morning. I did not do this. I sent her flowers and a Get Well Soon card. She phoned me a number of times from hospital before going home to Uckfield to recuperate. She sent me several sad and pathetic love letters, all to the effect that I was still the only man in her life and that I remained the man she was going to marry.

A few weeks later I was in London on holiday. I drove down to Uckfield and met her for lunch. I told her it was good to see her but that I did not want to get back together. After lunch I drove her home and kissed her goodbye. She went into the cottage. She told me later that, on entering the cottage, she said,' It is over!'

It had been over since August. I worked that Christmas in Belfast. I sent Fiona a Christmas card and phoned to suggest we meet for lunch when I was in London. She agreed. When I got to London and called her, she would not take my calls. I had thought we had remained friends. I got that wrong.

Later in 1974, driving to London from the Belfast-Liverpool ferry, I stopped in Liverpool to call on one of Fiona's old friends from university. We had a cup of tea. She told me that I was the first normal boyfriend Fiona had ever had. I told her I could not cope with Fiona's demands that I should put her life and career ahead of my own.

In the spring of 1976, when I had just started working for the *Sunday Times*, I decided to look Fiona up to see how she had been doing. She was working for the weekly magazine *Reveille*. We met at 7.00 p.m. in the bar at Dolphin Square, where she was living in the family's flat. We had two drinks. Then we crossed the garden to her apartment. By the lift, we met the Tory MP for Reading, who knew Fiona.

We sat in her apartment and talked until 9 p.m., when, by prior appointment, one of her colleagues from Reading arrived. I said good-night and left.

That evening, she told me that had not suffered an ectopic pregnancy late in 1973. After I had turned down her final ultimatum in September, she had slept with one of the many men who had been lining up all year. He had infected her with gonorrhoea, damaging one of her fallopian tubes, which had had to be removed.

I did not react with anger to this news. The young woman telling it to me was not somebody I knew any more. I didn't care. The Fiona of the early-morning monologues of misery and pain was long gone. This was the new Fiona.

She also referred to recent psychiatric problems she had undergone. She told me the man who had infected her with gonorrhoea did not want to marry her. They had lived together for two years in Reading. Then, when she got the job in London, he told her that they should split up but that it would be all right for them to continue to sleep together from time to time.

We met once more, for a lunchtime drink in a pub at Waterloo later that spring . We did not meet again, because I did not like the Fiona of 1976. She had changed. She had become coarsened by the world of tough, rough-talking journalists, what I call the 'bogus machismo' that so many journalists adopt.

Shortly after my return from Washington DC in 1984, I had two long telephone conversations with an MI5 contact whom I have called Jonathan Simpson. Speaking about my MI5 file, he told me there was nothing damaging *per se* on it, except that there were a lot of question marks which, taken together, created a damaging impression. He specifically referred to Martin Dillon. Something in what he said indicated to me that Fiona had left one of the question-marks on the file. Dillon I knew about. Fiona I did not.

On 10 December I sent her a brief one-page letter asking to meet her. I did not receive a reply. In January and February 1985 I wrote again, four letters in all. These letters were longer and contained explanations for what had gone wrong between us and expressions of good will towards her.

Her response was to go to the High Court for an *ex parte* injunction to prevent me from contacting her. I went to a Legal Aid solicitor, who told me that it was massive overkill to go to the High Court for an injunction. Fiona's affidavit contained three main allegations: that I belonged to the Provisional IRA and that she had told the police this in 1974 in the belief that I proposed to bomb her sister's wedding, so that Special Branch had provided protection at the wedding (that, perhaps, had been the question-mark); that I had tried to strangle her in the spring of 1976 as we walked through the gardens at Dolphin Square; and that when our relationship had ended I had repeatedly harassed her and her friends, including the friend in Liverpool whom I had briefly visited for a cup of tea.

My view was that Fiona had made up these allegations to provide a background of prior misbehaviour to justify her application for an injunction.

In particular, I had not tried to strangle her as we walked through the gardens of Dolphin Square. She had not asked for help from the Tory MP for Reading whom we met at the lift directly after this alleged attempted murder. When Fiona's colleague from Reading arrived as arranged at 9.00 p.m., she did not tell her colleague about the 'attempted murder'. When I had gone, she did not dial 999. She had no tell-tale red weals on her throat to suggest attempted strangulation.

I made an application to the Legal Aid Board for funds to oppose the injunction. The Board replied that I suffered no damage because of the false allegations in the affidavit and accordingly Legal Aid was not available to challenge the injunction.

I did not even suspect the existence of the Macdonald Hull allegations until after I had spoken to my MI5 contact, Jonathan Simpson, in April 1984, after my return to London.

Her allegations to Special Branch that I was a senior Provisional IRA terrorist and that she believed I would launch an attack at her sister's wedding were duly noted on my MI5 file, where Goodman saw them a decade later.

When Goodman learned of Ms McInerney's allegations from the New York police in February 1984, he remembered the allegations already on file and believed he had a pattern of violent conduct against women which he could use against me as leverage.

Since the allegations were false, the leverage failed. I had chosen to end relationships with each of these ladies when they had not wanted me to do so. Their allegations were payback. It is still painful today that young ladies for whom I had once cared very much could make such baseless allegations.

The MI5 file also made me out to be an alcoholic. It has been my misfortune that all these false accusations were collected by MI5 and passed on to the CIA in the summary of my file as though they were true. When I met Corson in 1987, he said, 'Some of

48

those summaries can be worse than the files themselves.' In effect, Corson was confirming what Jonathan Simpson had told me in April 1984: 'There is actually nothing there – just a lot of question-marks.'

Both Ms McInerney and Ms MacDonald Hull were only 5 ft 6 in height and weighed around 125 pounds. I am 5 ft 10 and weigh around 200 pounds. I should have expected to succeed if I had attempted to murder either woman.

Both sets of false allegations were to prove devastating to me, even though no action had been taken following Ms Macdonald Hull's allegations of early 1974. If Britain's Special Branch had ever had the remotest suspicion that they were true they would have acted. Instead, they passed the allegations on to MI5.

No action was taken following Ms McInerney's allegations of January 1984 either. But they, too, were sent to Goodman, who, seeing the note of the previous allegations on the summary of my MI5 file, thought he could use them as leverage to make me work for the CIA against my will. Without these allegations, he might well have felt the game was not worth the candle and I should never have been plunged into the nightmare he created.

In October 1984 the former editor of the *Sunday Times*, Harry Evans, then living in New York, upon hearing what the CIA had done to me, called me on the telephone. Harry Evans is a generation older than me. I was still stunned that a woman I had loved had been able to go into a police station and tell barefaced lies about me. I asked Harry Evans how she could have done it. He replied, 'There are certain women who do this sort of thing and that is all there is to it.'

My Finnish friend, Juha-Pekka Rentto, paid no attention to Goodman's orders that I be avoided. We spoke every day. Each conversation began with Juha-Pekka saying: 'Goodman said this about you to so-and-so . . . ' He persuaded Trisha van Klaveren, one of the girls whom Goodman had persuaded to go into hiding, to speak to me on the telephone. She told me she had telephoned her parents in California and asked what she should do. They told her to do what Goodman said.

I asked Trisha: 'Do you believe that what Dr Goodman told you is true? Can you believe that I would harm you in any way?'

'No.' She burst into tears and sobbed that Goodman had her

future in the palm of his hand. He could make it or he could destroy it. She was frightened.

Meanwhile, a Dr McGill telephoned me non-stop, telling me I was suffering from a mental breakdown and that I should check myself into a hospital I had never heard of, the Psychiatric Institute. Georgetown University Hospital had given me the name and address of a low-cost medical centre where I could ask if doctors there would assist me in my objective of ending my dependence on doctor-prescribed central-nervous-system stimulants. I met Dr McGill there. He told me he worked full-time at St Elizabeth's Hospital, the large public mental hospital in Washington, where poor people went. He had no interest in helping me with the problem I had. I took a personal dislike to him. Had he been willing to help me get off the doctor-prescribed stimulants, I should have attended him for as long as it took, but I should have had to bite my lip to do so. When later I asked Dr McGill why he, a doctor at St Elizabeth's Hospital, was pestering me to check myself into a quite different hospital with which he had no connection, he replied, 'I know people there.'

When I met Joe Trento in October 1986, he told me that the Psychiatric Institute is a hospital which the CIA uses from time to time.

Perhaps the most extraordinary exchange I had with McGill on the telephone in these weeks went as follows:

I said, 'You keep telling me that I am mentally ill and have been for three months. I don't think I am, but, as you have told me, that could be part of the illness. Why don't I just fly to London and check into a hospital there? That makes more sense to me than what you are telling me to do.'

Dr McGill replied, 'Oh, no, you mustn't do that! *They* don't want you to leave.'

I think we both knew who 'they' were – Goodman and the CIA – but this was the first and only time that Dr McGill referred directly to *them*. I wondered just who was supposed to be mad. Harkness House was on at me every day to get out of the US and out of its hair, but *they* did not want that at all.

The Dr McGill phase ended when I got a call from him at around 3 p.m. on Friday, 6 April. Dr McGill said he had had enough of all the shilly-shallying. He gave me the name of a doctor at the

Psychiatric Institute, its address and specific instructions where to report. He told me I had one hour to check into the place. If I had not done so within the hour, they would be sending people to take me there.

I put the phone down on him and got out of the apartment at once. I walked to the subway station at Roslyn, Virginia, and took the train deep into the wholly black area of north-east Washington. There I went to St Anselm's Benedictine Monastery and asked to speak to the British abbot, Father Leonard. In the late twentieth century in the capital of the Free World, I sought sanctuary in a monastery from the United States Central Intelligence Agency.

Abbot Leonard and I spent more than two hours in his office discussing the previous two weeks. The abbot, then in his mid-fifties, chain-smoked throughout. He believed me. He felt my position was hopeless. I should have to leave the USA because I had no way of undoing all the damage that had been done to me. In the meantime I could stay at the monastery for as long as I needed.

I only needed a couple of days. After the interview with the abbot, I phoned Mrs van der Workeen at her apartment in New York. Like me, she was appalled, but not surprised, by Dr McGill's ultimatum. We agreed that staying at St Anselm's was not a long-term solution. Mrs van der Workeen said, 'You have to go back to the apartment. If they do lock you up, Van and I will hire lawyers in New York and get you released within 24 hours, *even if you are saying you don't want to leave.*'

I stayed at the monastery until Sunday afternoon. Then I returned to the apartment in Arlington. I had switched the telephone off just before I had left on Friday. I did not switch it back on until ten that night. No sooner had I switched it on than it rang. It was Dr McGill. Where had I been? He had been calling me all weekend. I didn't tell him. I told him to stop threatening me. I quoted Mrs van der Workeen's promise to me, without identifying her. 'Now leave me alone!' I said, and I put down the phone.

I got little sleep that night because I was expecting the men in white coats to come and pick me up as Dr McGill had threatened they would. They did not come. I never heard from him again. When CNN started digging into my case, they located Dr McGill at a hospital in Florida, but he would not talk to them.

3

Untenable Tenure

'The first thing you must realise is that power is collective. The individual has power only in so far as he ceases to be an individual.'

from *Nineteen Eighty-Four*, GEORGE ORWELL

The following day, Monday, 9 April, Goodman changed tack completely. That evening somebody came to the apartment, but it wasn't men in white coats. It was one of Goodman's students, Craig Allen. Goodman had failed with the big stick. Now he would offer me the big carrot.

I had met Craig at the start of the Foreign Studies programme back in September 1983. He was a tall, slim, friendly young man from Michigan, at least a decade younger than me and fresh from his primary university. But we became friends. It was through him that I got my apartment in the Fort Bennet Apartments. At the start of the autumn semester, when I was looking for permanent accommodation, I had chanced upon him in the student-accommodation office. He told me he had just taken an unfurnished apartment in Arlington and it had been one of two he had been offered. I went out there and took the second apartment.

Craig had found another young student to share but hadn't the means to furnish his apartment. I had the money to furnish mine. I went through the second-hand furniture ads in the Metro section of the *Washington Post* and then hired a van. One evening in early September 1983, Craig and I drove the van all over suburban Washington, Maryland and Virginia, viewing, buying and collecting furniture and Persian rugs.

In the first semester we had attended a couple of classes together and, although my life almost immediately centred on CSIS, Craig would hang out with me when I was at home in the apartment. There was no furniture in his apartment, so we would shoot the breeze over a case of beer at my place. My favourite American beer is Stroh's, from Detroit, Craig's 'home beer', as it were. We usually watched the Monday night American football game when the season started, often with a couple of other neighbours like Assad Shah, an Afghan political refugee who lived in my apartment block and who, like Craig, had a job waiting tables at the Marriott Hotel in Roslyn, Virginia, about half a mile away.

One Saturday night at the start of the semester the previous September, Craig and I threw a party in my apartment. Most of the MSFS students came, as did Paul Cole and Paul Stairs. In short, Craig Allen, when he turned up that night in April 1984, was a good personal friend. Perhaps that is why Goodman chose him as a go-between.

At the time Craig started calling around nightly, for two weeks Goodman had failed to get me under his direct control in a CIA-favoured mental hospital. I had refused to play. Harkness House, fearing a huge public scandal if I were, frantically wanted me to leave the USA and resign the tenure of my fellowship. They had refused to pay me the twice-yearly $5000 fellowship stipend, which had been due the previous week.

McGill having failed, Goodman sent Craig Allen to me, every evening, to say how sorry Goodman was, and how it could all be made better. As the days passed, and as I refused offer after offer, Goodman gave Craig instructions to talk about two things: I must complete the MSFS programme and graduate; and after graduation I must work for the CIA, inferentially under the cover of my journalistic career.

I wanted something else: my independence and my integrity.

I could see that my attitude made no sense to Craig. In his terms, the offers Goodman was telling him to put to me were very generous. If only Goodman would make him such an offer, he told me.

During Craig's last visits, it was my joining the CIA that Goodman focused on. Craig said Goodman would look after me when I had graduated. He would find me a job and get me the right to live and work in the USA. I said no to everything, including the US Green Card.

Some years later, when I told Joe Trento of these conversations, he told me that the CIA was allocated 500 Green Cards each year and that Goodman had access to this supply as part of his job.

Apart from the more independent-minded foreign students like Juha-Pekka Rentto and me, the students on the MSFS programme *wanted* Goodman to sponsor their lives. Their relationship to him was at all times one of fawning dependency. They were supplicants for his favour. Unlike MI5 or MI6 in the UK, the CIA was as open as any other department of the US Federal Government. Goodman's students *wanted* to be recruited by the CIA. The MSFS programme was their stepping-stone to a secure government job.

I knew that all the wonderful offers Goodman made to me via Craig in these night-time meetings had strings attached. How could Goodman, a supposed academic, arrange important staff posts for me at any of my choice of prestigious American newspapers? *Qua* university professor, he could not do that. *Qua* long-time CIA officer, he could.

When I kept saying no, Goodman believed that I was haggling, seeking better terms. It was almost pathetic in those final nine days. Craig would come around to the apartment for a few beers and a chat, as he had always done. Never before, though, had he come every night without fail. During each visit he would relay to me the latest offer from Goodman, accompanied by expressions of Goodman's high regard for me and his deep regret at all that had happened. If only I would see my way clear, he would be my biggest friend and benefactor for life. He would undo all the damage he had done to me. He would always take care of me. He would always be there for me, part of the furniture of my new life. I had only to say yes.

On 16 April, Craig came with Goodman's final offer. I could name my own terms. I could have anything I wanted, the pick of US newspapers, a job as a senior foreign correspondent – perhaps the plummiest job in journalism – and money would not be a problem. I listened silently as Craig laid out before me what Good-man believed was an offer I could not refuse.

I was sick of the charade. Without giving it any thought, I said to Craig that he could tell Goodman to do the other thing.

Why? For one thing, Goodman's ever-more-extravagant offers showed beyond reasonable doubt that he did not believe – and could not possibly have believed – the allegations he had made about me to Harkness House. It was difficult not to suspect that he had made his allegations solely with the intention of cornering me like a rat and then offering me recruitment to the CIA on generous terms as a suddenly attractive way out.

Craig Allen seemed genuinely astonished that I should reject the final offer. I had liked Craig. He was a good young man, a fine specimen of American manhood. It is often said that Americans have no sense of irony. Craig had one, though. We shared a lot of good times together. I recognised that in coming to visit me every evening he was not only fulfilling his orders from Goodman: he was genuinely trying to help me. He found it inconceivable that I did not want to join the affluent and privileged group of young people whom Goodman was grooming for their new lives in the glittering shadows.

That last night, Craig and I had a few more beers together. I have no recollection what we talked about, except that it wasn't Goodman and what had been going on for the previous three and a half weeks. At around 10.30 p.m., Craig left. I was never to see him again.

The following morning, my brother-in-law in Kent rang to tell me that earlier in the day my sister, his wife, had been rushed to hospital in great abdominal pain and that she was scheduled for emergency life-saving surgery that night. There had been no history of any illness. It came as a complete shock. The prognosis did not sound good.

I went straight into Washington and bought a ticket to London on that night's flight. Margaret Mahoney and Professor Garretson had got what they had wanted. I was out of the USA. Their problem was solved. Mine had hardly begun.

I arrived at Heathrow Airport at 7 a.m. on Wednesday, 18 April. My brother-in-law and my six-year-old nephew met me at the terminal and told me that my sister was still alive. Surgery had been postponed at the last moment for further tests. When they operated they removed her gall bladder, on which they found a cancerous tumour.

Before flying from Dulles, I had written to inform Professor Garretson that I was leaving the USA because of a family medical emergency in Britain. A week later, a letter from Professor Garretson,

addressed to me care of my sister in the hospital, instructed me to
resign the tenure of my fellowship.

I was astounded. Professor Garretson was exploiting my sister's
grave illness as a stratagem to force me to do what I had refused to
do during the previous month – to resign.

My sister's serious illness was a shattering blow for the family.
We hoped for the best but prepared for the worst. My sister, whose
three children were aged 16, 9 and 6, believed she was about to die
and leave them all behind.

That weekend I telephoned my MI5 contact, Jonathan Simpson.
I outlined to him what had happened in the USA. He told me to
give him the weekend to look into it. We then had two long telephone conversations on Monday, 23 April. After them I had
a clear, if at that stage incomplete, understanding of what had
happened.

I knew that Goodman had telephoned Harkness House when I
had been in Britain in March. I now knew what he had said about
me. I knew that Harkness House had cancelled my US visa. I knew
I could not return to the USA.

Without the information that Jonathan Simpson had given me,
and the information that William Corson would give me in the
future, I should not have had anything approaching a coherent
picture.

At that stage, however, it was clear that one person could undo
all the damage if he were minded to do so. That was Sir Douglas
Wass, the chairman of the London Harkness Fellowships Selection
Committee, which had interviewed me in December 1982 and had
chosen me as a Harkness Fellow.

Sir Douglas was 60 years of age. Until a few months earlier, he
had been the Head of the UK Home Civil Service and Joint Head of
the entire Civil Service. He had chaired the bureaucratic body that
oversaw MI5, Britain's domestic security service. He had a far higher
position within the British Intelligence community than Goodman
had in US Intelligence. He could verify what had happened by
consulting his former colleagues in MI5.

I decided to contact Sir Douglas. My thinking was that he would
investigate, find Goodman's allegations false and tell Harkness
House, which would welcome me back.

I was wrong on both counts. First, Sir Douglas would not help me, even when he knew that I had been an innocent victim. Second, Harkness House chose to do nothing when it learned the truth.

I looked through the literature published by Harkness House in the UK and saw that one of the members of the Selection Committee that had been chaired by Sir Douglas was Mary Goldring, a well-known journalist at the BBC. I did not know that Ms Goldring was a close personal friend of Sir Douglas.

Ms Goldring was a journalist, and no journalist ignores even the most extraordinary accounts of wrongdoing. Sometimes they are true. Extraordinary accounts are the stuff of journalism. That a CIA officer should want to recruit a journalist to work as a spy for the Agency under the cover of his career as a journalist is not even extraordinary for journalists. We are all well aware of the way spy agencies operate.

Ms Goldring would not find my account of what had happened incredible. I hoped she would agree to see me and give me a fair hearing. If she did that – and I knew that she could verify via Harkness House in New York the fact that Goodman had telephoned it while I had been in Britain in March – then, armed with the knowledge that I was telling the truth, she could approach Sir Douglas on my behalf.

I telephoned her at the BBC. I told her very briefly what had happened and she agreed to meet me the next morning, 2 May, at her house in Sloane Avenue, Chelsea. I arrived as requested at 10 a.m. I sat for three hours in her drawing-room, setting out every-thing that I knew. I told her that, in my view, only Sir Douglas could sort everything out.

The meeting with Ms Goldring was everything I had hoped it would be. She would later tell my friend, Alex Coxen, that she had been profoundly impressed, that I was clearly 'brilliant' and that she had been able to verify almost all I had told her. She took me to a nearby restaurant for lunch. When she ordered a bottle of wine, I demurred, saying that I should not drink alcohol because of the allegations that I was an alcoholic. She replied, 'Of course you are not an alcoholic. That is obvious. There are signs, and you have none of them.'

We drank a bottle of white wine. I left her at 3.30 p.m., or 10.30 a.m. New York time. When Margaret Mahoney reached her office at Harkness House in the following hour, she found Ms Goldring on the telephone from London wanting to talk to her. After that conversation, Ms Goldring left a note for me with my brother-in-law. It said, 'Ms Goldring believes you are right and that this is something that only Sir Douglas Wass can deal with.' So far, so good.

The following morning, on the telephone, Mary Goldring told me, 'The telephone lines have been burning between London and New York since I spoke to you!'

Ms Mahoney had confirmed to her that Goodman had, indeed, telephoned Harkness House in March while I had been in Britain and made the allegations that I had detailed to her. She told me that Harkness House had already been in turmoil after Howland Sargent's death so soon after Mrs van der Workeen's resignation. She had not been replaced, so that, when Howland Sargent had died, there had been nobody left at the tiller when Goodman had made his call. Ms Mahoney had panicked.

Ms Goldring said that she had then spoken to Wass about me and told me, 'Douglas is very worried about what is going to happen to you.'

Mary Goldring told me that she had also spoken to a senior staffer at the London office of the Harkness Fellowships. She had just returned from New York and wanted to see me urgently. Ms Goldring said that the Harkness official had found Garretson, on her visit to New York, to be an immensely arrogant man who had refused to talk to her. She had been unable to find out what had been going on.

The impression I got was that the Harkness official in London wanted to help me. I got that badly wrong. I telephoned her. She did, indeed, want to see me urgently. I went in to her office at once. I got a shock. She formally denied everything that Margaret Mahoney had confirmed to Ms Goldring. There had been no telephone call from Goodman. Nobody had made any allegations against me. The Harkness Fellowships and the Commonwealth Fund had put no pressure on me to resign the tenure of my fellowship. But the Harkness official added, without irony, that it would be best for me to resign my tenure.

I refused to resign. Yet, with no visa, I could not return to the US. Where, I asked the official, did she and her colleagues expect me to live?

'You can live with your sister,' she replied.

I told her that my sister was seriously ill in hospital, awaiting an operation for cancer. She and her three young children lived in a three-bedroomed house. I was sleeping on the sofa in the lounge. That was a short-term arrangement. I also pointed out that no newspaper would employ an alleged maniac said to have raped and tried to kill numerous women. Her only reply was to say: 'I hope you don't give up your career in journalism.'

Almost three years later, the *Sunday Express* published a freelance article of mine. I was paid £300. Other articles I submitted were not published. The London Harkness official, on the basis of this one article, wrote in that year's *Harkness Fellowships Newsletter*: 'Denis Lehane now works for the *Sunday Express*.'

I was no longer in any doubt that Mahoney and Garretson in New York had no intention of reconsidering their policy towards me. 3 May 1984 was my 14th consecutive day outside the USA. The rules of the Harkness Fellowships stated that, if a Fellow on tenure in the USA were to spend more than 14 consecutive days outside the USA, his tenure would automatically be at an end.

I had spoken to Garretson on the telephone on Friday, 27 April. He had cockily confirmed that my US visa had been cancelled and that there was no way I should be allowed to return to the USA.

'You have been the victim of a strange series of coincidences,' he said. 'But there is nothing you can do about it now. All you can do is write to me resigning the tenure of your fellowship on grounds of family ill health.'

I declined to resign, pointing out that the academic year was almost over and that there was no reason why I could not return in September to begin the second and final year.

He laughed. He told me that there was nothing I could say to him that would make the Commonwealth Fund change its mind. 'You must just put this all behind you and get on with your life,' he said.

I replied, 'How?'

He said, 'Oh, that is for you to work out.'

The following morning, since I was now in breach of the Harkness Fellowships' rules by being outside the US without permission for more than 14 days, I wrote Garretson a brief note, which I sent to him via the London office of the Harkness Fellowships, in which I resigned the Fellowship. Not the tenure of my Harkness Fellowship but membership of the body of Harkness Fellows. I did so because I had been told clearly that I should not be allowed into the USA to finish my tenure.

Garretson replied accepting my resignation not of my Fellowship but of its tenure.

Ms Goldring would later say that as far as Mahoney and Garretson were concerned I had ceased to exist when I had got on the airliner at Dulles and flown to Britain to be at my sick sister's bedside.

The Civil Service is divided into two unequal parts. One part, the Foreign and Commonwealth Office, is the Foreign Civil Service. All the rest is the Home Civil Service. Each government department is headed by an elected politician as Minister. Inside each department work the civil servants whose job it is to translate into reality the wishes of the elected politicians. The theory is that all civil servants are apolitical and carry out the instructions of the politicians no matter what party is in power.

At the top of the Civil Service hierarchy in each ministry is the Permanent Secretary, whose role exactly mirrors that of the politician at the head of the department. Each Permanent Secretary, such is the British obsession with class, rank and titles, automatically gets a knighthood. As Head of the Home Civil Service, Sir Douglas Wass was the bureaucrat to whom Britain's domestic spy service, MI5, reported. Sir Douglas was, in short, the conduit through whom the Prime Minister of the day would receive reports from MI5.

This is why Wass, although recently retired, would be in a position to assist me in sorting out the mess Goodman had caused. No one could do it better. Until a few months before, MI5's Director had been reporting directly to Wass. By comparison, Goodman was a low-ranking operative.

Douglas Wass came from an ordinary working-class background in the north-west of England. His parents were Arthur and Elsie Wass. During his childhood they moved to Nottingham in the East Midlands. There Wass had done well at school and, in 1941, at the age of 18, he had gained a place at St John's College, Cambridge, where he had studied mathematics.

Upon graduation in 1944 Wass went directly into the British Civil Service, where he remained until he reached the mandatory retirement age of 60 in 1984.

Behind these dry facts lies a most extraordinary story. In 1941, when Britain was at war with Nazi Germany, Wass chose to go to university rather than fight for his country. During the Second World War, all British universities were reduced to a wartime emergency level: most university candidates were instead joining up. To go to Cambridge in 1941, Wass had to obtain a deferment. When he graduated three years later, he obtained a second deferment.

Wass would never serve a day in Britain's armed forces: neither in wartime nor in the mandatory two years' national service that followed in peacetime. In his entry in *Who's Who*, Wass describes his wartime service thus: 'Served war, 1943–46: Scientific Research with Admiralty, at home and in Far East'. This 'military' service involved using his mathematics to calculate the losses that Britain's merchant shipping had suffered owing to enemy action.

After the war, four million young men of Wass's age who had fought for their country returned to Britain and were demobilised. Many joined the Civil Service. Such war veterans invariably achieved promotions to senior positions over the heads of those who had not fought. In 1964, after 20 years in the Civil Service, Wass had achieved only a single, routine promotion from trainee to non-trainee status. He had remained on the lowest rung of the Civil Service ladder.

Yet his life had not been without incident. In 1954 the retiring, bookish Wass had shocked all his colleagues with an action which was striking, because nothing in his previous 30 years had given any indication that he was capable of boldness. For his summer vacation that year, Wass spent two weeks in Communist Yugoslavia.

It was the height of the Cold War. Stalin was not yet cold in his grave. In Britain, food was still rationed. Winston Churchill was Prime Minister. Ordinary people did not consider going anywhere abroad for their summer vacations. In that era, the notion of visiting an essentially unknown Balkan Communist state would have been bizarre for anybody. For a British civil servant, it was astonishing.

Wass would not have been allowed to take such a holiday had he not been at the very lowest rank in the Civil Service. He was so insignificant that it did not matter that he was exposing himself to Communist recruitment. Wass had no access to any secrets the Soviets might want. There seemed no likelihood that he ever would.

On his return, Wass brought with him a Yugoslav wife whom he had met on holiday. Mrs Wass was the former Miss Milica Pavičić. They were to have a son and a daughter.

Such a bold and – seemingly – romantic act on Wass's part was at odds with his previous life and with the life that would follow. It astounded his colleagues. He had no reputation as a ladies' man. His sudden marriage to Miss Pavičić did not seem to be a good career move.

For the ten years following his marriage, Wass was still not promoted. He remained on the lowest grade in the Civil Service after the entry-level 'trainee' grade. Then, at the age of 40, in a dramatic six-year period, he received four promotions. In those six years he made up and then some for 20 years of failure.

Sir Douglas was retired. He had no full-time job. Yet he was always too busy to see me. On 30 June 1984, a lovely, sunny day, I went around to his house in Wimbledon uninvited. His teenage daughter opened the door. I told her who I was and asked to see her father. She went to him in the garden, as I waited outside the front door, and returned to say he could not see me.

I asked my friend Alex Coxen to speak to Sir Douglas for me, because I wanted a detached view of the thing. He spoke many times on the phone to Mary Goldring, but every time he tried to speak to Sir Douglas he was rebuffed. Alex said that he found it unpleasant and scary to try to speak to Sir Douglas. Later that summer he told me: 'The thing that most disturbs me about this is the way everything is being done behind closed doors.'

In October 1986 Alex Coxen would recount to CNN all that he had witnessed in these months. He would also reveal how, unknown to me at the time, Professor Garretson had made a trip to London in June of that year. He knew this because Mary Goldring had met the professor during this trip and discussed me with him. Alex said:

> Mary Goldring told me that the man she called a senior Harkness official from New York had come to London and that she had been very angry at the way Denis had been treated. She told me that this man had confirmed to her that everything that Denis had told her was true. She told me that she was glad to hear this because, even though she had confirmed what Denis had told her in telephone calls to people in New York, she realised that she still a small doubt that Denis might have had a mental breakdown.
>
> After speaking to this man, she told me, that small doubt had

been removed. She knew that Denis had been telling the truth and that he had not had a mental breakdown.

I told her that I was very pleased to hear it, too, because I had also had a small doubt that Denis might have had a breakdown in the USA.

I spoke to Sir Douglas on the telephone on Monday, 14 May. The first words he said to me were: 'Denis, I beg of you, you must see a psychiatrist.'

At the time, given what Goldring had been saying to Alex, this was strange. Yet my reply was: 'I have no problem with that.' Despite my agreement, he kept repeating the point. I had to interrupt him to repeat my answer. He then said that he would do everything in his power to help me – everything, that is, except approach his former colleagues, the one thing that might have worked. I replied, 'If you won't do that, I don't see how you can help me.'

Wass did not reply to that. Instead, he talked about my US visa: 'Ms Mahoney will not have you back and so you cannot use that visa. You have other visas in your passport. You will be able to use those visas should you ever need to return to the USA.'

My reply was that the fact that I had visas in my passport meant nothing. The visas did not guarantee that US Immigration would let me in. Every time one presented one's passport, they checked the blacklist. I had already been told I was on that list. I told Sir Douglas this. He merely repeated himself over and over again, saying I should try to use my other US visas.

I got the impression that Sir Douglas had been told to persuade me to give up trying to undo what had been done to me. I must not make trouble for the CIA. If I went on making trouble, I should be discredited as a madman.

Sir Douglas delivered a series of statements as though they were orders for the future conduct of a refractory teenager. His job was to tell me how to behave and mine was to do what I was told. At one point, apparently astonished that I was not proposing to follow his instructions, he said, 'Surely you don't doubt my *bona fides*?'

I replied at once, 'You are a civil servant. I am a journalist. Of course I doubt your *bona fides*.'

In 1987 at the Maudsley Hospital, London, Dr W. C. Warwick pronounced me sane.

4

The Lobotomy Man

'The scientist of today is either a mixture of psychologist
and inquisitor, studying with extraordinary minuteness the
meaning of facial expressions, gestures and tones of voice,
and testing the truth-producing effects of drugs, shock
therapy, hypnosis and physical torture, or he is chemist,
physicist or biologist concerned only with such branches
of his special subject as are relevant to the taking of life.'

from *Nineteen Eighty-Four,* GEORGE ORWELL

More than a decade later, at some point in 1995, I happened to see
a television documentary on psychiatry on the BBC. It started with
a man in his sixties, with silver hair, in a dark suit, using a wooden
pointer on a large diagram of a human brain. He was lecturing to
students of psychiatric medicine on a procedure called a prefrontal
lobotomy.

Those who have seen the chilling film based on Ken Kesey's
novel *One Flew Over the Cuckoo's Nest* will recall that a prefrontal
lobotomy is the operation on the brain of Randal P. McMurphy,
the Jack Nicholson character, which renders him a vegetable. This
barbaric procedure was once as routine in psychiatry as cold baths
and strait-jackets. The brain is opened and the surgeon makes
incisions into the prefrontal lobes. Few, if any, reputable psychiatrists would approve of such a procedure today.

The opening sequences of this documentary were riveting: the
programme-makers were ridiculing the elderly lecturer, who was
shown cracking crude jokes about mentally ill people and what he
used to do to their brains. He was a grotesque comedy turn.

This powerful piece of television journalism set the stage for the
critical look at psychiatry that was at the heart of the documentary.
The sequences were all the more compelling for me because I

recognised the Lobotomy Man. I had met Dr Paul Bridges in July 1984, after I had told Sir Douglas Wass that I was willing to undergo a psychiatric evaluation.

After my conversation with Sir Douglas on 14 May, I had consulted my GP, Dr Parsons, about undergoing a psychiatric evaluation. He was strongly against it. He said, 'If you tell a psychiatrist what you have told me, he will find you mentally ill. I know you are not mentally ill and never have been, but a psychiatrist will not know you. Because he does not know you as I do, he will automatically conclude that you are mentally ill. That is the way they work.'

In his later interview with CNN, Dr Parsons would elaborate on this view:

> The problem with psychiatrists is that they only get what is, in effect, a snapshot of the patient when they interview him. It can often be very misleading, indeed wrong. A general practitioner gets to see the patient over a number of years and gets a much more detailed picture of him. Denis had been my patient for almost ten years when he told me what had happened to him in the USA. I knew what he did for a living. I saw that he was the same man he had always been. There were never any grounds to find him mentally ill, but it did not surprise me when Dr Bridges, who did not know him at all, decided that he was. Dr Bridges only got a snapshot of Denis. I had the full picture.

I agreed with Dr Parsons' opinion, but I also feared that to refuse to undergo a psychiatric evaluation would signal that I had something to hide. By the end of June 1984 I had concluded that Sir Douglas was not going to help me. Seeing a psychiatrist was the last card I could play.

In theory, I hoped, no competent psychiatrist could conclude from my story that I was mentally ill. I was not claiming that little green men had abducted me into an alien spaceship and had done medical experiments on me. As Dr Parsons would later tell CNN, given my career and background there was nothing inherently incredible in my account that a CIA man had wanted to recruit me and, when I had declined, had sought to protect his reputation with his superiors by falsely alleging that I had committed serious crimes of violence against women.

In reality, for many psychiatrists, as soon as one mentioned the

CIA one might as well be talking about little green men in alien spaceships. Anyone who makes any sort of reference to wrongdoing by the CIA is instantly rubber-stamped as insane. That initial rubber-stamp, without anything so diligent as an attempt to verify the facts, is thereafter used as the cornerstone of all subsequent 'diagnoses'. It is the basis for the deadly statement: 'The patient has a long history of psychotic mental illness where delusions of persecution predominate.'

I did not know this in June 1984. Perhaps I was naïve. But I was in an uncomfortable position. I had reason to doubt Sir Douglas' *bona fides*, and I had begun to wonder whether I could count on Mary Goldring. I concluded that it would be better to submit to a psychiatric evaluation than not to do so.

I asked Dr Parsons to refer me to a psychiatrist. By some mis-chance, he referred me to Dr Paul Bridges. The Lobotomy Man was a consultant at Guy's Hospital, a large general hospital on the south side of London Bridge. I saw him on the morning of 4 July 1984. In a consultation which lasted less than one hour, I outlined to him essentially what I had told Mary Goldring at her house two months earlier. I also showed him the letter that Garretson had sent to my sister's hospital bed instructing me to resign the tenure of the Harkness Fellowship.

This letter impressed Dr Bridges. He said it indicated clearly that something had happened. At the end of our meeting he said that he could not come to any decision on the basis of what I had told him. He invited me to admit myself to Guy's Hospital so that he and his team could undertake a thorough evaluation. I con-sented. Later that afternoon I checked into the hospital. I was astonished to find that it was a mixed ward separated only by curtains. I did not know that in the cash-strapped British National Health Service all wards were mixed wards. I found it distasteful.

A young Irish doctor, Dr Deirdre O'Brady, introduced me to the head nurse, Mike Briggs, who then conducted the first interview with me. Again I outlined what had happened in the USA. At the end of the interview, unprompted, Mike Briggs said, 'Denis, I have dealt with many paranoid people, but on the basis of what you have just told me you demonstrate no symptoms.'

Shortly afterwards I had the first of many sessions with Dr O'Brady. The Lobotomy Man was not based at Guy's Hospital: he would only come in once a week to conduct a meeting with the full team. I mention this because the consultation I had had with Dr Bridges was the only one-on-one session I had with him. Deirdre O'Brady and Mike did all the groundwork. Like her colleague, Dr O'Brady did not consider me to be mentally ill. She once said to me, 'Mr Lehane, you are much too sane.'

One of the interrogation techniques used by the KGB in Communist Russia was to get a prisoner to repeat over and over again his account of what had happened. I soon began to feel like a victim of the KGB. A week after I had been admitted, the Lobotomy Man arrived in all his pomp to sit on his throne, surrounded by Deirdre O'Brady, Mike Briggs, Jeannette Reid (a social worker), and other nurses.

During the previous week I had talked every day with Dr O'Brady, once with Ms Reid and also with several of the nurses. I had told all of them the same story. The team meeting I attended with the Lobotomy Man was an interrogation. Why, he asked me, would fine, upstanding, respectable people like Ms Mahoney and Professor Garretson have treated me so badly?

'Because that is how they are,' I said.

'I see,' replied the Lobotomy Man. Not a normal 'I see' but a drawn-out, disbelieving 'Ayee–ee see–ee!'

To every answer I gave, the same response came from the Lobotomy Man: 'Ayee–ee see–ee!'

Perhaps he was not intentionally contemptuous. His nurses had told me that he was ever so distinguished in his field. Maybe he was, but he seemed to me to be an arrogant man who specialised in belittling his patients *de haut en bas*. Sadly, I was to learn that this was typical of his profession. If there were ever a flag day for distressed psychiatrists, I should not buy a flag.

His dozen team members treated him with reverence and awe. He was God surrounded by His archangels, cherubim and seraphim. I was the poor 'sinner' upon whom He sat in judgment. The interrogation continued for maybe half an hour. Again I went through my story. He did not believe me. Towards the end, he began saying: 'It doesn't hang together.'

I agreed that it did not make a lot of sense to me either, but what had happened to me had the character of a hit-and-run road accident. I had been walking along the road without a care in the world when a car had come up behind me, mounted the pavement and run me over. The fact that I had not seen the car coming and that I did not know its colour, make or registration number said nothing about me. I could not expect to know these things in such a situation.

'Ayee–ee see–ee! Bu–ut, it do–es not ha–aang too–getthh–err!'

The Lobotomy Man held that my failure to present a motive for the actions of Goodman, Mahoney, Garretson *et hoc genus omne* at the Commonwealth Fund implied that there was something wrong not with them but with me.

It was humiliating for me to be subjected to such ridicule in front of strangers. It was the first occasion when I experienced what it is to be a member of the underclass, routinely mistreated as *Untermenschen* by doctors like the Lobotomy Man. I was thoroughly sickened by the Lobotomy Man's interrogation.

At length he, too, had had enough. He dismissed me curtly with the words: 'You are clearly suffering from paranoia. Happily for you it is something we can treat. Three weeks' treatment with a major tranquilliser and you will be well again.'

To which I replied, 'I don't think I am suffering from paranoia.'

He replied, 'Ah–hh! That is a symptom of paranoia!'

If so, most of the seven billion people who believe they are not suffering from paranoia are paranoid. It was an instance of the sophistry and hocus-pocus which underlies the worst sort of psychiatry.

The drugs which the Lobotomy Man prescribed for me did not act on the mind: they acted on the chemistry of the brain. It would come as a shock to me to realise that psychiatry is not a science. It is a primitive, mystical art-form practised by modern-day shamans.

The Lobotomy Man had scheduled me for the last grilling of that week's Grand Rounds. At the conclusion of my interrogation, I was angry. As the team, led by the Lobotomy Man himself, streamed out of the room where the interrogations had taken place and walked the length of the ward to the exit, Dr O'Brady detached herself from the procession and sought me out. She said, 'Mr Lehane, I am sorry. I know you are not paranoid. You must be feeling completely alone at this moment.'

It was a great kindness. I had a longer meeting with her later in the day and she told me what lay behind what had happened that morning. With my permission, the Lobotomy Man had spoken to

Sir Douglas Wass on the telephone about me. Remarkably, Sir Douglas had told him that no allegations of violence had been made against me in the USA.

The Lobotomy Man, relying solely upon Sir Douglas's word, not checking the truth of it with me, not even arranging for one of his seraphic host to telephone the New York Police Department to verify that the allegations had been made, had confidently diagnosed me as paranoid. This failure by psychiatrists to check any of the facts would occur again and again over the coming years, and would finally come very close to killing me, leaving me permanently disabled.

The Lobotomy Man could easily have arranged for one of his cherubs to telephone Mary Goldring. She had told me on the telephone on 3 May that Ms Mahoney in New York had confirmed to her that Goodman had indeed repeated Ms McInerney's allegations to her at the Harkness office.

The Lobotomy Man, an upper-class creature with the old-school-tie mentality, had no difficulty in accepting Sir Douglas's *bona fides*. For him, if the recently retired Head of Her Britannic Majesty's Civil Service said that a man was suffering from delusions of persecution then that was the end of the story. Not only that: the Lobotomy Man saw no reason to advise that man of what Sir Douglas had said to him. If Dr O'Brady had not broken the rules by telling me, I should never have known.

Almost three years later, the prominent Liberal Member of Parliament Simon Hughes would write to the Mayor of New York, Ed Koch, to ask him about Ms McInerney's allegations. Koch's office would write back that on 30 January 1984 Ms McInerney had lodged a complaint of attempted murder by me at an unspecified time, place and date in September 1983. That letter from the Mayor's office in New York proved that what Sir Douglas had told the Lobotomy Man in July 1984 had been untrue.

Dr O'Brady was right. I did feel alone, awfully alone, after the Lobotomy Man had sat in judgement upon me and found me to be insane. I faced a stark choice. I had checked in voluntarily a week earlier for an evaluation of my sanity. That evaluation had ended. Nothing stood in my way should I decide to leave the hospital, except that I should leave with the label *Insane!* around my neck, like a modern-day leper.

So I chose to stay. I did so because the Lobotomy Man had told me, in front of all his team, that I could be cured of my 'paranoid psychosis' by what he presented to me as a relatively easy process. Three weeks of treatment with an anti-psychotic tranquilliser, he had told me, and all my 'delusions' would go away. It seemed to me that, if I went along with the Lobotomy Man, I should have to endure no more than three further weeks in the hospital.

But what if the 'delusions' did not go away? On the evening of 11 July 1984 I was officially insane. Nothing that I said could be taken to be true. But Alex Coxen was not officially insane. Nor was Mary Goldring. So I asked both to come in as a matter of urgency and speak to Dr O'Brady. Both agreed.

Mary Goldring came two days later in the afternoon. After speaking to Dr O'Brady, she came to see me. I was sitting in the ward. She was taken aback by what she found. She had clearly had no previous experience of a mixed National Health Service psychi-atric ward. What she found was about 30 patients, men and women – most of them, though not me, in their nightclothes covered by dressing-gowns – and a handful of nurses, not in uniform, sitting around twiddling their thumbs.

'Don't they talk to you?' Ms Goldring asked me incredulously. She had expected all sorts of proactive programmes which would occupy our day. Alex, who had visited me a number of times there, had remarked on one occasion that he did not understand how I could handle the boredom. Mary Goldring did not realise that what she saw was the norm for NHS psychiatric in-patients.

I told her that all that happened was that we were given medic-ation two, three or four times a day. Otherwise, we were left to sit around all day, day after day, while the medication took its course. Although Mary Goldring did not tell me so herself that day, she was shocked to find that the bright and alert person she had met for the first time two months earlier had been transformed into a slow and sedated zombie. What did she expect, I wonder? I had been taking the maximum dosage of a powerful anti-psychotic tranquilliser for 48 hours when she met me. That is what such drugs do to people: they slow down their thought processes and leave them groggy.

Mary Goldring told me it did not matter that the Lobotomy Man had misdiagnosed me. I should accept his treatment willingly, because it would help me. I could see that behind her words was the conviction that I needed help and support to deal with the terrible trauma that had been inflicted on me by Goodman and her friends in the Commonwealth Fund. She clearly believed that such help and support would be readily available under the National Health Service and that the Lobotomy Man would tailor that treatment to my needs. To my dismay, it did not seem to matter to her that the Lobotomy Man, solely on the basis of Sir Douglas's untruths, had falsely labelled me insane.

Public psychiatric health services in Britain are poorly funded and provide a minimum of care. In the Lobotomy Man's ward in Guy's Hospital in July and August 1984, some of the patients were given electro-convulsive therapy – electric-shock treatment where electrodes are placed on the outside of the skull and a large voltage is administered. This 'therapy' was delivered not in specially equipped theatres but in the public ward, on the bed, with just a flimsy, half-transparent curtain separating the person getting the electric shocks from the rest of the ward.

One little elderly lady, called Daisy, who got the electric shocks on a regular basis, used to scream in terror every time they did it to her, 'Stop! You're torturing me!' As well as terrifying poor little Daisy, it was distressing and frightening for all the patients in the ward.

'She doesn't mean it,' an obnoxious staff-nurse said to me after one such particularly distressing incident. Maybe she doesn't, I thought, but just supposing Daisy was being tortured, or believed she was being tortured, what, then, would she say to alert people to her torture? She would say, 'Stop! You're torturing me!' And she would say it with the full power of her elderly lungs. That is what she did each time they gave her electric shocks on the bed behind the curtain. The nurses held her down as she screamed.

Having been diagnosed as insane because I thought I was not insane, I was getting off lightly compared with Daisy. *One Flew Over the Cuckoo's Nest,* however, told me that the Lobotomy Man and his eager coterie would not hesitate to do to me what they were doing to Daisy and others. And worse.

By Friday, 14 July, Dr O'Brady had spoken to both Mary Goldring and Alex Coxen. Alex had told her what he had learned from me and from Mary Goldring. He was unequivocal: Ms Goldring had confirmed to him that the substance of my account was true. Dr O'Brady was pleased to have his confirmation of my account. Dr O'Brady told Alex: 'I don't have any difficulty with Mr Lehane's account of what happened. The CIA is capable of anything.'

Dr O'Brady, like Mike Briggs the chief nurse, had never seen anything in me or my account to justify any psychiatric label. One psychiatrist (unfortunately the boss) had concluded that I was insane, while another, on the basis of the same information, had concluded I was sane. It is a fundamental principle of all health care, even in the public health services, that where a patient is not happy with one doctor's diagnosis he is entitled to a second opinion.

Almost three years later, Joe Trento and CNN arrived in my life, with independent confirmation of the truth. By then I was also armed with the letter that the office of the Mayor of New York had sent to Simon Hughes to confirm that Ms McInerney had made allegations of attempted murder against me in January 1984. With these confirmations, I went to a different London Hospital, the Maudsley, and sought my entitlement to a second opinion of my sanity on the basis of my account of what had happened.

I was interviewed at length by a lady consultant, Dr H. W. C. Warwick. She cleared me of any insanity and said that she felt that I should benefit from some psychotherapy to deal with the consequences of what had been a major trauma in my life. Two weeks later, I got a note from her saying that this would not be possible. I later learned that the Lobotomy Man, Paul Bridges, had intervened – without having examined the patient a second time – to overrule Dr Warwick.

Worse, at the time the Lobotomy Man intervened to overrule Dr Warwick at the Maudsley he knew that what Sir Douglas Wass had told him had been independently challenged. I know this because Dr O'Brady, after interviewing Alex Coxen and Mary Goldring, had reported to the Lobotomy Man that their interviews had contradicted what Wass had told him in early July.

It must be emphasised that the Lobotomy Man's label of insanity was based solely on the information from Wass that there had never been any allegations that I had attacked any women in the USA.

When I saw Bridges for his weekly sitting-in-judgment session of Tuesday 1 August, after the magic three weeks of the prescribed anti-psychotic, I had not changed my tune by one note. He had told me that all my 'delusions' would go away after three weeks of this drug. None of them had. The evidence from the interviews Dr O'Brady had conducted with Alex and Goldring supported my account. Either I was sane or the Lobotomy Man had got it wrong about the effects of the drug on a delusional psychotic. Faced with this dilemma, he concluded that Sir Douglas had indeed misled him. That gave him a way out.

He told me that Tuesday afternoon that I was not insane after all. However, he added, I was in what he called 'a paranoid state', which I understood to mean that I was not paranoid at all but had exhibited all the symptoms of paranoia. And in what way had I exhibited this 'paranoia?' By asserting that allegations of rape and attempted murder had been made against me when, as the Lobotomy Man now knew, they had indeed been made.

5

A Proud North Cork Blueshirt

I bear the name of ancient Irish kings. Bernard Cornwell, researching the historical records of the Dark Ages of these islands for his *Warlord Chronicles Trilogy* based on the Arthurian legends, came upon a sept of fifth-century Irish kings based in the valley of the River Blackwater in North County Cork. He called them the Ui Liathain (which could mean 'the Grey Ones') and their followers 'the Blackshield Irish'.

If you trawl the tourist shops of Nassau Street and its environs in central Dublin looking for a heraldic emblem for the Lehanes, you will not find one. Those came with the Normans in the twelfth century. Lehanes had been in Ireland for many, many centuries before then. After the years of the Great Hunger, 1845 to 1851, when Ireland's population was halved by starvation, disease and emigration to not much more than today's five million, the native Irish decided to anglicise their names. So Lehane was born. Until then it had been O Liathain. The Ui Liathain had alternated with the Eoghanacht as kings of Munster between the sixth and ninth centuries. The stronghold of the Ui Liathain was Ceann Toirc (Kanturk). We are no longer kings but we are still there.

Joe Trento of CNN has described me as 'a poor Irish peasant'. Perhaps I am. I was born the second child of Nora and Rick Lehane in September 1949 in the south-east London suburb of Greenwich. My parents spent most of their lives in south-east London, but their home was always the ancient barony of Duhallow in the valley of the River Blackwater, with the Boggarah Mountains looking down.

Their parents, my grandparents, had 30 children between them. All but three sons had to leave to find work in Britain, the USA, Australia and Canada. They did not want to go but had no choice. By 1922, centuries of British rule and an economically unnatural partition of the country had left the 26 counties of the new Irish Free State economically unsustainable. Only accession in 1973 to what is now the European Union provided the basis for the country to build itself up and, in the 1990s, launch the Celtic Tiger. For the first 70 years of independence, Ireland's main export was her people. My parents were just two of these exports.

My father was the second of 16 children of a poor agricultural labourer and his wife, Hannah and Denis Lehane, of Dromalour, Kanturk, North Cork. He was born on 12 November 1922. My mother, Nora, the 13th of the 14 children of Con O'Connell, another poor agricultural labourer from Kanturk, and his wife Mary Ann, was born on 17 January 1923. Nine days earlier the new independent Irish Free State had come into formal existence. My mother was the first O'Connell to be born into a free Ireland in more than 750 years. The only flag flying throughout the state was the green, white and orange tricolour of the newly-independent Ireland.

The world into which my mother and father were born was a traditional, conservative, Irish agricultural community. Kanturk, their home town of about 2000 inhabitants, is the capital of North Cork. Each week in Kanturk on a Thursday there would be a mart where all the farmers from the surrounding areas would come to buy and sell their animals. The only industry, and hence the only source of employment, was agriculture.

People had lived in Kanturk, living much the same lives that the O'Connells and Lehanes lived, for thousands of years. The branch of the great Celtic nation, the Gaels, who composed the vast mass of the people of Ireland in 1923, had started coming to Ireland 1000 years before the birth of Jesus Christ, mainly from Galicia, the land of the Gaels, in northern Spain.

In 1946, in Greenwich, Nora O'Connell married Richard Lehane, a man from Kanturk whom she had known before she had left for London. Their first child, my sister Mary Ann, who had thick, curly, brown hair, was born on 18 February 1948 and died in hospital five days later. My mother was devastated. She did not understand why her child had had to die. She never really recovered from the death, and my father began to doubt the Catholic faith into which he had been born.

The following year, I was born. My father, despite his grief for the loss of his elder daughter, would instruct his two surviving children into that faith, teach them the Catechism and take them to Mass each Sunday and on Holy Days of Obligation, but he himself had ceased to believe.

My first memories date from the time when I had just learned to walk and was placed, as all children were then, in a playpen. I remember distinctly being annoyed that I could not climb out of it to walk and crawl about as I wanted to. I remember later, when my mother was pregnant, accompanying her to the ante-natal clinic, where, on one occasion, the doctor let me climb up to my mother lying on a bed so that I could listen to the heartbeat of my unborn sibling. I was two years old.

My mother would tell me, before such visits or when we met family and friends, to say that I wanted a baby sister with dark brown curly hair. At the time I did not understand but I said it as I was told.

In March 1952 my mother gave birth to a little girl. She was not Mary Ann. This realisation only served to aggravate my mother's pain. Perhaps for the first time, she understood that Mary Ann was gone for good and could not return. My mother felt completely alone. I know that for the rest of her life she always thought of Mary Ann. She was always with her. February would be a terrible month for her. Once, in 1971, as if in passing, my mother said to me: 'My little girl would have been 23 today and she would be married with her own family by now.'

All through my childhood my mother would be struck down by periods of debilitating illness. She suffered with increasing severity from bronchitis and asthma. She needed to have a large cylinder of oxygen in the bedroom, often spending days or weeks on end only able to breathe with the oxygen. Her stays in hospital became more frequent and lasted longer. My father did not how to cope with her. She felt he was cold and unkind. Their mutual incomprehension grew and their marriage fell apart. It was a relief when they separated in 1965 and later divorced.

In 1935, when Nora O'Connell was twelve years old, the nuns who ran her school in Kanturk sent for her mother, my grandmother Mary Ann O'Connell. My grandmother assumed that there was something seriously wrong, though she had no idea what it was. In the Catholic Ireland of the 1930s, priests and nuns were treated like living gods and goddesses. The Mother Superior quickly cut to the chase when my grandmother went to see her. Her daughter, Nora, the Mother Superior said, was a gifted child and should go to university.

The Mother Superior said that she would make sure she did go to university but to do so she intimated that it would cost Con and Mary Ann O'Connell £100. In 1935, that was a lot of money. Ireland, like every other European country, had been devastated by the aftermath of the 1929 Wall Street Crash. There was mass unemployment. To a man like my grandfather, £100 was a fortune.

However, my grandmother had been born Mary Ann O'Herlihy. The O'Herlihies of Kanturk were a very rich family. They had made their fortune in the goldfields of South Africa at the turn of the century. Among other things, they ran a road-haulage business. I do not know whether the O'Herlihies were ever asked for the £100. My assumption is that they were not. If they had been asked, they would have given the money willingly.

There was much discussion in the O'Connell family. Most of Nora's siblings were adults living and working in Britain. The oldest, Neil, was well established. All the brothers and sisters living in Britain said they would each chip in to make up the sum of £100. But it did not happen.

Con and Mary Ann decided to turn down the Mother Superior's suggestion, because they felt that it would be unfair to all the other children were Nora to be singled out for such special attention. So, having decided against sending Nora to university, they decided there was no further point in her staying on at school. A few months later, she went to work as a parlourmaid in the house of a rich doctor in Kanturk. The doctor had a daughter of Nora's age at school, whom Nora would help with her homework.

I did not hear that my mother might have gone to university until my Aunt Imelda, the last of Con and Mary Ann O'Connell's 14 children, told me in 1987, shortly after my mother died. I was stunned. My mother had never told me. I immediately thought back to the day when I had received my Oxford degree in an impressive ceremony in the Sheldonian Theatre, with my mother looking on from the balcony. How proud she must have been to know that her son had been able to have the university education that she should have had.

How my mother's heart must have leapt when she learned what

the Mother Superior had called in my grandmother for! What new and exciting life did she envisage ahead for her? And what a crushing disappointment it must have been for a twelve-year-old child to learn that her parents had turned the opportunity down! The older she grew and the more she learned about real life, the more she would have felt that loss. It is not surprising that she kept it all to herself.

I was brought up in Deptford, where my parents had lived since their early years in Greenwich. Deptford had a large expatriate Irish community centred on the Catholic Church in Deptford High Street. The Irish had been there for more than a century when I was born. It was not really a ghetto because British people lived there too, but there was a distinctively Irish flavour to the place. Half the pubs were Irish and only Irish people drank in them. The other half were British and only British people drank in them. There was a natural segregation.

Looking back on those years I can see that the Irish were trying to build a small part of Ireland in Deptford. Nobody ever leaves Ireland for good. They always intend to go back one day soon, even if, like my father, they spend half a century away, or, like my mother and too many others, they never go back at all. There were Irish shops where the Irish would do their shopping even if the British shops were cheaper or closer.

The Catholic Church was an Irish Church. The parish priest and his assistants would always be Irish. There was a primary school run by the priests and nuns and the Irish sent their children there. My mother, going against the grain, would not send me to that school because, she felt, it was too rough after one of my older cousins was so badly beaten there that part of his hair went white overnight. So I went to the British primary school at Lucas Vale. When it was time to leave after I had passed the 11-Plus exam she applied for me to go to the posh Roman Catholic grammar school, St Joseph's Academy, but they would not have me because I had not gone to the Catholic primary school.

We chose Irish doctors and dentists, no matter how bad they were, just as long as they were Irish. Again my mother went against the grain by choosing a non-Irish doctor – but he was Jewish and so not really British. Dr Sidney Lindsay used to have bowls of sweets for children when our parents took us to see him. When I was just two years old, my mother bought me a blue Naval-style overcoat, complete with officer's peaked cap. Dr Lindsay called me 'captain' ever after. He was an honorary Irishman. He was also very good.

No such luck with the dentist, however. He was, indeed, Irish. I first met him when I was ten years old and had broken some teeth playing football in a practice match between the school first XI, of which I was a member, and the third XI. He patched up the broken teeth that night but he also gave me 14 fillings without an anaesthetic. Those were the days! It is unthinkable today that a ten-year-old child would be given one filling without an anaesthetic, but then it was common practice. I have been terrified of dentists ever after. But we went to him because he was Irish. That was all that mattered.

It was and is sad. The word for Ireland among the Irish of the diaspora, whether in New York, London, Sydney or Toronto, is always the same: 'Home'. Nobody says, 'I am going to Ireland this summer.' They never name the town or village or county they come from. They always use that small word. They always say: 'I'm going home this summer.'

Having passed the 11-Plus examination, I attended Brockley County Grammar School in the neighbouring suburb of Lewisham. When I was 15, in June 1965, my parents were legally separated (in those days the first legal step to a divorce, which occurred later). My mother was granted custody of me and my 13-year-old sister. I was placed in a children's home. By the end of the year, my mother had been granted a council flat in Nunhead, south-east London.

After the legal separation, my mother told me that she could not afford to keep me at school: I had to go out and get a job. I was doing very well academically. My ambition was to read for a degree at Oxford. I did not want to leave school, so I did not leave. Instead I got a job as a petrol-pump attendant at Gosnell's Service Station, Bermondsey, working at nights and at weekends. Bert Dodds, a mechanic there, got the job for me. He was the brother of Mrs Nell Savage, a friend of my mother. I was paid four shillings an hour at the start, which later rose to 5s. an hour.

My usual routine would be to get home from school at around 4.30 p.m., change, have something to eat and then get on my bicycle in time to clock on at the service station in Bermondsey at 6 p.m. The bicycle ride was 45 minutes each way. The journey to and from school was 35 minutes. We would close the service station at 11 p.m. My duties then would last another 20–30 minutes. Having clocked off, I rode through the night to get home just after midnight. I woke at seven the next morning and was at school for nine. At weekends, I worked a full shift, 3 to 11 p.m. on Saturday and 7 a.m. to 3 p.m. on Sunday. I fitted my school homework into this schedule.

I never for one moment felt deprived or put out by this life. I enjoyed it. I lived a full life at school. I captained the rugby team for two years. I held various house positions, secretary, vice-captain and captain. In my final year I was school captain.

My mother suffered a massive stroke and died on 16 May 1987. I was in Cambridge that day, trying to earn the £2,500 for a private operation to remove the cataracts which were turning her blind. I telephoned my sister's home at just after 5 p.m. My elder niece answered. She told me to wait a second and then put my father on the line. He said simply, 'Denis, your mother is dead.'

I told him that I would call him back in a little while. I put the phone down and wept, then called him and arranged to return to London immediately. My sister and her husband met me at Liverpool Street station. My sister buried herself in my arms and sobbed. We drove to her home in north Kent. When I went into the living-room, my two nieces and my nephew were sitting there with red eyes from weeping. My father got up from his armchair, collapsed in my arms and wept. His body was wracked with pain. All my life I had known him as a physically and mentally tough, hard man. I was moved. I had not expected the reaction. I knew that he and my mother had never ceased to love each other despite the separation and divorce, but I had never felt it so deeply before.

I had not been able to pay the £2,500 for the operation my mother needed to regain her sight in January 1987 when she told me for the first time that she needed one. Four months later I could not pay for her funeral. She should have been buried in the family grave in Kilroe, Kanturk. I did not have the money for that. There are three sorts of graves: the family grave like the one in Kilroe, a pauper's grave for people who have no money and no family to bury them, and a public grave where one is allocated a small piece of ground by the local authority with no regard for the wishes of the relatives. My mother received the last of these at Falconwood, Kent, where she had never been and where nobody belonging to her was buried.

The rituals and ceremonies of death are an important and powerful element of Irish culture. When a member of the community is dying somebody always remains with them so that they do not depart alone. When my grandfather, Con O'Connell, had died in his 86th year in March 1974 in Kanturk Hospital, his nephew, Danny Linehan, had sat with him. At three in the morning, my grandfather had awoken and, seeing Danny there by the side of the bed, had said, 'Danny, I'm going now. Good luck and God bless!'

As they shook hands, Danny had replied, 'Good luck and God bless, Con!' Thereupon my grandfather had died.

After death, the remains are never left alone. When the undertakers have done their duties, the remains are returned to the family and are put in the best room in the house, with the coffin open. Somebody is with the body at all times from the moment it is brought to the house till the time comes for burial. It is our way. It is the way we have lived and died in our land for some 3000 years.

This did not happen with my mother. I could not pay to have her sent back to Kanturk as she was entitled to be. Instead she was buried in an unknown cemetery. The local authority, like all bureaucracies, paid no heed to human needs and desires. It was three weeks before they allowed my mother to be buried. The night before the funeral, I was in my father's house. I broke down and wept uncontrollably. I feared that I should make a show of myself the next day at the funeral.

I did not do so. A very kind and gentle English Catholic priest said prayers with a small group of close family around before the coffin was closed. Then at the graveside he said more prayers. I gave the gravedigger ten pounds. He was Irish and I was grateful for that. My sister gave the priest the same amount. It is an interesting view on our different priorities.

In Kanturk, the coffin would have been carried to the grave – 'shouldered' – by male members of the family. In Falconwood this did not happen. It was painful. Nothing in my life had prepared me for the pain of my mother's sudden death.

I felt such shame and humiliation that I had not been able to take mother back to Kanturk as I should have done. But with the unbelievable pain came hatred. It is glibly said often enough that hatred and pain are two sides of the same coin. No, they are not. They are two quite different states of mind. More than three years after I had landed at London Airport from Washington I felt hatred for those on both sides of the Atlantic whose misconduct had deprived me of the means to give my mother a proper Irish funeral in her own land among her own ancestors. The Lord God Almighty may forgive and forget. I won't.

My father returned to Ireland in 1999 after 58 years away. He had started his working life aged twelve, indentured to a farmer as a labourer. In London he had been employed as a construction worker, acquiring the trade of plasterer. He had to give up work after two major operations on his spine in 1978. He died in Kanturk in May 2007 before this book was published. For both my parents their final memories were of a son destroyed.

It was into this Irish consciousness that I was born.

I do not hate Britain and the British. I never have. For the first almost nineteen years of my life, I had no difficulty with the idea that I held dual nationality, that I was both Irish and British. In the long summer holidays in Kanturk my friends would be my Irish cousins and neighbours. The rest of the year, most of my friends were English. When I became older, in Kanturk I would go dancing to showbands in the local dance-halls at the weekend and have the occasional summer romance.

In London, all the girlfriends I had were English. My all-boys' grammar school would team up with an all-girls' grammar school a few miles away. We would get together for the annual school play and to go around local public houses singing carols at Christmas. The girls were lovely and I have fond memories of them.

Despite not infrequently being called an Irish bastard, often by friends, I was never conscious of being hated. My religion made me slightly different because my own faith, in those days of the old Roman religion, forbade me to attend the daily Anglican morning service or the religious education classes. But we London Irish were joined in this by the sons of Poles who had come to Britain during World War II and by Jewish boys.

I do remember I was irritated by the master who ran the school rugby first XV shouting at me from the sidelines: 'Come on, Lehane, where's your Irish spirit!' because being singled out embarrassed me. It was not racism, but it was not helpful. Anyway, that master's surname was Kelleher, so racism would have been a bit difficult to prove.

It is true that when Ireland played England at rugby there was never any question but that I would support Ireland, but that did not seem odd to me. Protestants in Northern Ireland, fanatically committed to the Union, would do the same. To me it was no different from the sons of people born in Wales and Scotland supporting those teams when they played England.

Between 1966 and 1968, as well as playing rugby regularly in my school first XV, I also played for the old boys' teams in the school holidays. The teams would travel all over north-west Kent for away games, and my older colleagues were happy to sing the Irish rebel songs I taught them as the coach returned through the beautiful Kent countryside.

Thus it was, in those more innocent times, that the raucous, south-London accents of a coachload of rugby players could be heard singing refrains such as –

> 'And we're off to Dublin in the green, in the green,
> Where the helmets glisten in the sun,
> Where the bayonets flash and the rifles crash
> To the echo of a Thompson gun!'

But with the start of the unrest in Northern Ireland, singing rebel songs soon became impossible. The conflicting Irish and British loyalties inside me had not been noticeable before. Now that internal conflict grew more troublesome, as it did with most Irish people born in Britain.

Ireland and Britain have been at war – often bloody, terrible war – for mor e than eight centuries, during most of which Britain has denied that the Irish as a nation actually exist and has tried to stamp out our ancient religion.

Despite this war and the terrible things each side has done to the other, Britain is Ireland's closest neighbour. The British and Irish people, personally and as nations, get on together. In January 2008, almost 80,000 people packed into the largest sporting stadium in Europe, Croke Park – hitherto a bastion of the anti-British Gaelic Athletic Association – and cheered the playing of Britain's national anthem before a rugby match between Ireland and England.

Long ago, I heard an Irish rugby international explain on television that the Irish team much preferred to beat Wales because, in defeat, the English are so sporting, full of praise for their victors even when the victory was a fluke, whereas in defeat the Welsh were always bitter and twisted, which pleased their Irish victors no end.

The Prince of Wales has visited Ireland. He has had a guided tour of St Andrew's Resource Centre in Pearse Street, Dublin, where I wrote this book. And, yes, he did ask people there, 'And what do you do?' The Princess Royal has visited Ireland many times. Her Majesty Queen Elizabeth, it is strongly rumoured, will make a state visit here in 2009. All but a few crazies, who will be dealt with by the authorities, will applaud her visit.

I live in a traditional inner-city docklands community called 'Monto'. The name comes from Montgomery Street which, in the late nineteenth century, had the highest concentration of brothels in the British Empire. It features in James Joyce's *Ulysses* as 'Nighttown'. It is said that the then Duke of York, later George V, used to visit Montgomery Street when he was a young naval officer on leave in Dublin.

The brothels have gone and the street has been renamed Foley Street, and it may be that the story about Queen Elizabeth's grandfather is a myth. What is true, however, as anybody who has read Harold Nicholson's biography of George V knows, is that he had a lifelong love of Ireland and the Irish north and south, Catholic, Protestant and Dissenter. Moreover, he exercised a decisive influence on Lloyd George and Churchill to make them agree to the independence Ireland gained in 1922. His granddaughter will receive a genuine *ceud mile failte* from the Irish people when she visits Ireland this year.

The Queen's proposed state visit here will serve to underline that the Irish and the English, despite all that has happened between them, are naturally and happily friends.

My English birth, under the law as it then was, made me a citizen of the United Kingdom. My Irish parentage made me a citizen of the Irish Republic. In 1968 my mother got me a British passport so that I could visit Canada, but in 1970, when I was an adult, I obtained an Irish passport. The horror started by MI5 in the 1970s, and the sudden death of my mother in May 1987, led me to send back my British passport. One can only have a single loyalty.

The truth at the core of my identity is that I am Irish. In June 1815 the people of Duhallow were praying for a victory for Napoleon at Waterloo. That a large part of that British army was Irish, including the North Cork Militia of my ancestors, and that its commander was as Irish as any of them, even though he always protested that he was English, only heightens the inherent complexity of relations between the two peoples.

Three of my great-uncles fought, and one was killed, in the British army in the First World War. There was no conscription in Ireland and all three volunteered because Ireland's then unchallenged political leader, John Redmond, promised them that their service would secure Home Rule for Ireland.

Home Rule was due to become law later in 1914, but was postponed till the end of the First World War. It was not delivered when the war ended. Redmond's political career, and the cause of constitutional nationalism, was destroyed. It was a tragedy for Britain and Ireland, as was the war of independence and its consequence, the civil war.

My political antipathy towards British policy in Ireland does not make me hate the country where I was born and reared. I like and admire Britain and the British. Shakespeare is my favourite poet and playwright. I still follow the fortunes of Millwall Football Club and listen to Sports Report on BBC Radio, as I have done all my life at 5 p.m. each Saturday. I miss cask-conditioned, hand-pulled English bitter. I miss the Oxfordshire, Kent and Sussex countryside. I miss small, quiet village pubs where one can get excellent Sunday lunches for a reasonable sum.

Because of who and what I am, I cannot accept that six of Ireland's counties continue to be part of the United Kingdom, any more than the British people living in the rest of the country would accept the secession of Cornwall, Devon, Somerset, Dorset and Wiltshire to the Irish Republic or France.

There is no dispute among the vast mass of the Irish people, apart from the Unionists, that Ireland should be reunited within the Irish Republic. The only dispute is about means. My political views may seem extreme in Britain, but they are mainstream in Ireland.

6

A Speech and its Consequences

'There are three peoples in the world who are mad for freedom: the Poles, the Afghans and the Irish.'

GERMAN CHANCELLOR HELMUT KOHL
interviewed by the *Irish Times*

I got my place at Oxford University.

By no stretch of the imagination was I a self-made man. Nobody ever is. We all need other people to help us along the road of life. At every stage, I had been assisted by other people and forces quite outside my control. Had Bert Dodds not helped me, I should not have got the job at the petrol pumps and I might well have had to leave school. He did, so I didn't.

In Britain at that point there existed a well-established programme whereby the children of the poor and working classes could, on academic merit alone, without money, go to the finest university in the world. The programme was established by the 1944 Education Act. Without it, I could not have gone to any university, let alone Oxford. Today, I should not have been able to do so because successive governments, Tory and Socialist alike, have abolished the programme.

In Fleet Street, as in the rest of Britain, the indefensible terrorist war in the North of Ireland, which the Provisionals had increasingly brought into Britain itself, had created an inevitable polarisation. The British people and many, perhaps most, British journalists had come to see all Irish people as thick, ignorant Provo bombers.

Tens of thousands of ordinary Irish people who had no connection with the Provos had since 1975 been held without trial or access to a solicitor for seven days while the British Special Branch police worked them over, all quite legally, under the Prevention of Terrorism Act 1975. As an anti-terrorist measure it was useless. As a means of alienating ordinary Irish people from their British neighbours, it was very effective.

I had never had any sympathy for the obscene tactics of the Provisionals. But, like the majority of Irish people, I believe in their goal – a united, independent, 32-county Irish Republic. All but a handful of British people want Britain to leave Ireland but, while their troops are engaged against Irish terrorists there, all British people are passionately patriotic on their behalf. Who can blame them? I don't. The British are right to support their troops wherever they are fighting.

The middle of August 1969 was to become the defining point of my life, as it was for many, many other Irish people. The government of the Irish Republic mobilised the entire army and reserves – some 32,000 well-equipped and well-trained soldiers – and sent them to the border. The British had a few thousand garrison troops, not deployed to resist the army had it crossed the border and resumed control of the separated Six Counties.

Northern Irish Protestants in the uniforms of the British Queen had been attacking Catholics, including children, as they had many times before. This time, the government of Ireland said it had had enough. The Taoiseach, John Mary Lynch, made a speech explaining the decision to mobilise our forces and send them to the border. Deputy Lynch was widely – and erroneously – reported to have said, 'We cannot stand idly by.'

It was electrifying. Every Irishman, Catholic, Protestant and Dissenter, knew (or thought he knew) what Deputy Lynch meant. Most Irish people thought the army was going to be sent into Northern Ireland to take control of the Six Counties: that Ireland was going to war with Britain to expel her finally from our land.

I was under no illusions. Although there were relatively few British troops there, I knew that Britain would not accept a *fait accompli* and that it would rapidly send more troops in. That, in short, Britain would fight. But I was excited as the thought of going to war makes young men excited. I assumed the Irish army would be in Belfast and Derry by dawn the next day, that a general call for volunteers would be issued and that the final chapter in the long Anglo-Irish war was at hand.

I made hurried plans to travel from London via Paris to Kanturk so that I could volunteer. I believed it was my duty to do so. I expected that my friends and relatives of fighting age would get together in Kanturk and go to Cork City to enlist. I knew the British would fight – that is what they do, and they do it well – but I believed our army would win the war. I did not expect to survive. I was 19. I had two fears. My first fear was that, when the fighting came, I should discover that I could not cope with it, that I should prove to be a coward. Secondly, I feared that I should be killed in some remote corner. I wanted to die in the final charge up Stormont Hill which took that Unionist cathedral and then blew it into little pieces.

Three years later in Belfast, I learned the answer to my first fear. The second was never put to the test. Lynch did not send the army into Northern Ireland. Instead, Britain sent in thousands of its own troops to regain control of the situation lost by the local Unionist government.

More than a decade later, when I was a journalist, I learned that, had the Irish army crossed the border in August 1969, there would have been no war because it would have done so with the agreement of the British government.

The then Labour Prime Minister, Harold Wilson, had long been a supporter of a united Ireland and, like the bulk of British politicians of all parties, had detested the Ulster Unionists. When the violence broke out that August, he had told Lynch that, since the Irish army was well equipped and well trained, with a reputation for acting as peacekeepers in world trouble spots for the United Nations, Britain would acquiesce in its presence in Northern Ireland under UN auspices as the nearest appropriate military force, to separate the warring communities. 'Once there,' Wilson told Lynch, 'you will never leave and a united Ireland will come about in due course.'

The Irish Cabinet debated this offer till late in the night. It voted to reject it by nine votes to seven, with Lynch in the majority. The decisive factor was the conclusion that it would be impossible to coerce the million Protestant Unionists who hated the very idea of a united Ireland ruled from Dublin.

Among the minority who had been in favour of accepting Wilson's offer was Charles J. Haughey, a young and ambitious politician. He was disgusted by Lynch's refusal to accept the invitation to 'liberate' Northern Ireland. In the months that followed, Haughey and others collected some £100,000 with which they purchased arms and ammunition to found the Provisional IRA.

None of this was known to the ordinary Irish person at the time. Lynch's speech gave the clear impression that the Irish army was going into Northern Ireland and everybody held their breath or, like me, made preparations to get to Ireland. But nothing happened. The Irish army stayed south of the border.

Today, almost 40 years later, I look back to that time and I am amazed at what happened and how people, myself included, reacted to events.

I returned to Oxford University in October for my second year there. I did not feel any different from how I had been before the eruption of violence in Belfast and Derry. My automatic assumption that I would enlist in the Irish army, had it crossed the border as Lynch indicated it would do, was no more strange to me than the idea of an Englishman joining up if the Soviet Union had landed forces in Britain. Indeed, if that had occurred I should almost certainly have joined up myself.

I stand for the independent free Irish state of 32 counties, with a president and parliament elected by universal suffrage, where Protestant, Catholic and Dissenter can live in peace and prosperity together. That makes me in Irish politics a Blueshirt. The term is derived from the civil war which erupted immediately upon the departure of the British from most of Ireland in 1922. The native Irish government was attacked by dissidents who refused to accept the 1921 Anglo-Irish Treaty. The dissidents were defeated.

A decade later the political representatives of those who had lost the civil war won a general election and formed the government. A large section of those who had between 1922 and 1932 been the government and had defeated the dissidents in the civil war organised themselves into a military grouping which, for a time, was subsumed within the main opposition political party.

Its members wore blue shirts. The organisation was closed down after just over a year in existence and the political party with which it had been united resumed its independence, but the tag has stuck in Irish politics. It describes those of a deeply conservative, usually agrarian and rural philosophy, represented during the civil war by Presidents Griffith and Cosgrave and Generals Collins, Mulcahy, Dalton and O'Duffy.

I accept such a label. I fear God, love my country and keep my word. I do not accept that any county, or group of counties or lump of the country, can secede from the *Saorstat*, the indivisible Republic of Ireland. Because of sweeping demographic changes in Northern Ireland, today there is probably a bare majority of Catholics. In years to come, the majority will increase and, after a constitutional referendum in Northern Ireland, partition will be ended and an independent, united Ireland will be re-established. The long quarrel with Britain will be over.

At least four fifths of the Irish people (all except the Northern Unionists) and every Dublin government of every political hue here since the first modern administration established in January 1919, believe exactly the same as I do. Politically, on the national issue, I am in the mainstream.

On Thursday, 9 March 1970, I made a major speech at the Oxford Union on Northern Ireland. They all laughed at me. Some 800 of Britain's future leaders simultaneously burst out laughing a second after I ended the speech and sat down. It was the most humiliating experience.

I had finished the speech with a quotation from Commandant-General Padraig Pearse, Commander-in-Chief of the Irish Volunteers (*Oglaigh na hEireann* in Irish) during the 1916 Easter Rising in Dublin. The quotation was from a speech Pearse had made in Dublin in 1912 about Home Rule, when it seemed that Britain's political leaders were yet again going to renege on their promises to the Irish people: 'If we are cheated again by the foreigner, there will be war in Ireland.'

Pearse used the terms 'the *gall*' and 'red war' in his speech. I translated 'the *gall*' into 'foreigner' because nobody in the chamber would have understood the meaning of the quotation without it, and omitted the 'red' because of the tenor of the chamber, which had become heated and volatile.

I had torn up my prepared speech after Viscount Lewisham had got them all cheering and stamping their feet with an inane (and insane) speech attacking 'the infernal power of the Roman Catholic Church', and nonsense like that.

I was on next. The speech I had prepared was completely useless in the atmosphere that had been created by his lordship's greatly appreciated rhetoric. So I tore it up, stood up and spoke off the cuff. I told the assembled future leaders of Britain the truth about Northern Ireland. I told it like it was. I stood up in my borrowed dinner-jacket and said simply that my home was in North Cork, that partition, not civil rights, was the issue at stake in the north of my country and that, unless partition was undone very quickly, unless Britain withdrew from Northern Ireland and a free and independent 32-county Ireland was established, there would be a new IRA war in which thousands would die and tens of thousands would be wounded. I quoted Pearse and sat down.

There was a brief moment's silence and then they all burst out laughing. Not muffled titters either: it was thigh-slapping stuff. It lasted for about five minutes until the Union President got them to shut up by calling for 'Order' over and over again like the Speaker of the British House of Commons. I felt horrible. It took all the courage I could muster not to run out of that chamber when they were all laughing and jeering at me. For days, if not weeks, I was deeply embarrassed just to walk around the town of Oxford, in the belief that people would point me out and laugh at me.

It was my own fault, really, I suppose. After Lynch had decided – wrongly, in my view – not to send the army into the North in August the previous year, there was nothing for me to do. There-fore I went on a trip overland to Turkey, as I had intended before the August crisis had erupted. The incoming President of the Union was Gyles Brandreth. On my way back, in September, from the Greek fishing village of Kavala, I wrote to him asking for a debate on Northern Ireland when we returned.

Brandreth would later enjoy a successful career as a television personality, as well as an undistinguished political career as a Tory MP, brutally terminated in the 1997 New Labour landslide. In September 1969 that was all ahead of him. He turned me down. He said he saw no reason for a debate on the North of Ireland. When we all returned to the university in October, I made a total – and very public – nuisance of myself each Thursday night at the Union about the issue. Each week I tried to get that week's debate adjourned so that we could discuss Northern Ireland. Each week Brandreth would squash me. He did so for the same reason they all laughed at me the following March: the Northern Ireland problem had been solved and was not on the front pages or anywhere else in the papers. The abiding image in British consciousness was of British Tommies in full battledress getting tea and sandwiches from adoring Catholic matrons in Belfast's Falls Road and Derry's Bogside in August 1969. Northern Ireland wasn't an issue any more. It was over. All solved.

The following term the new President of the Union, Guy Harkin, gave me my debate on the motion 'This House believes that the best interests of Northern Ireland would be served by supporting the Unionist Party.'

I opposed the motion. The Oxford University student newspaper, *Cherwell*, of which I was Features Editor that term, wrote of my speech: 'Denis Lehane (Pembroke) broke the time-honoured conventions of the Society with his patent sincerity, although his delivery was palsied.'

That was all it said of my speech. I was a joke. I have often wondered, as the years have passed and the deaths have mounted up to more than 3500, and the wounded to at least ten times that many, more than justifying my prediction, how many of those who laughed that night were to have a relative – a father, brother or husband, or a son then unborn, in the British army or administration – killed or wounded in that war I had predicted that night and which they had all found so thigh-slappingly funny.

One of the undergraduate speakers proposing the motion that night, Clive Stitt, was from Pembroke College, too. He was a Protestant Unionist from the North of Ireland. He was in his final year, one year ahead of me. In the four and a half terms that we had been members of the same college (which had in round terms about 300 members in residence) we had never spoken to each other until that night.

We had had a cursory conversation before the debate. In the debate, Stitt spoke immediately after me. Picking up from what I had said, he said that partition had been a terrible mistake and should never have happened. What a strange thing for a Protestant Unionist to say! His British upper-class public-school listeners had no idea what he was talking about. I did. It is, and remains, curious that Stitt should have said such a thing, because in 1921 the only practical alternative to partition had been for all of Ireland to be given independence, which is the antithesis of the Unionist position which Stitt advocated that night.

What could it mean? A Protestant Unionist that night in March 1970 stating unequivocally that there should have been a united independent Ireland in 1921? That is what he said, at any rate. His 800 listeners did not understand him. They had not understood me. We understood each other, though, Stitt and I. I always felt sorry for him after that night. He wanted partition no more than I did. He did not want to be part of Britain. He wanted to be what I had been ever since my birth – a citizen of a free Irish state. There were plenty of British Intelligence supporters at the formal dinner before the debate. I recall an exchange with one of them at that dinner. We had been discussing the mobilisation of the army by Prime Minister Lynch in August and I had quite naturally said that his decision not to invade the occupied North had been wrong.

'Our troops would have thrown your army back at the border,' I was told.

'You didn't have any troops on the border,' I replied.

The reality is that we had 32,000 troops and they had a few thousand garrison troops spread all over the North. The man was talking tosh. I knew it. He did not. 'Twas ever thus with John Bull.

MI5 was responsible for the North of Ireland. It had come to the same conclusion about an imminent and terrible war that I had expressed that night. But it was supposed to be a secret. MI5 was very interested in what it had heard about my speech. It wondered why I held such views. MI5 knew that the Provisional IRA had been founded at Christmas 1969, just over two months before my speech, after a split in the 'Irish Republican Army', a terrorist organisation. In August 1969, the Catholic, nationalist population in the North were defenceless in the face of rampaging Protestant mobs given tacit or open support by the local police. Only the sudden intrusion of regular British troops had saved the Catholics from massacre.

Years before, this self-styled 'IRA' had come under the control of Marxists who wanted a political solution to partition and who had sold all the gang's weapons in 1966 to the 'Free Wales Army'. Over several days at Christmas 1969 at a secret meeting, the Northern elements had argued vigorously for a return to violent action. They had lost out and seceded. Thereafter, the majority at that meeting became known as the Official IRA and the seceders as the Provisional IRA.

The Provisionals were committed to launching just such a war as I predicted that night. Behind them were powerful government politicians in the South, led by Charles J. Haughey, who immediately raised £100,000 to buy weapons to send north to the new Provisionals, the creation of which they had instigated. But all of this was unknown outside the Provisionals, the Dublin politicians and British Intelligence.

However, I should later learn that, after my activities at the Oxford Union since October 1969 and my speech of 9 March 1970, MI5 had wondered whether I might be one of the new Provisional IRA. What stupidity! If I were a Provo, the last thing I should have been doing was to draw attention to myself in such a public way for seven months.

MI5 were not the only ones who had heard about my speech. So had one of my tutors, Dr Paul Hayes of Keble College. I was attending weekly tutorials with Dr Hayes. I knew him well. He was 'a character'. I had had dinner with him. His field was twentieth-century politics, and his particular interest was in Benito Mussolini and Italian Fascism. He was a young don in his thirties who had been active in undergraduate Conservative politics. He was on the right wing of the party.

His surname, Hayes, is Irish and betrays connections to my own southern province of Munster, if not County Cork itself. I have Hayeses in my own close family in Kanturk. The blood coursing through Dr Hayes' veins was as likely as not as Irish as mine. When I went to see Dr Hayes for my regular tutorial the week following the Oxford Union debate on Northern Ireland, he had that week's issue of *Cherwell* ostentatiously open in front of him. He was assiduously reading it, when I entered his room. I was supposed to conclude that he had been reading about my speech before my arrival. Yet the report of my speech was barely three lines and made no reference to any substantive thing I had said. Nevertheless, Dr Hayes spent a large part of my hour-long tutorial questioning me about my speech. And he knew everything that I had said. He had certainly not got it from *Cherwell*. How did I know about this new war about to erupt in the North of Ireland, Dr Hayes asked me? I'd made it up, I replied. He asked whether I knew any of the people who were going to wage this new war. 'No,' I replied.

I have discussed this 'tutorial' and the speech that had provoked it with other Irish people many times over the years. I recall the response of one young lady I told it to in October 1987. 'But you said only what any Irish person could have said that night. It was obvious what was going to happen!'

Not to those who heard my speech, it wasn't. Or to MI5. My listeners thought I was laughably mad. MI5 thought I was part and parcel of the events then taking place to set up the Provisional IRA. At that time, I had no reason to believe that I should ever live in Belfast, let alone that just over two years later I should get a job as a journalist there and spend more than two years reporting on 'the Troubles' at the most intensive period of the terrorist war. Had I had any intention of going to Belfast, I should certainly have kept my gob shut that night and should not have made such a nuisance of myself in the preceding seven months.

The Oxford Union is a famous debating society with a long and distinguished reputation for debating serious issues of contemporary significance. My country was about to fall into a blood-filled tragedy and I wanted to tell my fellow-undergraduates the truth of what was going on in what under international law was part of their country.

I cannot stress often enough that my views on the North of Ireland are indistinguishable from those of the vast majority of Irish people. The Irish people don't want partition. They don't want Britain to rule in any part of Ireland. The upper-class children who laughed at me that night in March 1970 were wrong to laugh. I got it right. I did not advocate a 'new IRA war' in Northern Ireland that night. I predicted one. There is a big difference.

What I said clearly was that unless the British government addressed partition, the only issue that had existed in Ireland since 1921, there would be war. As the report in *Cherwell* said, I spoke with sincerity. I meant what I said. I had the right to do that. But the head-bangers in MI5, including Paul Hayes, whom I could almost have called a friend, decided to label me as a probable self-styled 'Provisional IRA' terrorist.

That is when it all started. The MI5 file, a summary of which was to be sent to CIA headquarters in 1983 on my arrival at Georgetown, and from there to Goodman, was opened then after my speech at the Oxford Union predicting a war which indeed broke out scant months later.

Apparently, British Intelligence was not the only significant listener to my speech that night. A young American Rhodes Scholar, William Clinton, may well have been in the chamber that night. Clinton was at Oxford between October 1968 and June 1970. He has repeatedly stated that it was by attending debates at the Oxford Union in these years that he first became interested in the problems of Northern Ireland.

For some time at least, he stayed in a house with one of the other speakers that night, Christopher Hitchens of Balliol. But Hitchens, the leading light of the Oxford Revolutionary Socialist Students at the time, put forward a classic Marxist solution to the problem, and that was his only appearance there on that subject. I was the one who had been causing all the trouble since the previous October and had already appeared at one debate. What, I wonder, did Clinton say to himself when my speech ended: 'Why are all these people laughing so loudly at this man, and why does he seem so convinced that he is right and they are wrong?'

It is strange to think that that speech by a 20-year-old undergraduate not only led to the complete destruction of that undergraduate's life 14 years later but also may have introduced the US President who played so crucial a part in the 1998 Belfast Agreement to the Irish question.

Without me at Oxford, there would have been no debates at the Oxford Union on Northern Ireland for the young Bill Clinton to attend.

7

Belfast

'You are prepared to betray your country to foreign powers?'
'Yes.'

from *Nineteen Eighty-Four*, GEORGE ORWELL

I turned up in Belfast just over two years after my speech at the Oxford Union. I had worked on the student newspaper *Cherwell* as an undergraduate, and when the time came to leave the university in the summer of 1971, I had decided to pursue a career in journalism. I had got a good degree and could have stayed on, or gone elsewhere, to pursue my studies with a view to a career as an academic but the idea never appealed to me. I wanted to get out into the real world.

In 1971 a major British newspaper, the *Daily Sketch*, had folded and as a consequence the journalists' union, the National Union of Journalists, had leant on the other newspapers not to recruit graduates to their trainee schemes that year. Even the Reuters news agency was constrained to cut back on the numbers of graduates it recruited and, instead, to employ journalists who had lost their jobs on the *Daily Sketch*. There were not many trainee schemes for graduates anyway. As a result, the competition was fierce. Each of the few schemes available attracted up to 1000 applicants.

Thomson Newspapers, which then owned *The Times* and the *Sunday Times* plus many regional daily newspapers, did not recruit any graduate trainees in journalism that year. My ambition centred on the *Sunday Times*, which, at that time, five years after the appointment of Harry Evans, had become the most exciting and innovative newspaper in the English language. This, therefore, was a blow.

I applied for the Reuters' graduate trainee scheme and got a long way in the application process. The interviews had taken place in December 1970 and January 1971 and other students I knew who had applied received their rejections shortly after that. I was told that Reuters could not give me a definite answer until they had agreed a figure of trainees for that year with the National Union of Journalists. The agreement, when it came, was for eight trainees as opposed to the usual 16. After that agreement had been sealed, in June 1971 I got my rejection. As a result, I worked initially for a weekly property newspaper, *Estates Times*, but my ambitions lay in serious national newspaper journalism.

Early in 1972 I applied to Thomson Newspapers for a place on their graduate trainee scheme. In 1970, the scheme had recruited 16 graduates, in 1971 none. In 1972 it had eight places on offer. About 800 graduates applied. The way the scheme worked was that those on the first shortlist, based on the application alone, were seen by the personnel director at Thomson House in the Gray's Inn Road, home of *The Times* and the *Sunday Times*. If one passed that interview, one was allocated to one of the Thomson Group's regional daily newspapers for the second interview, more or less at random for almost all the applicants.

The NUJ had an agreement with the national newspapers by which graduates were not allowed to work on national newspapers until they had spent at least two years on non-Fleet Street newspapers, which meant the provincial dailies and the London weeklies. My Gray's Inn Road interview was with the head of personnel for Thomson Newspapers, Arthur Wenburn. At that interview he asked me if I should be interested in going to the group's Belfast newspaper, the *Belfast Telegraph*, an evening newspaper and the only such evening newspaper in Northern Ireland. I said I should be very interested. I received an interview there in April 1972. I got the place on the scheme.

The *Belfast Telegraph* took two graduates that year, a British Protestant and me. Traditionally a Unionist newspaper, the *Belfast Telegraph* was publicly committed to equal opportunities for Protestants and Catholics, a key issue in the conflict in Northern Ireland after more than 50 years of pro-Protestant sectarian bias in employment, as in public housing. By choosing me, an Irish Catholic, along with a British Protestant, the newspaper fulfilled its obligations under the principle of equal opportunities for

Catholics and Protestants. I doubt very much whether there were any other Irish Catholics on that final short list. I was the beneficiary of positive discrimination.

I know that at least one graduate who was short-listed for Belfast, Sally Anne Thomas, would have rejected the offer if it had been made. I had known Sally Anne at Oxford and I met her at Belfast's Aldergrove Airport after my interview. The planes had been delayed. Sally Anne had had an interview about an hour or so before me. We had a few drinks in the bar. Sally Anne had not liked Belfast, with its heavily-armed British soldiers and police saturating the city centre, where the *Belfast Telegraph*'s offices were behind 'a ring-of-steel' fence with soldiers body-searching everyone who passed through.

She told me she had already been offered a place on the BBC graduate scheme and had decided, after seeing what Belfast was like, to take that. She had no wish ever to return to Belfast again. I, on the other hand, did want the job. As well as being in Ireland, Belfast was at that time one of the major news stories in the world. On the other Thomson regional newspapers, the successful graduates would spend their time covering flower shows and small-time town-council meetings. In Belfast I should be catapulted into major journalism at once.

I met Martin Dillon at the *Belfast Telegraph*. Martin was one of the few Catholics on the editorial staff. We became friends. At that time there was a phenomenon called 'apparently motiveless murders'. These seemed to crop up almost every day. Martin and I got together to investigate them in our own time. Our intention was to produce a series of articles for the *Belfast Telegraph*. One thing that prompted me was the routine of the *Belfast Telegraph*'s reporters when talking to the police press office about each murder as it occurred. At that point the only terrorist groups known positively to be operating in Northern Ireland were the so-called Official and Provisional IRAs. After each body was found, the *Belfast Telegraph* reporters would routinely ask the police press office if it believed the murder had been committed by either of the self-styled IRAs. The reply would invariably be, 'We are keeping an open mind on that.'

This gave the impression, when printed in the newspaper, that the killings could have been the work of republican terrorists. As the victims were invariably Catholic and equally invariably were found dumped deep inside the Protestant heartlands of the Shankill Road and East Belfast, such a theory was implausible.

Martin and I investigated the murders. By early 1973 we had produced a series of articles for publication in the *Belfast Telegraph* which showed that some 150 'apparently motiveless murders' during the previous three years had been committed by Protestant loyalist terrorists, principally the paramilitary Ulster Defence Association, which had invented a non-existent cover as the Ulster Freedom Fighters. They had launched what they regarded as a retaliatory campaign against the Catholic community in Belfast. The loyalist terror groups had conceived a strategy of killing Catholics as a way of hitting back at the two self-styled IRAs.

The *Belfast Telegraph* refused to publish the articles. I sent them to Penguin Books in London. One of its senior editors, Neil Middleton, flew over to Belfast to see us and commissioned us to write a Penguin Special about the loyalist murder campaign. For various reasons, Martin did not contribute to the writing of the book. I did it all. But we had both worked equally hard on the research and there was never any question that Martin's name should not be on the book. I worked on the book quickly. It took me a little over three months. It was called *Political Murder in Northern Ireland*. It was published with huge publicity in October 1973.

The book caused a sensation. Immediately after publication the head of the Catholic Church in Ireland, Cardinal William Conway, Archbishop of Armagh, publicly referring to *Political Murder*, called on the British government to ban the Ulster Freedom Fighters and a smaller loyalist terror group, the Red Hand Commando. The government banned both.

Political Murder made my reputation as an investigative journalist. I was nominally a trainee journalist but I had broken the biggest news story in Northern Ireland. During the previous three years of terrible self-styled IRA violence, there had been much talk of a possible 'Protestant backlash'. *Political Murder in Northern Ireland* showed that such a Protestant backlash, far from being a hypothetical future possibility, had been in operation since 1970. Never again would the *Belfast Telegraph* write that the police were keeping 'an open mind' as to whether the self-styled IRA had murdered a Catholic and dumped his body deep in enemy Protestant territory.

After the publication of *Political Murder,* what I saw as a ham-fisted attempt to recruit me by the British was made via Martin Dillon. At least they did not threaten to murder me. Instead, Martin kept inviting me for drinks with British couples whom I did not know and had no wish to know. Once a British doctor at the Belfast City Hospital gave me a great deal to drink and then tried to get me to disclose information about terrorist activities that he seemed to think I knew. After the meeting somebody I knew looked up this man's personnel file at the hospital. It had a single sheet of paper in it, saying that the doctor was 'a serving officer in the British army and his personnel details are at the Musgrave Park Military Hospital'.

Martin Dillon also took me for drinks at the home of Colin Baker. Martin said that Colin, an Englishman then in his thirties who was a news reporter for Ulster Television, was keen to meet me. He plied me liberally with drinks, presumably to loosen my tongue. He said that, if I told him all I knew about British Intelligence activities, he would help me write a book for Penguin about the subject. He said that there were six journalists working in Belfast at that time who were assets of British Military Intelligence and that one of them I 'know very well. Very well.' My response was to ask Colin Baker why he, a reporter with UTV, should know anything significant about British Intelligence activities. I asked him about his background, but he refused point-blank to tell me anything about himself. He struck me as a typical middle-class Englishman – the sort of person who would have attended a state-funded grammar like myself or, at best, a minor fee-paying school. After we left Colin Baker's house, I asked Martin Dillon how he knew him. He said Baker had been a reporter for the then-defunct London tabloid newspaper the *Daily Sketch* in August 1969. Baker had been behaving suspiciously, according to the soon-to-be Provos in the Lower Falls Road, and had been taken prisoner. 'They were going to shoot him as a British army spy, but I persuaded Andy [a commander on the Provo 'Army Council'] to let him go.'

My reply to that was, 'Well, Martin, there's your answer! What on earth are you palling around with him for?' There was no answer to that. I told Colin Baker it would be difficult to trust him as a co-author if I knew nothing about him. He said, 'Never mind all that,' and repeated his offer: if I turned over to him all that I knew about

British Intelligence activities in the North, he would help me to write the book. These are not normal conversations between complete strangers. I turned him down flat.

I had an angry and terse conversation with Martin after this. I told him that it was clear to me that he had been told by British Intelligence to introduce me to all these strangers. I told him that the attempt to get me involved with British Intelligence was absurd, that I wouldn't work for them, and that he was to tell the British to stop trying to woo me. I wasn't woo-able, I told him. They did not bother me thereafter.

Back home in Kanturk, about as far away from Belfast geographically as one could get, one of my aunts had asked Commandant Michael Keating, a veteran senior officer in the war-of-independence IRA who had also fought against the new government in the civil war, whether he could provide protection for me in Belfast. Michael Keating was well in his eighties when I went to Belfast. However, I learned years later that he was, indeed, involved in the new Provisionals and had sent instructions that I was to be protected in Belfast. Such an instruction from him would have been taken very seriously.

As it happened, I did get heavy-duty protection ordered by a member of the Provisional IRA's then 'Army Council', 'Old Andy' (his son was 'Young Andy'). Old Andy lived at the foot of the Catholic Falls Road. I used to visit him there once a week. Sometimes Martin Dillon would accompany me. I had been repelled by the Provisionals' so-called 'Economic War' in the North, where they planted bombs in city centres, often killing or maiming innocent civilians whether Catholic or Protestant.

I used to ask Old Andy why on earth they were doing such things and berated him for such a mindless policy. The genuine IRA of the war of independence had not done such things, I used to tell him. The old IRA had engaged in guerrilla attacks or ambushes on British military forces and had never considered bombing the heart out of Irish towns. Old Andy would sit there listening to my complaints without defending the policy. Martin Dillon once said to me, 'God, Andy thinks you're a great man! He's saying the same things to the Army Council that you say to him, but he is always overruled.'

Old Andy intervened twice in my time in Belfast to stop Provisionals killing me. The first who wanted to kill me was Martin Meehan, the Provisionals' 'Officer in Command' in the Ardoyne. The second was the Provo 'Quartermaster' in the Old Park area. After the second attempt, Old Andy said to me: 'You know I have given you complete protection in Belfast but it would be advisable not to go into Ardoyne because Meehan is very angry with you.'

Martin Meehan was angry because in *Political Murder in Northern Ireland* I had poured contempt on him for the cold-blooded murder in 1971 of three British boy soldiers, one aged 18 and two aged 17. When the Provisional campaign had hardly begun, British troops were allowed to go into Belfast bars when off-duty, because they did not fear attack. Meehan and his henchmen had spent the night drinking with these three youngsters in a Catholic bar, got them drunk and told them they would take them to a party where there would be plenty of available women. They took them out to a spot in North Belfast, where they ordered them to kneel and shot all three in the back of the head. This is not how real Irish soldiers should behave and I said so. It was an atrocity. Meehan and his henchmen were despicable.

Martin Meehan did not like my views. I despised him and all like him. He died in 2007 and was feted as 'a veteran republican'. To me, he was always a mindless killer. The Provisional IRA in my period in Belfast were a rabble. In the war of independence, the old IRA had been led by educated and able men and women. In Belfast in the 1970s those who called themselves the Official and Provisional IRAs were armies without an officer caste, or even functioning NCOs, a true working-class army with few in positions of power, such as Old Andy and Young Andy, who had the intelligence and understanding to conceive a plausible military strategy.

The strategy which the Provisionals, with their 'Economic Warfare', pursued was a non-strategy. It was founded on the absurdity that if they planted enough bombs in their own country the foreign enemy, Britain, would withdraw. During the truce between the two IRAs on the one hand and the British on the other in the summer of 1972, the Provisional leadership, such as it was, had secretly met the British Secretary of State for Northern Ireland, William Whitelaw. The Provisionals' delegation was headed by their leader, an Englishman called John Stephenson who had no Irish blood in his veins and was a mentally unbalanced Walter Mitty character:

even the Provisionals realised this eventually and expelled him from their organisation.

So bereft of leaders of true calibre had the Provisionals been in the summer of 1972 that they had to ask Willie Whitelaw to bring the 22-year-old Gerard Adams out of captivity in Long Kesh internment camp so that he could take part in the discussions. The Provisionals, led by John Stephenson, had thought they were meeting Whitelaw to discuss the terms of the British surrender to them.

They got a shock. Whitelaw told them that the British Army of the Rhine – the main concentration of British forces of some 150,000 men – lost far more servicemen to military accidents in North Germany than the Provisionals were managing to kill in Northern Ireland. Whitelaw derided them in terms not unlike those I used to use towards Old Andy.

It is almost 40 years on since those days, but the abiding contempt and distaste I had for the Provisionals then has not diminished. For me, Old Andy and Young Andy, who were magnificent Irish patriots of the same calibre as those who had fought in the war of independence, were, alas, the rare exceptions which proved the rule of Provo incompetence and mindless atrocity.

On 1 January 1974 a new devolved power-sharing government between Protestants and Catholics took effect. The Ulster Unionist Party and the nationalist Social Democratic and Labour Party governed in coalition. In the nationalist areas, and some Unionist ones, there was a feeling of hope.

One of the first decisions of the new government was to order a freeze on domestic rental properties. I had an apartment on one floor of a large old house in a posh part of south Belfast. Two Catholic nurses had apartments on the first and second floors. In February 1974, the landlord informed us that the rent would be increased the next month. I spoke to the SDLP's Austin Currie, the Housing Minister who had ordered the freeze on rents, and he said the landlord could not do this. I told the landlord and he withdrew the rent increase. The two nurses were most impressed by my access to the highest levers of power!

The terrorists of both sides were excluded from the government, unlike after the 1998 Belfast Agreement, but even so a strong, perhaps majority, element in the Unionist population rebelled at the idea of Catholics having their hands on any levers of power. This opposition all came to a head in May when the Unionists called a general strike. The strike was enforced by the UDA terrorists and was very effective. Northern Ireland was paralysed.

The British government of Prime Minister Harold Wilson lost its nerve and eventually capitulated to the strikers by ending the brief power-sharing government and imposing direct rule from London. For the last ten days of the strike, the North of Ireland had been on the brink of total anarchy and civil strife. We *Irish Independent* journalists had booked into a hotel in the city centre because we had not been able to guarantee that we could travel in to work each day because of the UDA road blocks throughout the city.

Each morning I awoke in the hotel room thinking that I might not live to see the next sunrise. It is the sort of thing young men can do without worry. As the British government sat back and did nothing to support the new Northern Ireland government, in the Catholic areas of Belfast – particularly in the Falls Road – local community leaders began to organise militiamen to defend their areas if inter-communal fighting broke out and the traditional armed loyalist mobs, backed by the heavily-armed Protestant police, attacked.

The militiamen were a wholly defensive body, supported by all community groups in Catholic areas with the one exception of the SDLP. The only bodies in Catholic areas that had the weaponry and organisation necessary for such a militia were the two IRAs. I made a decision to join the militia when the fighting began. It was no big deal. What else would I do: sit on my hands in the hotel while my friends in Belfast's Catholic nationalist areas were subject to overwhelming Protestant loyalist attack? Such an idea was absurd. When the British government surrendered to the loyalists, the need for the militia ended. Yet my willingness to join was assiduously noted on my MI5 file for the CIA's Goodman to see almost a decade later.

I had never intended to spend more than two years in Belfast before pursuing my career, perhaps with the *Sunday Times*. The collapse of the honest and honourable attempt by the main Unionist and nationalist non-violent political parties to rule Northern Ireland implied that the killings and the bombings would continue indefinitely. I was sickened by the mindlessness of it all. By 1975 I had had enough. I worked in Dublin for a few months, then got a job in Britain. I would return many times to Belfast over the following years, but whatever value I might have notionally had for British Intelligence ended when I left Belfast.

In 1977 I got a job in the elite corps of lobby journalists based at the House of Commons, where I attended press briefings at 10 Downing Street each morning with the Prime Minister's press officer. In the Palace of Westminster itself I had unrestricted access to all MPs. To get such a post I had to pass a positive vetting. Had there been anything at all on my MI5 file which indicated that I was, or had been, a terrorist, I should not have been given the job.

As Jonathan Simpson would tell me in April 1984, there was nothing on the file against me, just a lot of question marks. It was what Martin Dillon had told me. I used to visit the homes of terrorist leaders, Provisional IRA and UDA. I was regarded as politically unreliable. All this meant was that I was doing my job and the British could not rely on me to push their propaganda line. It meant, in other words, that I was a journalist who reported the truth without fear or favour at all times in all circumstances. That did not stop me passing the positive MI5 vetting for the job in the parliamentary lobby at Westminster. MI5 may not have liked me because I had refused to be recruited. But that did not make me a terrorist. It made me a good journalist. That is all.

William Corson, in an interview with Joe Trento in February 1993, identifies various individuals whom the Intelligence community hoped to protect from danger by setting me at a disadvantage. One was Vincent Browne, a journalist born in the south-west of Ireland in the early 1940s. At University College, Dublin, his political views had tended towards extreme republicanism. He had joined the *Irish Press* group, founded and owned by Eamon de Valera as an organ for his Fianna Fáil Party, and was appointed Belfast bureau chief shortly after graduating. He covered the civil rights unrest in 1968 and the outbreak of violence in August 1969.

Browne cultivated a close personal and professional relationship with David 'Daithi' O'Connell, a southern-based hard-line militarist who had been one of the key founders of the new, activist Provisional IRA in December 1969. He remained a close friend and confidant of O'Connell until the latter's death some two decades later.

It was this relationship which attracted MI5 to Browne early on. MI5 was aided by Browne's spectacular private life, minutely chronicled by the Dublin-based satirical magazine *Phoenix*.

Martin Dillon, whom William Corson calls my 'co-author', was at that time close to the Provo officer commanding the Lower Falls, 'Old Andy', who lived in the Lower Falls and was a close friend of another Belfast Provo commander and key Army Council member. 'Young Andy', his son, was leader of what the Provos called an 'Active Service Unit'.

Dillon had been a senior member of the Official IRA, which, in 1972–4, rivalled the Provos. He had told me that when he had been sent for training at a Palestinian Liberation Organisation terrorist camp in the Middle East, he had been detected by MI5, and that on his return to Belfast, 'leverage' – he would be shot dead if he declined to work for British Intelligence – had been successfully applied.

Dillon had studied to be a Catholic priest but had no other educational qualifications. He got a job as a reporter with Belfast's small-circulation Catholic morning newspaper the *Irish News*. From this position, he cultivated Old Andy.

8

Unperson

'Why would the CIA be interested in the likes of you, Denis? Look at the state of you! You are just somebody sleeping rough on the streets of Dublin. Why, in God's name, would the CIA bother with the likes of you?'

Chief Psychiatrist, Grangegorman Asylum, Dublin

In March 1981 I took a call in New York from Simon Freeman, a colleague at the *Sunday Times*. He told me that I had won a British Press Award for 1980. An excited Harry Evans, the editor, had come out of his office on the 6th floor with the official notification in his hand, saying, 'Simon, we've won seven British Press Awards. You've got one, Denis has got one . . . '

By the time they gave us the awards at a luncheon at the Savoy Hotel in April the following month, Harry had left the *Sunday Times*. Rupert Murdoch had bought both the *Sunday Times* and its sister paper, *The Times*, and Harry had been appointed to edit the latter. It was the end of an era of great investigative journalism. Harry would last barely a year at *The Times* before Murdoch fired him. He never edited a newspaper again. He moved permanently to New York, where he still lives. I had myself left the *Sunday Times* in May 1981 to join the *Daily Express*.

In October 1981 the editor of the *Daily Express*, Arthur Firth, who had hired me earlier in the year, was suddenly fired. He had hired me because his brief was to take the paper up-market and he had nobody on his staff, he told me, who was capable of writing articles longer than 1000 words. Arthur was replaced by a man from the *Daily Mirror*, whose brief was to take the paper down-market to challenge the *Mirror* and the *Sun*. That is not my sort of journalism.

I was at a watershed after Arthur Firth had been fired. I was 32. I had got a good degree at Oxford, and had then gone into journalism, where I had done very well very young. I was set up for life in the business in England if I wanted it, but I did not want it. Early in 1982 I decided also that I had no wish to continue living in England. Belfast had changed me. I had always known I was Irish, but I had never felt it so much as I had during my two years there.

I had felt revulsion at the sight of English troops on Irish streets, and had felt sick each time I witnessed the almost always fruitless but routine destruction of Irish people's homes when they were searching for weapons. I had never had any sympathy for the obscene tactics of the Provisionals but, like the majority of Irish people, I believed in their goal – a united independent 32-county Irish Republic. My dilemma was that I could not support the Provos because of their mindless terrorism, but I could not share the patriotism of the British against the Provos. It was time for me to leave Britain for good. I decided to seek a new career in international relations.

I chose programmes at three major universities. I applied for, and was accepted by, Columbia University, New York and the School of Foreign Service, Georgetown University, Washington. My application to Harvard's John F. Kennedy School of Government was pending when I accepted Georgetown. To fund my two-year studies, I had applied for and won a 1983 Harkness Fellowship from the Commonwealth Fund of New York.

The Harkness scheme was inaugurated in 1925 when it was called the Commonwealth Fund Fellowships. Its founder, Edward Harkness, wanted to foster international fellowship and understanding between young people who would, when in their middle years, be the leaders of their countries in various fields. The promotional literature which I was sent in 1982 was explicit:

As it was when Edward Harkness established the program 58 years ago, this goal is expressed in the Board of Directors' inaugural statement in 1925 that 'international understanding can be forwarded in no more practicable way than through the provision of international opportunities for education and travel to young men and women of character and ability. Such men and women, potentially leaders in their own country . . . '

The achievement of this goal requires the rigorous selection of candidates on the basis of outstanding intellectual and personal gifts, a demonstrated capacity for leadership, and receptiveness to the ideas and manners of a different society. The Fund's success in this program is demonstrated by the high esteem in which the Fellowships are held, the distinction of earlier Fellows . . .

In my time, the Harkness Fellowships aimed to rival in prestige the Rhodes Scholarships scheme that enabled bright young US postgraduates to spend two years at Oxford University. In this intention those running Harkness had lamentably failed. Joe Trento calls Harkness 'the sister program' to the Rhodes Scholarships: just as Rhodes scholars travel from the US to study in Britain, Harkness fellows travel from Britain to study in the US. Yet in prestige and importance the Harkness programme lags far behind the Rhodes Scholarships.

Allan Goodman had never heard of the Harkness Fellowships or the Commonwealth Fund of New York when I arrived at Georgetown. William Corson and Joe Trento, however, may well be correct in stating that Harkness, like the Georgetown MSFS programme, has been used by the CIA as a source of recruits. As my friend Paul Cole never ceased to say to me, Goodman is just one of 16,000 CIA employees.

Goodman asked me shortly after I arrived on his programme to provide him with the promotional literature from which I have just quoted. I gave it to him.

Goodman was very interested in the promotional literature: so interested that, a few weeks later, he travelled to New York to meet those running the Commonwealth Fund, principally its President, Margaret Mahoney, and the Director of the Harkness Fellowships scheme, Howland Sargent.

Goodman offered them three or four guaranteed places on his MSFS programme. Margaret Mahoney and Howland Sargent were very pleased with the offer. Goodman was very pleased that his offer was accepted. It met the needs of both sides. Their treatment of me put paid to that arrangement.

All students were regarded seriously as potential assets. As my own story shows, potentially valuable assets were not supposed to be able to get away. On the other hand, many MSFS students were rejected because they were not good enough to be of use to the Agency.

The Harkness Fellowships can in no way be compared to the Georgetown set-up. They were not quite as grand as their literature made out, but they were grand enough for that literature not to seem absurd.

Of course, individual Fellows may well have been 'talent-spotted' by Howland Sargent, but that happened at Oxford too. When it happened at Oxford (and I am vehemently opposed to it), it involved only a relative handful of students. The vast majority went about their lives unaware that such things went on.

In April 1984, when Professor Garretson told me I must put 'all this' behind me and get on with my life, I immediately asked him, 'How?' He replied, 'That is for you to work out.'

More than a quarter of a century later, I have yet to work it out. That brief exchange, over in a few seconds, set the scene for a life straight out of Kafka. Garretson's words assumed that my situation, as he and his confrères had created it, was not at all grave or damaging and that anybody who put their mind to it could easily and swiftly overcome the sort of minor damage I had sustained.

Minor damage? I had been sacked from my employment in the USA because I was presumed guilty of the most serious crimes of violence. Because I could not return to the USA, I could no longer live in the apartment I had rented in Arlington, Virginia. I was thus homeless as well as unemployed. I needed to find work so that I could rent somewhere to live. I could scarcely disguise the truth that I was unemployed and that my employment had ended suddenly for some reason. I should be seeking employment in the context not just that I was unemployed and homeless but also that a great many people, in both the USA and Britain, knew that allegations of multiple rape and assaults on women had been made against me and taken seriously by, among others, the police in New York and the Commonwealth Fund.

Mary Goldring told me several weeks later: 'Denis, you have known great success in your life. This is just the other side of the coin.' If I had known success when Ms Goldring first met me in 1984, that success had been based on addressing the realities of the world as it is, and not as we might want it to be. It was in that frame of mind that I addressed the realities as they then existed.

And on that basis, what had been done to me – and was not going to be undone – was devastating, not just to the life I had led before Goodman's attack, but also to my future life.

Those who had caused my problem, and those who were not going to do anything to put it right, were rich and privileged people from affluent backgrounds. They had no idea of the real world. I had lived in that real world all my life. I knew its rules. I knew its prejudices. I knew its faults and pitfalls. They did not. How could they, from their backgrounds?

Very few of us live in vast mansions situated in hectares of lush parkland, waited on hand and foot by servants. Some people do, but the rest of us live quite differently. How many of those of us who live in modest circumstances would not want to exchange them for a mansion in the country with the servants and every-thing? Most of us. But most us live where we do because it needs more than 'putting one's mind' to something to actually get that mansion in the country.

When I met Mary Goldring, she had a large townhouse in fashionable Chelsea plus a house in the country to which she repaired at weekends. They weren't the product of her starting with nothing and 'putting her mind' to it. They came from the great wealth she inherited as the only child of rich parents.

People like Mary Goldring tended to tell me to ignore what had happened. In 1987 a very important British Establishment figure, who had direct personal access to very powerful people at the very peak of the US Intelligence world, refused to help me when approached by somebody with equally impeccable Establishment credentials to rescue me. He sent me a terse note which stated: 'There are some things in life we just have to accept.'

Easy for him to say. He was not the one in the mire. In the actual world, they are many, many things that one is expected not to accept.

As the summer of 1984 ended, I had been labelled insane after 'a thorough examination' by a suitably qualified psychiatrist, the Lobotomy Man. His deputy, Dr Julian Natterjack, had been on his summer holiday when I had checked into Guy's on 4 July. He returned almost three weeks later and asked me to tell him what had happened. His manner was gentle and frank. He was the complete opposite of the Lobotomy Man. He treated me with the respect that the Lobotomy Man singularly had not. I told him what had happened. When I had finished, he told me that it was an extraordinary tale but that he had no reason not to believe me. This surprised me. I told him that his boss had found me to be insane on the basis of the same account. He said he knew this but that I should not pay too much attention to that, that had been a couple of weeks before and since then Goldring and Alex had been interviewed by Dr O'Brady and the Lobotomy Man might take a different view the next time I saw him. This, too, surprised me. I had had no indication that this might be the case. Dr Natterjack then said to me: 'As far as I am concerned, the only thing wrong with you is that you cannot accept humiliation.'

Had it been up to me alone, I certainly would have put it all behind me and got on with my life. But I failed. The evidence of this failure lay all around me for years.

At the start of the new millennium, I was fighting for my life with heart failure in hospital. Six months later, I was sleeping in a cubicle each night in a dormitory with another 100 members of the permanent underclass in a hostel for homeless men, surrounded with wire netting to prevent me getting at my neighbours and to stop them getting at me.

That I now live in a pleasant apartment in a housing-association development is largely due to the kindness of my then GP and others who nominated me for a place here.

When I landed at Heathrow on 19 April 1984, I was aged 34, unemployed and homeless. The homelessness was not of immediate concern. Various family and friends would put me up for exactly a year before I had to sleep rough in the streets. The unemployment was the devastating factor. When I had resigned from the *Daily Express* in March 1982, in round figures I had been getting £20,000 a year plus a company car. I was a well-paid senior journalist at the top of my profession. Such a journalist should not have become suddenly unemployed for no good reason. One does not walk into a senior post in journalism from the ranks of the unemployed without an explanation for being unemployed. The only explanation I had was not regarded as credible. Therefore everybody I approached chose to ignore me. For a quarter of a century I have tried and failed to find work.

Of course, my strong desire to be employed was not enough. In each application I had to state clearly and cogently my working history and my present circumstances. Nobody even replied to my applications where I told the truth as to why I came to be unemployed and homeless. I had no control over that. I became a member of the underclass – an unperson, erased from the records of the Harkness Fellowships and unable to find work in my former profession. I have remained an *Untermensch* ever since.

By April 1985, I was living in a bed-and-breakfast hotel in Blackheath, south-east London. In Ireland the local authority has a legal obligation to house all homeless persons. Not so in Britain, where social welfare will do no more than pay for homeless men to stay in bed-and-breakfast accommodation. In practice, the rates paid are far below what most bed-and-breakfast hotels charge. As a consequence, many thousands of homeless men in Britain sleep rough in the streets. There are not enough hostels for the homeless.

A homeless family had been placed in a swanky four-star hotel, the Clarendon, on Blackheath the previous week. I thought it was simple: one booked into a hotel and then asked the Social Security Department to pay the rent. Boy, did I get that wrong! I picked a hotel out of the *Yellow Pages*. I moved in, paid a week's rent with the last of my money and then merrily presented myself at the Department of Social Security at Blackheath the next morning.

I was interviewed by a young lady barely into her twenties. She screamed at me hysterically and asked me how I had dared to move into any accommodation as a homeless man without first seeking her permission. It was only then that I discovered that in law I had no entitlement to accommodation of any kind and that, even if the Department deigned to pay for me to stay in bed-and-breakfast accommodation, it would only pay a derisory rent, far below that charged by any reputable hotel, including the one I had booked into. The rates that the DHSS would pay were only accepted by flop-houses, and they were all full.

Why did that come as a surprise to me? I was 35 years old. I had not led a sheltered life. I thought that I was worldly-wise, even cynical. Yet I had blithely moved into a clean and decent bed-and-breakfast hotel believing that the social welfare people would routinely pay the bills. What was wrong with me? Surely it should have been obvious to me that if I could do that everybody else would and there would be nobody sleeping rough in the streets anywhere in Britain? What could I have been thinking?

Well, I guess that part of it was that those people sleeping rough were just qualitatively not like me: they not only deserved to be sleeping rough in the streets in a British winter but had chosen to do so rather than move into the equivalent of the nice bed-and-breakfast hotel. Subconsciously, I did not associate myself with such people. It wasn't snobbery – simply a matter of perception.

I still regarded myself as the ambitious, successful journalist I had been before a rogue CIA agent had brought my career to an end. I did not feel any different and my friends had told me that to them I did not seem any different. Yet I was different. Though I did not realise it, I was precisely the same as the men sleeping rough on the streets.

For a year I had been the recipient of charity from family and friends. Therefore I had not recognised that I was essentially no different from the man who slept in the doorway of a shop in London's Oxford Street. But the truth was that those men and I were identical: we did not have the means to keep a roof over our heads. It was a truth which came suddenly and as a shock early in 1985.

No one seemed bothered by the fact that I should thenceforth be living and sleeping on the streets. I don't really have the words to record how painful it was to learn that nobody cared enough about me to give me accommodation.

Of course, the truth is that many kind people had cared. That is why it had taken a year before I descended into the underclass and finally had to sleep rough. But at the time it did not seem that way.

During my encounter with the young bureaucrat that February morning in 1984, I learned that when the permitted housing allowance and my unemployment benefit were added together I had just enough to pay the weekly bed-and-breakfast rent at the hotel. But this meant I went hungry. I stole food, but it was not enough.

When I had met Mary Goldring for the first time in early May 1984 at her Chelsea townhouse, she had offered me money to buy clothes. All my clothes and belongings were in my apartment in Arlington, Virginia. I had declined the offer. A year later, when I had been reduced to stealing food to survive, I telephoned her and said, yes, I should like to borrow some money to buy food. She declined, on the ground that I had not 'behaved' myself.

I had never gone without food in my life before – no more than Mary Goldring had. At that time the traditional British cod and chips cost £1.40. I did not have the money for that any night of the week. If I had had seven friends who cared enough about me to invest £1.40 per week in me, I could have had a hot, nourishing meal of fish and chips each night. With the breakfast I got at the hotel as part of the rent, I should have had enough to eat.

But I did not have one friend. It was in those early months of 1985 that I learned just how limited and conditional is human friendship. Friendship had always been important to me. I had liked being a friend and having friends. Now it seemed that all that had been an illusion: that I had been living in a false dream-world where everybody else had known the rules but me. It hurt.

A decade and a half later, the Irish national newspaper *The Examiner* made it a condition of my being considered for some modestly paid casual work that I cooperate with it in publishing what had been done to me by the CIA and British Intelligence. I did not want to do it but, having first refused, I changed my mind because I was desperate for the work. To augment its own story, the paper insisted that I provide an account myself of my experiences. I wrote some 2000 words. The paper published it all except for one line: 'The definition of a man with no friends is a man who sleeps rough in the street when he would prefer not to.'

I never learned why that line had been cut out. It could not have been for lack of space. For me that was the most important line in the entire piece. A man with no friends is a man with no life worth living. And I now know that what Danny Glover tells his fellow *Untermensch* in New York City in *The Saint of Fort Washington* is true:

'All those people in their fine clothes, with their good, well-paid jobs, nice homes and cars, who go about their lives, carefully walking around us, the underclass, who they pass on their streets every day as though we don't exist on the same planet as them . . . to them, we really don't exist, we're just bums who won't go out and get a job.'

Those fine people do not know that they are no different from us. Until November 2002, when I was offered my present apartment by a Dublin housing association, I had a very few clothes, all of them second-hand, charitable gifts from people who had never met me, all of them basic and shoddy. I slept each night in a cot in a cubicle in a hostel for homeless men. I had no nice home and car, no well-paid, satisfying job, no wife and children to love and be loved by. I never will have these things. I had nothing. I did, however, know something that all those people in their real world who walked around me on the streets every day did not know. I knew that every one of them – albeit unwittingly – was only a hair's breadth away from being like me. They all genuinely believed that their individual destinies were in their own hands. They were wrong. I was once one of them. But when disaster came there was nothing I could do to prevent my rapid descent into destitution.

Anybody who has become suddenly unemployed can testify that after a few months looking for work without success a chilling reality arrives: there is no logical reason why the unemployed man should ever work again, or why the pattern of rejections should not continue indefinitely. This has nothing to do with the time that has passed since the unemployed man had last worked. Of course, the longer one is out of work, the more one is likely to fail when up against qualified candidates already in work whose expertise is up to date. And, of course, too, there is a serious stigma to unemployment which increases in proportion to the time a man is out of work. But these things are not what I am talking about. They are something else that the unemployed man has to deal with.

After a certain number of failed applications, the unemployed person suddenly realises that his destiny is completely out of his hands, and always has been. He looks back on his life and career and sees that what he took to be his achievements and successes in life were not due to his own efforts and talents alone. He realises that today, unemployed and homeless, all he can do is apply for work and present the best possible case to the would-be employer for being hired. After that it is up to the would-be employer.

It was a shock to realise that, outside journalism, I had no other skills to commend me. I was an unskilled labourer in a world that needed skilled labour. In the Britain of the mid-1980s, there were more than three million of us registered as unemployed and looking for work. No matter how good one might be, if no vacancies existed it would be hard to get work.

At that time, the Conservative government of Prime Minister Margaret Thatcher was dealing with a strike by the National Union of Mineworkers. When the battle was over, the government closed most of the country's coal mines. In South Wales, for example, long a major centre for coal mining, not a single mine was left open.

I watched this with dread fascination. Hundreds of thousands of coal miners, who knew no other trade, were suddenly unemployed. One cannot be a coal miner when there are no coal mines. Their unemployment was softened by lump-sum redundancy packages worth, say, £40,000. Aside from that, the miners were like me: there were no jobs available for people trained as miners, just as there were none available for me as a journalist. We were suddenly unskilled labourers – the least wanted category in the job market.

In 1984 there were 25,000 jobs in British journalism. Of these, only 2,000 were in the national newspapers, the elite segment where I had worked. And the few vacancies in national newspapers were for young, inexperienced journalists at the start of their careers. The opportunities for an experienced journalist in his mid-thirties, as I was, were few.

Being unemployed and homeless did not help. I sent off hundreds of letters seeking work in the immediate aftermath of my return from the USA. I had a couple of interviews but, as is usual in such cases, they were just a chat to get acquainted in case, at some future date, a vacancy for which I was qualified cropped up. I got a few weeks' work as a casual sub-editor here and there, but never enough to live on.

All my past history and experience as a journalist meant nothing. I was just one of scores, probably hundreds, of journalists seeking casual work. I was much too old and too experienced to suit the opportunities that existed.

What I needed desperately was regular, paid employment of any kind so as to be able to rent somewhere, however modest, that would be secure and give me a base on which to build. I wrote many letters asking for work. Somebody once saw me hammering out these letters on a small Brother portable typewriter. He had seen me doing so for weeks. What, he asked, was the point of such letters? I replied, 'The point is that somebody, somewhere will read one of them and decide to help me.' The questioner was not convinced. He thought I was out of my mind.

'This is not a story for the *Daily Mirror*,' wrote the patrician liberal, Paul Foot, to whom I had written in July 1984 seeking help in getting work. In writing to Foot, I had not sought publicity in his newspaper but work, so that I could overcome what had happened. Foot, a scion of a grand British liberal family long in the House of Lords, was born into riches. I did not know him personally: just by reputation as a crusading journalist. He, at least, I figured, would understand my predicament. I was wrong. Foot's dismissal of my plea for help turned out to be the norm.

R. W. Apple Junior, the distinguished London correspondent of the *New York Times*, did not reply to me at all when I wrote to him. What he did do, however, was read all the material I had sent him and then pass it on to a man he had known well for many years. This man, Apple knew, could find out if the story was true or not. He was William Corson, a former Lieutenant Colonel in the United States Marine Corps then aged 58. I should meet William Corson just once, in February 1987.

Early in 1985 I had never heard of him. I later learned that he had spent a lifetime in the United States Intelligence community, where he remained an influence. As a young man, Corson had volunteered for the US Marine Corps. He had fought in the Korean and Vietnam Wars, latterly as a tank commander. Between those wars he was recruited by the CIA and had obtained a doctorate in Chinese, while remaining a member of the Marine Corps. South-East Asia would become his specialist field of knowledge. In his closing months in Vietnam, in 1968, he worked in Washington on Systems Analysis in the area of Pacification and Insurgency in the South-East Asia Programs Division. His recommendations were bitterly rejected by the then US President, Lyndon Johnson.

The CIA grew out of the Second World War's Office of Strategic Services, then the only US Intelligence agency dealing with foreign threats. After the end of the war, faced with the new threat from Stalin's Soviet Union, the US Congress quickly passed, and President Harry Truman signed, the National Security Act of 1947, which gave the Central Intelligence Agency its charter.

The CIA needed to expand rapidly to deal with the Soviet threat. William Corson was one of the first wave of recruits to the Agency. He served in Japan, China, Indonesia, Thailand, Burma, Laos and Cambodia during the Cold War. During one such posting in 1956, at the start of a round of golf with the local Station Chief of the

Communist Chinese Intelligence Service, with whom he played golf every Friday afternoon without caddies so they could talk privately, the Chinese officer casually threw a package into Corson's golf bag as they left the first tee, saying: 'You might find that of interest.'

They played 18 holes of golf with no further discussion of the package. On his return to his office, Corson found that his Communist Chinese colleague had given him a copy of a secret speech given a few months earlier to the Central Committee of the Communist Party of the Soviet Union by its then General Secretary, Nikita Khrushchev. This was the speech in which Khrushchev denounced Stalin and Stalinism. It was the first crack in the monolith of Soviet Communism. The Central Committee under the Soviet Constitution was the ruling body, the parliament or congress, of the state but had, under Stalin, been used as a rubber stamp for the dictator's policies of terror.

Khrushchev had been an apparently loyal follower of Stalin until the dictator's death in 1953. He had won the internal struggle to become the leader of the Soviet Union, but to friend and foe alike he had been regarded as just another loyal apparatchik until this secret speech. One incident during this speech serves to illustrate its significance, inside and outside the Soviet Union. The Central Committee comprised some 500 members gathered in an auditorium to hear what they had assumed would be the usual meaningless catalogue of Soviet Communist jargon. At one point, when Khrushchev outlined the years of terror and oppression under Stalin, he was heckled from the floor.

'What were you doing during all these years, comrade?' the heckler shouted.

'Who said that?' demanded Khrushchev. The hall was silent. Nobody spoke a word. The heckler had no desire to identify himself. Finally Khrushchev said: '*That* was what I, too, was doing, comrades!'

This secret speech would cause an earthquake within Russia. Hundreds of thousands would be released from the Gulag. For a time there would be a Russian cultural renaissance. Writers such as Pasternak and Solzhenitsyn would briefly flourish. But that Friday afternoon, when the young William Corson played golf with his Communist Chinese friend, not one word of the speech had reached the West.

Corson sent the speech immediately to the Director of the CIA, Allen Dulles. Later, a copy of this speech was leaked to the Moscow Bureau Chief of the international news agency, Reuters, which made great play of being the first Western body to have received it. Not so: the CIA had it first from Corson. At the time, though, it suited the CIA for the world to believe that Reuters broke the news.

William Corson subsequently became the personal CIA officer in the White House to Presidents Eisenhower, Kennedy and Johnson. When President Kennedy was assassinated in Dallas in November 1963, William Corson was his CIA liaison. President Johnson was sworn in as US President on the presidential aircraft, *Air Force One*, that Friday afternoon. He inherited the dead President's team, including William Corson. On 23 November, President Johnson called William Corson into the Oval Office. They were alone. The President said: 'I have just appointed the Chief Justice of the Supreme Court, Earl Warren, to head a public presidential committee of investigation into President Kennedy's assassination. It will find that Lee Harvey Oswald killed him acting alone. But I want to know what really happened. I want you to find out for me. I think the Soviet Union was behind Jack's assassination but, if the American public ever found out that their young hero president was killed by the Soviets, it would lead to World War III. I have to stop that at all costs.'

William Corson's conclusion was that President Kennedy had been killed by a dissident element within the CIA which had been bitterly opposed to the President's policy towards Cuba after the fiasco of the Bay of Pigs invasion in 1961. Chief Justice Earl Warren duly held his public presidential inquiry into the assassination. It found that Lee Harvey Oswald, who had been himself murdered on Sunday 24 November in police custody in Dallas, had killed President Kennedy while acting alone.

That is who William Corson was when he came into my life in 1985. No member of the US governing elite had more power, knew more secrets, knew where more bodies were buried. It was as the personal CIA liaison to President Johnson that he travelled and served extensively in Vietnam. He split with President Johnson over the war in Indochina, which he came to believe by 1968 was unwinnable. That year he published a critically-acclaimed and best-selling book, *The Betrayal*, on the unwinnable war. Five days before the publication of *The Betrayal*, William Corson resigned from the United States Marine Corps.

President Johnson tried, and failed, to have him jailed for the revelations in the book. After President Johnson left office in humiliation later that year, William Corson filled numerous senior CIA positions while ostensibly pursuing an academic career. He held a BBA, an MA and two doctorates, one in Communist Chinese money and finance, as well as fellowships at the Universities of Miami and Wisconsin.

William Corson was one of the few giants of the CIA who remained from its early turbulent years during the new Cold War of the late 1940s and early 1950s. By 1984, ostensibly in retirement, he remained available for service to his country via the Agency. He is thought to have played a leading part in a covert CIA operation to train and arm the pitiful Bosnian Croatian army so that it became capable of defeating the Bosnian Serb army and ending the war in Bosnia.

Corson believed that 'National Security is a goal, not an alibi'. It was in that spirit that he approached the news from Johnny Apple of the London bureau of the *New York Times* about Goodman's misconduct in the spring of 1984. He decided to alert Joe Trento of CNN to the story.

Joe Trento of CNN was one of the most distinguished US investigative journalists of the period. When he came into my life in 1985, he had been covering that CIA beat for 20 years. His exposés of CIA wrongdoing had earned him numerous nominations for the Pulitzer Prize. At that time, Joe Trento was a senior producer in CNN's Special Assignments Unit, working out of its Washington bureau. The Special Assignments Unit was an elite group whose brief was to go behind and beyond the breaking news stories. It produced critically-acclaimed documentaries that were aired at peak hours.

William Corson read what Johnny Apple had sent him and went into CIA headquarters at Langley, Virginia, where he booked out the Agency's file on me. He saw there that I was telling the truth.

I have often speculated on what might have happened once Corson saw that Goodman had done me great harm in the name of the CIA. Did he go to the Director to ask him how the wrong that had been done could be put right? It seems unthinkable that

Corson would have taken the action he did without having obtained the authority of the Director. If so, then I have reason to be grateful that the CIA – through Corson – was at that moment trying to do its best to put right the wrong that its rogue operative had caused in its name. And I do not think that anyone in the British security services, if it had been they who had caused harm to an innocent third party, would have gone to the lengths to which Corson went to help me. Whether or not I have cause to be grateful to Corson's superiors – and I do not think he would have acted as he did without having obtained their consent – I certainly have reason to be profoundly grateful to Corson himself, and I shall always honour his memory.

What I do know is that Corson called up Joe Trento at CNN and they met for lunch. Corson passed on the material from London, plus what he had gleaned from my CIA file. He urged Joe Trento to follow up my case. Joe Trento in turn went to his boss, Ted Kavanau, a CNN vice-president, and got the go-ahead to prepare a documentary film about my story. Then he set about finding me. It was not easy.

At that time I was locked up in an Irish lunatic asylum. The key, I was told repeatedly, had been thrown away.

9

Unpitied Sacrifice

When bad men combine, the good must associate;
else they will fall, one by one, an unpitied sacrifice
in a contemptible Struggle.

from *On the Causes of the Present Discontents*,
EDMUND BURKE, 1770

In April 1985 I took the bus from London en route to Dublin, via a few days in Cork City. A year after I had left Washington, I had been emphatically rejected by the world of British national newspaper journalism. The people I had approached there had all chosen to ignore me. Ireland is my home. The only reason I did not live there was that, like millions before me, I had had no prospect of work there. I didn't believe that my chances of work now were likely to be any higher than they had been in London but, if I had to live in the permanent underclass, I preferred to do it in my own country.

One night in May, I was sleeping rough under the portico of the Allied Irish Bank at College Green in Dublin. The bank was next to the Bank of Ireland, whose fine building had been the eighteenth-century Irish Parliament. Anybody who has had to sleep rough knows that the two important things are to have some layer between oneself and the cold ground (torn-up cardboard boxes that night) and to be sheltered from the wind and rain (by the portico). It was raining heavily and, while I was not getting the rain directly, it was none the less being blown into me by the wind. I had had difficulty sleeping because of this.

At around about 1 a.m., I had finally fallen asleep when I was woken by a man and a woman kneeling above me. They were volunteers from the Simon Community, an independent group of ordinary people who aid the homeless in Ireland. My visitors were part of what is called 'the soup run': they toured Dublin city centre where people like me were to be found.

As an undergraduate, in the summer months I had hitchhiked all over England and Scotland with friends, carrying a tent and sleeping bag in a backpack. Often, we would arrive at our destination so late at night that we would not bother putting up the tents but, if the night was clear, would sleep out in our sleeping bags beneath the stars. It had all been an adventure.

What I was doing when the Simon Community's volunteers found me that night was, I suppose, a sort of adventure, but it was qualitatively quite different from the undergraduate kind. Then it had all been fun, part of the joy of being young and alive. Now it was awful. Sleeping rough in the streets, one gains no real rest. The day is a 24-hour circle of misery. One wakes up exhausted, dirty and unhappy. One has no change of clothes, no basic toiletries like soap and towel or a razor. One packs up one's sleeping bag and then spends the day walking around town with nothing to do and no hope of anything changing. When darkness falls, one returns to one's pitch, beds down as best one can and tries to get some sleep.

Sleep does not come easily. It is filled with horrible nightmares, and when morning comes one has to start the miserable round all over again. The life of the homeless underclass is lived parallel to the lives of the ordinary people in the town all around them, who behave as though they do not exist. I used to wake up early, around 6 a.m., and then go scavenging. The best food was to be found in early-morning deliveries at shops before opening time. These deliveries would usually have been completed by the time I was up and about. One could count on milk and bread almost always, sometimes pastries, too. One particularly barren morning, I remember, the only food that I could find was a huge pack of yogurts. I took about half a dozen, which I ate with my hands. It was incredibly difficult. I made a mental note to steal a spoon somewhere so this could never happen again.

The life of a person sleeping rough is a sordid and demeaning one. It is a life of constant humiliation. Many people beg for money from passers-by in the real world. I couldn't do that. I was too proud. I preferred to steal from the early deliveries to shop doorways. In my mind at the time, such theft was honourable. To have begged for money was not. Odd, really, I suppose, but that is the way it was.

Anyway, in the early hours of that morning in the driving rain, I had been roused from my sleep by these two volunteers on the Simon Community's soup run. My irritation was dissipated when they told me who they were and gave me a cup of hot soup and some sandwiches. They also gave me the address of their head office in Marlborough Place, told me that I should go there when it opened at ten o'clock, and said they would leave a message for the day shift to expect me. They left me then to seek out others sleeping rough.

I was boosted by their visit. I went back to sleep as best I could. When daylight came, I packed up my meagre belongings and presented myself at the Simon Community offices. They had been expecting me. I was assigned to a volunteer who gave me information about where to get free meals in Dublin. Various religious orders of the Irish Catholic Church provide these. These 'penny dinners' for the homeless and the poor have a long history in Ireland. Next, the volunteers took me to the offices of the Department of Social Welfare, where I was registered; then to the Iveagh Hostel for homeless men, where I was registered for a week, paid for by the Department of Social Welfare.

James Joyce's father had ended up in the Iveagh Hostel. That first night I had no money to buy food in the canteen. So I sat there while the other men had their meals, then ate whatever they left on their plates. In that way I fed myself.

The homeless men were not allowed into the dormitory until 7.30 p.m. When I was at last allowed up into my assigned cubicle, I found wonderful clean white sheets and a pillow. It was the height of luxury to sleep in such a bed. My sleep that first night was blissful.

The following morning, I went again to the Simon Community offices. Again I went to the Department of Social Welfare, where this time I got a cheque which enabled me to buy basic toiletries. That night I did not have to scrape leftover food from the plates of other homeless men. I could pay for a meal. It was great.

A few days later, the Simon Community volunteer took me out looking for a bedsit to rent. At that time, May 1985, the Celtic-Tiger Irish economic boom was not even a gleam in the eye.

Ireland was a poor country. But, paradoxically, in those days there were plenty of bedsits to rent in the private sector and landlords had no problem accepting somebody whose rent was paid largely by the Department of Social Welfare.

Things are very different today in the wealthy Ireland of the twenty-first century. What was necessary in the spring of 1985, however, was a £50 deposit. I did not have that. The Simon Community paid it for me. A young female volunteer helped me get a small ground-floor bedsit in Harcourt Street off St Stephen's Green. I had a base in Ireland on which to build. Or at least I thought I had.

In 1987 the British government of Margaret Thatcher signed the Anglo-Irish Agreement with the Dublin government of Garret Fitzgerald. This treaty went a long way to providing for effective condominium with the Irish Republic of the six northern counties under British rule. The British believed that it would end the terrorist campaign of the Provisional IRA. The Irish saw it as a decisive diminution of Britain's presence in Ireland, a significant stepping-stone towards the eventual withdrawal of the United Kingdom from Ireland and her eventual reunification.

The architect of that treaty was a young Irish civil servant, Michael Lillis, five years my senior. I knew him. We had met in New York, where he was a senior figure in the Irish consulate there. I socialised with him and his wife Jane who, like me, was Irish born in Britain. Michael and Jane had met while undergraduates at Dublin's Trinity College at the end of the 1960s. I also socialised with a friend of theirs, Howard Stringer (now Sir Howard), who at that time was a producer in CBS Television News. He would, by 1985, be the President of CBS Television News. He later became President of Sony International.

I had made frequent visits to New York in the 1970s and early 1980s, on business and for recreation. It was in that context – that he knew me personally – that, after getting my bedsit in Harcourt Street, I wrote to Michael Lillis seeking his help. The Irish government should have been deeply concerned by what had been done to me, one of its citizens, and should have championed me against the US government. Of course, real life is nothing like that. Government bureaucrats in any country pay no more than lip service to the rules and proceed on the basis of realpolitik, not justice.

Nonetheless, I knew that Michael Lillis was an important man in the Department of Foreign Affairs. I had some reason to believe that he would do what he could to help me. I was completely wrong. Lillis refused to see me. Instead he referred me to a more junior official, Art Agnew, whom I met. The first thing I did when I met him was show him my Irish passport. He told me he had no need to see it. He accepted that I was an Irish citizen and entitled to his help. He told me that he was very sorry to hear what had been done to me but that the Irish government would take no action. He made a point of telling me that Michael Lillis would have nothing to do with me. His message was essentially the one that I had had to endure for more than a year: I should put what had happened behind me and get on with my life. He also queried whether I had not after all suffered a mental breakdown in the USA.

'You are clearly not mentally ill today, but how do you know that you did not have a mental breakdown in the USA? Perhaps you did have one but got better after you left,' he said to me. I may have been naïve but I had thought he genuinely wanted to help me. As previously with Sir Douglas Wass in Britain, his reasoning was impeccable. He, an official in the Department of Foreign Affairs, was not equipped or qualified to make any judgement on my mental health in the USA. He was satisfied that I was not mentally ill when I met him but he was in no position to decide whether what had happened had all been part of some random attack of mental illness which had abated after my departure from the USA.

I agreed to undergo a psychiatric evaluation arranged by Art Agnew to determine whether or not I had had a mental breakdown in the USA the previous year. In Dublin, away from the influence of Sir Douglas Wass, before Irish doctors, I did not believe I ran the same risk as I had run when faced with the Lobotomy Man. On the contrary, if the Irish doctors cleared me of any taint of insanity, I should be free to seek to rebuild my life on that basis and, I reasoned, the Department of Foreign Affairs, once reassured that I was not a madman, might be able to help me in some way.

Today I can see that I was a fool. At the time I did not see any alternative. It was another offer I could not refuse. So Art Agnew arranged for me to be seen at the Vergemount Clinic, Clonskeagh, in Dublin's southern suburbs. The doctor was a personable and friendly man. He did not instantly rubber-stamp me 'insane' when I told him my story. Instead, he invited me to check myself in while he undertook a complete evaluation.

The doctor decided that I should be certified insane and locked up on the ground that, while I had done nothing to indicate that I was a threat to myself or anybody else, I was a potential threat to other members of society and/or to myself and could not be allowed to live outside a lunatic asylum for the rest of my life.

The Vergemount Clinic is a non-secure unit. It has no facilities to lodge the incurably insane. It was decided to transfer me to somewhere that does. Upon hearing this from the doctor, I escaped. The doctor called in the police. I was free on the streets of Dublin for several hours while the police searched for me. I was chased through the back alleys behind Harcourt Street, where I gave the pursuers the slip by hiding in a basement.

I stayed in the basement for about half an hour after I had heard the pursuers run by. Gingerly, I left the basement. The coast was clear. Or so I thought. I turned a corner to make my way out of the area and ran slap bang into a police car. In the car was one of the nurses from the clinic and two uniformed policemen. I was prepared to try to fight my way out. There was a brief period of negotiation. I told the policemen that I should not go quietly into the secure lunatic asylum. They said that in that case they would take me to the police station, only a few minutes away. There the officer who had done the talking asked for details of why I had been arrested by the police. The reply was: 'The paperwork is all in order.'

It was too late to fight physically for my freedom. I was in a Garda station full of Gardai. I was put in a police car and taken to the Grangegorman Lunatic Asylum in north Dublin. It is officially 'St Brendan's Hospital' but it was what it had always been, a huge Victorian lunatic asylum housing almost 1000 of the poorest members of the Dublin underclass. All sorts of laws existed and still exist to protect Irish citizens from arbitrary arrest and incarceration. Those laws had traditionally never applied to the poor. I should never see a lawyer. I should never receive a copy of 'the paperwork' authorising my detention.

That I sought such things was taken to be in itself symptomatic of deep-seated insanity. I was immediately started off on a course of injections of a powerful psychotropic drug, forcibly administered by the warders. It swiftly reduced me to a shambling figure, dribbling from the mouth, unable to function normally. These forcible injections would last five months. I was lucky. The chief psychiatrist was an elderly, upper-class lady to whom I took an immediate and incurable dislike. In the estimation of the chief psychiatrist those five months should have been 50 years, if not more, because, as she calmly told me, I was so insane that I should never, ever be released. The chief psychiatrist, it seemed, was of the same school of psychiatrists as the Lobotomy Man in London: dedicated to abuse, insult, humiliate and degrade those unfortunates who, though incarcerated against their will, remain in law patients who are ill and in need of care and succour.

'Why would the CIA be interested in the likes of you, Denis?' she would declaim, ridiculing me. 'Look at the state of you. You're just somebody sleeping rough on the streets of Dublin. Why in God's name would the CIA bother with the likes of you?'

In December 1985, some six weeks after I had left the Grangegorman Lunatic Asylum, I had a brain scan in London. That brain scan showed significant damage. I was told that, had the drugs with which I had been forcibly injected continued for a further six months, my brain would have been irretrievably damaged and I should have become a vegetable.

However, that did not happen. I was saved by the unexpected arrival in my life of Dr William R. Corson of the CIA and Joseph J. Trento of CNN.

It was while I was in the echoing Victorian lunatic asylum of Grangegorman that Joe Trento finally tracked me down. He first spoke to me on the telephone in October 1985. Because I was locked up, it had taken some months for his researcher to find me.

I had been given a message to call him collect. I telephoned him from the office of the chief psychiatrist, who stood by the telephone listening to every word of the conversation. Joe Trento told me William Corson had confirmed the truth of my story, and that CNN would be making a documentary about what had been done to me.

Who knows what part that telephone conversation, overheard by the chief psychiatrist, played in the Irish government's decision to deport me to Britain and dump me on the streets later that month?

I do know that the chief psychiatrist did not want to let me go.

She had told me, 'You will never be released.' Somebody overruled her. She admitted that to me herself. She would have had to report the contents of that telephone conversation with a senior CNN producer to her bosses at Grangegorman who, in turn, would have relayed it to the officials within the Department of Foreign Affairs who had sent me there.

Perhaps some functionary in the Department decided it would be less embarrassing were I not to be locked up as though insane in a secure lunatic asylum in Dublin when CNN broadcast Joe Trento's documentary showing that I had been telling the truth and was not, therefore, insane. The Irish government would not get off lightly if CNN were to prove that one of its most nationalistically minded citizens had been unlawfully locked up for life and had been compelled to receive injections of powerful psychotropic drugs on the ground that he was dangerously deluded.

The timing is certainly suggestive. A week after the telephone conversation with Joe Trento, I was suddenly released from what I had been told was life imprisonment in the Grangegorman lunatic asylum in Dublin. One of the senior warders, Dinny Neville, was given a return airline ticket to London (for himself) and a one-way ticket (for me). He took me to Dublin Airport and we boarded an Aer Lingus scheduled service to London. In the arrivals hall, I was released from Dinny Neville's custody. Dinny pressed an English £5 note into my hand with the words: 'Go and buy yourself a drink, Denis!'

Legally, the situation was – to put it mildly – irregular. It is not lawful for any nation to deport one of its own citizens to a foreign country. Yet that is what the Irish government – my government – had done to me. It had forcibly removed me from my own country and dumped me on the streets of another country, with only a £5 note to support myself. The brute-force deportation had been, like the incarceration and forcible injections, entirely illegal.

What if I had actually been insane? Was what was done to me really the appropriate way to deal with a man so insane that he had been told he would have to be locked up for life? The Irish Ministry of Foreign Affairs had made the always-fatal mistake of pursuing two policies which, besides being morally wrong and contrary to every principle of natural justice and of constitutional law, were also mutually contradictory. The two policies could not both have been right at the same moment. If I were indeed insane, I should not have been deported from the country whose passport I held, and should certainly not have been set loose on the streets of London. On the other hand, if I were not insane, I should not have been locked up on grounds of insanity in the first place. The Irish Ministry of Foreign Affairs has much to answer for.

On the streets of London, I was a shambling, drivelling eejit of a creature, a long way from being a real human being. The impact of the drugs was horrifying. I had nowhere to turn for help in dealing with the effects. Dinny Neville's £5 did not last very long.

William Corson and Joe Trento perhaps did not realise it, and perhaps I have not properly thanked them for it, but they saved my life. Without that telephone call from Joe Trento, openly overheard by that wretch of a chief psychiatrist, I would have been kept on those pernicious drugs until I became a vegetable or died, or first one and then the other. The chief psychiatrist had made it quite plain to me that she was never going to let me out. Joe Trento's telephone call spiked her guns.

Before William Corson and Joe Trento appeared in my life, I was completely alone, abandoned by family and friends as a man who had gone mad in the USA – 'Poor Denis has trouble with his nerves.' After Corson and Trento, I had some hope at last. A man can undergo any amount of pain, horror and torture if he has that small amount of hope inside him. As things turned out, I was going to need it, because my life did not turn around at all.

10

The Establishment Runs a Mile

> To tell deliberate lies while genuinely believing in them, to forget any fact that has become inconvenient, and then, when it becomes necessary again, to draw it back from oblivion for just so long as it is needed, to deny the existence of objective reality and all the while to take account of the reality which one denies – all this is indispensably necessary.
>
> from *Nineteen Eighty-Four*, GEORGE ORWELL

I was in a terrible state when the Irish government forcibly deported me and dumped me on the streets of London in October 1985. My brain was mush because of the psychotropic drugs, and it would be two years before it returned to normal. Winter was coming. I had nowhere to live, no money, no clothes, no friends, no nothing.

I made no effort to contact Joe Trento, because my memory of our telephone conversation was a vague one, a sort of dream distorted by the drugs. I had and still have no memory of time passing in the Dublin lunatic asylum – just dreamlike memories of specific events. Given my condition when I arrived in London that October morning, CNN did not seem to be of any current importance to me.

Nine months later, purely by chance, in the pocket of a jacket I found the handwritten note I had been given the previous October in the Grangegorman lunatic asylum with the names and telephone numbers of Joe Trento and his researcher. I telephoned him. He was very keen to speak to me, he said. He told me he had continued to pursue my case in the intervening nine months and more than ever wanted to make a documentary film for worldwide broadcast on CNN. He would get to London with a film crew as soon as he could.

The CNN team arrived in London in October 1986, a year after we had first spoken on the telephone and more than 18 months after Joe Trento, acting on William Corson's tip-off, had started his investigation into what had been done to me. Joe spent a week in London. He shot six hours of on-camera interviews.

On the Saturday morning, we called on my longtime GP, Dr Parsons, who gave a detailed interview on camera in which he stated that I had never suffered any mental illness and that he had seen nothing on my arrival in London in 1984 that had led him to regard my account of what had happened as symptomatic of a mental illness. He said:

> What Denis told me was completely consistent with the life he led as a journalist. I had been his doctor for almost ten years and knew he had no history of mental illness. Denis had absolutely no symptoms whatsoever of any mental illness of any kind when he came back from the United States in April 1984. If he had had any symptoms, I should have treated them. I am a doctor. But he didn't have any symptoms, so there was no treatment indicated.

CNN also shot an on-camera interview with my old college friend Alex Coxen. Alex confirmed everything that he had learned from Mary Goldring and also gave his view of me as he had found me in April 1984. He said:

> I did not at any time believe that Denis was mentally ill. He was very upset because his Fellowship had been cancelled but he was not mentally ill. I had two small children when Denis came to stay with me. I should not have allowed him to stay with us because of the children if I had thought Denis was mentally ill.

During one of our long off-camera conversations, Joe Trento told me that in CNN's Washington bureau he had met an old friend of mine, Anthony Collings, a distinguished American journalist. Collings and I had met years before when I was working at Westminster as a London stringer for the US magazine *Newsweek* and Tony had been the London bureau chief. I had visited his London home. This was a stroke of luck. Joe Trento had ready access in his own office to a man who had known me before Goodman had misbehaved. Collings could give a detached and objective view of me.

Joe Trento told me that Tony Collings could not speak highly enough of me. He had been astonished at the very idea of my being mentally unstable, a drunkard or a man who beat up women. The picture that Tony Collings painted of me was definitely not the one that Goodman had spread far and wide in the spring of 1984 in Washington and New York. When Tony had arrived in Washington the previous year to work for CNN he had hoped to resume our friendship and was disappointed to find that I was not there. He was personally appalled at the story CNN was working on about a friend and former colleague.

Joe Trento used his visit to this side of the Atlantic well. He spoke at length on the telephone to an important witness to what Goodman had done to me, Juha-Pekka Rentto, the Finish student on the MSFS programme. Juha-Pekka had graduated from the MSFS programme and had returned to Finland, where he was teaching law at a university. Joe Trento offered to fly him from Finland, and put him up in a London hotel at CNN's expense, so that he could give us an on-camera interview. Juha-Pekka confirmed my account of events over the phone, but refused to fly to London because he feared that the CIA would make trouble for him.

He told Joe Trento:

I am safe in Finland. I know that Goodman cannot get at me here, but I should not be safe in London. Because of what Goodman did to Denis, my last months in Washington in 1985 were a nightmare.

Try as he might, Joe Trento could not persuade Juha-Pekka to come over, but it did not affect the programme CNN was making because he had Rentto on record saying that I was wholly innocent of Goodman's allegations.

Joe Trento had told me that, shortly after he had received the file on me from William Corson, he had telephoned Mary Goldring at the BBC. She had been in Paris but Joe Trento had left a message saying who he was and why he wanted to speak to her. She telephoned him as soon as she got his message. She had

confirmed as true all that had happened, from Goodman's initial
call to Ms Mahoney at Harkness House in March 1984 to the
subsequent conduct of Ms Mahoney and Professor Garretson.

Joe Trento concluded that Mary Goldring was sympathetic to
me and wanted to help me. He regarded her, in his own words, as
a friend of mine. When she later refused to see him at all, let alone
be interviewed on camera, Joe Trento revised his opinion. He said
her refusal to participate didn't matter, because she could not
withdraw what she had told him.

Joe Trento had been pleased with his London visit. When he
flew back to the USA, he and his team travelled to Massachusetts,
where he shot a long interview on camera with Mrs van der Workeen, who told him that I had not been drunk or in any way
mentally disturbed at the funeral of Howland Sargent.

He also spoke to Mrs Deirdre Leonard, another Harkness Fellowships official who had been at the funeral. She confirmed Mrs van
der Workeen's account. In Washington he spoke to many of my
fellow students on the MSFS programme. All of them confirmed
that they had heard Goodman's allegations but had never come
across any evidence to support what he had said.

Finally, Joe Trento decided to confront Goodman himself
on camera. He arranged to interview him about the MSFS programme in general. After about five minutes discussing the merits
and demerits of the programme, Joe Trento confronted Goodman
about me. He told me that Goodman had been 'bizarre'. He had
refused to discuss me on camera. While the camera was off he had
made 'outrageous' claims about me: he had said, for example,
that I had made a telephone threat to bomb the 1985 graduation
ceremony for the Masters of Science in Foreign Service at Georgetown, but had been unable to produce any evidence for such a
serious claim. As it happens, I had the perfect alibi. At the time
Goodman alleges I threatened to bomb the graduation ceremony, I
was locked up in Grangegorman lunatic asylum with no access to a
telephone.

Goodman tried to divert Joe Trento from the story by making
me sound like a lunatic. However, on camera he refused to say this.
Instead, he sweated profusely as the cameras rolled. Joe Trento
asked Goodman why the rumours about my having threatened
women all seemed to have originated with him. Goodman had

been unconvincing in his denials. He had agreed to go back on camera, but had then again refused to talk about me, so Joe Trento had turned the camera off, whereupon Goodman had resumed his personal attacks on me. He said Joe Trento should ring Detective Leinau in New York. Trento had done so, and had also called my classmates at Georgetown. All the interviews he obtained contradicted Goodman's account of events.

I had stressed in my on-camera interviews that I had no fundamental hostility towards the CIA as an institution. Joe Trento had concluded that I was an admirer of the United States, though I was naturally not pleased to have been mistreated at the hands of a rogue CIA agent.

Joe Trento investigated Ms McInerney's allegations and found no evidence to support them. He did find evidence that she had been having an affair with a detective in the New York Police, and that there was an IRA cell in the Police Department. He had also interviewed Ms McInerney herself, who had at first been reluctant to return his calls and had then given mutually-inconsistent accounts, mentioning also that she had had relationships not only with me but also with others.

Though there was no evidence of any violence on my part, rumours persisted that I was violent and out of control. Joe Trento traced all of these rumours to Goodman.

Joe Trento also discussed my case with a number of US and British Intelligence sources. He learned that MI5 had first decided to target me for recruitment after my speech at the Oxford Union in 1970. My pro-Irish but anti-IRA views had made me of interest first to the British and then to the US Intelligence community. My book *Political Murder in Northern Ireland* had also aroused their interest, because I had unearthed significant events that the Intelligence services themselves had missed. My relationship with Ms McInerney was also interesting to the intelligence world, because at that time any connection with anyone who had any connection with the Provisional IRA was watched very closely.

Joe Trento discovered that it was the British who had approached their US 'cousins' in 1983 with a request that I should be recruited. He discovered that the Georgetown and Harkness programmes had both been exploited by the CIA as recruiting grounds, and that Goodman was well known among students as a

CIA recruiter. He came across another student who also reported that Goodman had approached her to become a CIA asset.

He formed the view, as a result of these researches, that I had been telling the truth: Goodman had indeed taken amiss my adamant refusal to be recruited, and had decided to mount a campaign to discredit me. He traced all the stories that I had acted inappropriately, and in particular that I had been drunk at Howland Sargent's funeral, to Goodman. He visited several Harkness officials in Boston and in New York, who confirmed my account of events. Once Joe Trento had completed his researches and had verified my story in all respects, he began to write the documentary. He had proposed Anthony Collings, an old friend of mine from my London days, as the narrator. Ted Kavanau, a CNN Vice-President, had approved the documentary. Suddenly, however, Ted Kavanau's unit was closed down, and Kavanau warned Trento that documentaries about Intelligence matters – and particularly the documentary about me – should not be proceeded with: they were 'no longer of interest' to CNN. Trento himself lost his job with CNN when Kavanau's unit was axed.

Joe Trento left CNN – almost certainly a victim of his honourable desire to tell the truth about me. He did not let go after he left. He tried to get several other news media interested in the story, but none would touch it. In June 1987 he wrote to me that both he and I had been badly let down by CNN, and that he would do his best to see that my story was eventually told. He said he would not let them get away with it. 'Be brave. You will hear from me.'

He concluded: 'What the CIA has done to you is wrong. It is the most outrageous and unjust case I have ever come across in almost 20 years covering the CIA.'

The sudden ending of Joe Trento's career at CNN with no warning was as big a shock for me as it was for him. When we had parted in London at the end of October 1986, he had assured me that the documentary would be aired later that year. He had no idea that he was about to be booted out of CNN.

After the disappointing news that the CNN documentary would not be shown, I met William Corson. It was the only face-to-face meeting that we had, although I spoke to him on the telephone many times subsequently. During a long meeting on the afternoon of 2 February 1987, he told me, *inter alia*, that he had been assigned to work with the Provisional IRA in Northern Ireland in the 1970s and had worked closely with them for several weeks. 'The only thing I was told,' he said to me, 'was that I was forbidden to go out on operations with them. That apart, I could do whatever I wanted.'

Corson summed up to me that February afternoon in 1987 what had been done to me almost three years earlier in these words: 'Goodman had built you up to his superiors back at Langley to be such a big catch for the Agency that when you wouldn't play ball he had to destroy you.'

Corson was kind and sympathetic towards me but, in the aftermath of his friend Joe Trento's being fired by CNN, he felt the reality for me was bleak. He said, not unkindly but rather in sorrow for what he knew had been the consequences for me, 'Nobody cares!'

More than five years later, William Corson and Joe Trento had dinner with Sean McPhilemy, an award-winning London-based independent producer of television documentaries, and suggested to him that he make a documentary film on what had happened to me. Sean McPhilemy was keen to do so, and I met him. However, every major television company that he approached to broadcast such a documentary turned him down.

At the end of 2000, Sean McPhilemy was clearing out the files of his by then defunct company. He sent me mine. There I found an interview between Joe Trento and William Corson dated 26 February 1993. I had never even suspected its existence until it arrived with no warning. It is a fascinating account. Corson told Trento that he had first come across my case when he had received a letter from me giving a detailed account of what had happened to me. He had believed my account of how I had been recruited, because of his years as liaison to British Communications Intelligence. Nor was Corson surprised at the idea of Harkness being used to recruit an experienced journalist. However, he was surprised at my outrage at the attempt to recruit me, because most British journalists were willing to go along with the government.

Corson said I had become involved with a number of US officials, including Goodman, who had had 'less than admirable CIA histories'. IIe described the School of Foreign Service at Georgetown as 'a hotbed of Intelligence activity and recruitment'.

Interestingly, Corson confirmed that one of my fellow-students at Oxford had reported in on me and a file had been opened on me because I was suspected of being pro-IRA.

On receiving my letter, Corson had talked to Trento and had then contacted his old associates in British Intelligence. He had feared that the CIA or another Intelligence organisation might be using the IRA for operations, because it would be 'great cover'. My problems with the New York Police raised questions in his mind, and Trento had been pushing for more information on whether I was 'a nut or someone real'.

Corson called for a detailed assessment of the file, which revealed that in many ways I was my own worst enemy. But the real problem was that my credibility had to be destroyed because the Intelligence community was worried that I might have worked out whom the British had in place in the IRA community, and that I might betray that information either in a fit of anger or in one of what Corson called my 'more unfortunate relationships'.

In Corson's opinion, the British security services had decided that, rather than leaving me a credible journalist with an expanding influence and a successful career, they should buy me off. However, it had become clear at Georgetown that I was not easily manipulated.

Corson said that, once it was clear that I was not willing to play ball, I 'had to be controlled', by exaggerating all my faults. If I drank sometimes, make me a drunk. If I had unpleasant love affairs, give me a reputation as a batterer of women.

In answer to a question from Joe Trento about why Goodman would play a part in all this, Corson said that the CIA was wanting to be seen to cooperate with the British on anti-IRA operations, in return for which the CIA were allowed to recruit 'Third-Worlders' in England without let or hindrance. Corson confirmed that Goodman would broker new jobs with multinationals for his foreign students, in return for which, on graduation, they would be approached to spy in their home countries.

Corson said he had warned me to abandon my efforts to get to the bottom of the story. He had been told my professional life would be destroyed if I kept on trying to pursue the story. He told Joe Trento he felt very sorry for me because I was not 'grateful enough' to my 'betters' in 'not going along with their wishes'. I had got caught up in the IRA drama, which was as much a *Wilderness of Mirrors* as the old Cold War had been. Most Brits and Americans, said Corson, did not realise that there were double or triple agents in the IRA context.

My trouble, Corson said, was that to protect a valuable agent an Intelligence service would expend someone whom they considered less valuable – in this case, me.

Joe Trento asked William Corson how I had responded when Corson had warned me not to pursue the matter. Corson had laughed and had said, 'What would any good reporter say when you warned him off a story? It's like throwing out raw meat.' Corson said that a reporter as dogged as Joe Trento would be in jail in England. Which is exactly what happened to me, in the end.

Joe Trento was puzzled that Mary Goldring had not done more for me. Corson was blunt. He said you did not get to work for the BBC unless you had been vetted, and she was not going to sacrifice her career for 'some poor schmuck from Deptford'.

Joe Trento asked Corson whether I could simply expose the British Intelligence assets inside the IRA. Corson said that was my ace in the hole, exposing the system and how it worked. To Corson, that was at the heart of the story. But he said I could not break that news, because there was no TV station in Britain that would put the story on the air. As events turned out, no TV station in the US would put it on the air either.

Corson was astonishingly frank about the connections between the CIA, British Intelligence and the IRA. He said, 'The CIA uses the IRA, as did the KGB. Oliver North kept his bank accounts in Ireland and moved weapons through the IRA. The CIA in turn used its people in the IRA to report information back to the Brits about IRA activities.' And where did I fit in? 'Lehane was a gnat in all of this.'

As well as the unfortunate Sean McPhilemy, Joe Trento and William Corson tried several British-based independent documentary film-makers. None of them would dare to produce a film. So the Corson interview would remain in Sean McPhilemy's file until at the start of the new millennium, his business in ruins thanks to British Intelligence, he was clearing out his old files and chose to send me mine.

I was distressed by the cancellation of Joe Trento's documentary and felt sorry for him because he had lost his job – in part, at least – because of me. In April 1987 I wr ote to Ed Turner at CNN, explaining that the documentary was ready to be run and asking him to run it. At that point I was not aware of the pressure that the CIA had put on CNN head office to prevent the documentary being run.

What was of concern to the CIA was not me – it didn't give a tinker's damn about me – but the revelations that the CIA had a long-standing operation at Georgetown University's School of Foreign Service, that it used the Harkness Fellowship programme as a recruiting ground, and – worst of all – that Goodman, one of its recruiters, had destroyed my career without a lawful excuse.

I can see today that there was no chance of that documentary running. In April 1987, I had not seen that. Perhaps I was too close to the thing. Had CNN broadcast the programme world-wide, it would have helped me. Ed Turner replied in the first week of May. He confirmed that Joe Trento had spoken to him, but he refused to run the documentary. He did, however, send me his best wishes and good luck. I had had such letters before. I should get them afterwards. I call them 'F*** off and good luck' letters.

CNN had investigated my case and found it to be true and interesting, but it had decided, under pressure from the Intelligence community, to suppress the inconvenient findings of Joe Trento's 18-month-long investigation.

My father had been present for all of the CNN interviews back in October 1986. At one point when I was doing something with the cameraman, he had approached Joe Trento. He said, 'Surely all the things that Denis said the CIA did to him can't possibly be true?'

My father himself told me about this. He said that Joe Trento had laughed and then said, 'Believe it or not, the CIA has done worse things to people that what it has done to Denis. Yes. Everything that Denis says the CIA did to him is true.'

Until that time my father had believed me insane. He had seen me go into Guy's Hospital and knew that the Lobotomy Man had labelled me insane. After that exchange with Joe Trento, he realised for the first time that I had been telling the truth for two and a half years. It profoundly affected him. I showed him Ed Turner's letter in the first week of May 1987. He said, 'You have had no luck.'

Worse was to come.

In 1956 Roger Bannister, an Oxford undergraduate, was the first man to run a mile in under four minutes. It made him instantly famous. The world record did not last long. Today an average international middle-distance runner would expect to break four minutes for a mile regularly. But that first four-minute-mile went into the history books and Bannister's name will always be remembered, even though he never won an Olympic gold medal, while hundreds of better runners have long been forgotten.

Sir Roger Bannister became a neurologist. In the early summer of 1987, he was Master of Pembroke, my college. All of the university's more than 30 colleges and halls are independent private institutions. Some of these colleges are immensely wealthy owing to ancient grants of land which in the twentieth century became high-priced real estate. Others were not so fortunate. Pembroke College is one of the less fortunate ones. It used to be one of the smallest Oxford colleges – perhaps even the smallest before World War II when the then Master, Dr Homes-Dudden, lived to be more than 100 and for many decades refused to appoint new fellows when incumbents died or retired.

In my time Pembroke was in the middle rank among the colleges. At any one time there would be 300–350 members of the college resident in Oxford undertaking academic studies, the vast majority being undergraduates, as I was between 1968 and 1971, studying for their first degrees. Just as Oxford and Cambridge, untypically, are wholly private bodies not ruled by the government so, too, the status of the students is different. Upon being awarded one's place one becomes a member of a college. Matriculation into the university as a whole, which occurs when one arrives in Oxford at the start of the Michaelmas term in October, is a procedure consequent upon being awarded one's place at one's college. Undergraduates are termed 'junior members' of that college. Upon being awarded the bachelor's degree, one becomes a middle member. On being awarded one's master of arts, one becomes a senior member. The principle is that one is a member of the college for life once one has been awarded a place there. The college is a small and intimate environment. Virtually everybody knows everybody else. When people graduate and go out into the world, they are kept fully informed of the life of the college, are invited back at regular intervals for formal dinners – 'gaudies' – and are invited to the annual college dinner in the Michaelmas term.

A yearly magazine is published and sent to all members. There are appeals to members for funds. Such appeals are frequent for a college like Pembroke because its endowments are small. The over-all ethos is one of a family of elite members of society bound together by common ties of affection for the college and mutual respect. That I had won a Harkness Fellowship had been published in the annual magazine under the category of prizes won by members of the college the previous year. It had been entered there by my old tutor, Dr Piers Mackesy, Tutor in Modern History, who had been one of my three sponsors for the Fellowship. Dr Mackesy had been in his post for a quarter of a century and was perhaps the most distinguished authority internationally on the American War of Independence and on military history.

I had greatly enjoyed, and benefited from, my three years as an undergraduate at Pembroke. I had grown to love and cherish the college. As well as my being part of Pembroke, it was part of me, it went with me wherever I went.

After the death of my mother, shortly after CNN's cancellation of Joe Trento's documentary, I contacted Dr Mackesy at Pembroke to ask whether Sir Roger Bannister might be willing to see me. Though CNN had refused to run Joe Trento's documentary, for the first time since I had left Georgetown in April 1984 I had evidence to support my story. Dr Mackesy was encouraging.

Accordingly, I wrote to Sir Roger asking him to grant me a meeting so that I could tell him what had happened to me. It was an appeal for help to 'the head of the family' from 'one of the family members'. I hoped he would try to help me. I was wrong. He wouldn't even give me a hearing. I did not think my approach to Sir Roger was inappropriate. Nor, while my actual circumstances were unusual, did I think that he would respond by refusing even to see me.

My specific request for help, had Bannister granted me an audience, would have stood a very good chance of success. This is because two members of the college were uniquely well-positioned to act. They were the elderly J. William Fulbright, a former US

Senator for Arkansas, and the much younger Richard Lugar, the sitting Senator for Indiana.

Senator Fulbright was, for various reasons, the college member best placed to help me. He was an immense figure in the United States political establishment. Born in 1905, he had gained his first degree in political science at the University of Arkansas in 1925. He had then attended Pembroke as a Rhodes Scholar. By 1987 he was an Honorary Fellow.

When Fulbright returned to the USA after Pembroke, he studied law at George Washington University in Washington In 1936 he returned to Arkansas where he lectured in law and was from 1939 to 1941 the President of the University of Arkansas. He entered politics in 1942 and was elected to the US House of Representatives.

Arkansas then was one of the most backward and undeveloped states in the Union. It was a deep-South state where racial segregation was firmly entrenched. In 1960, when President John F. Kennedy wanted to make Fulbright his Secretary of State, the move was blocked by the Democratic Party's black caucus in the House of Representatives. The black Democrats, elected to northern constituencies by black votes, would not accept the segregationist Fulbright as Secretary of State. So he remained in Congress.

He had been elected to the US Senate in 1944. He served there until 1974, becoming a member of the Foreign Affairs Committee and one of the best-known and most influential members of the Senate. His legislation establishing the Fulbright Program for students of all nationalities was passed by the Senate without debate in 1946. Its first participants went overseas in 1948, funded by war reparations and foreign loan repayments to the USA.

This programme, which bears Fulbright's name, has made a major impact throughout the world. To date there have been more than 250,000 Fulbright grantees. Fulbright's major impact was in the conduct of US foreign relations. He served as Chairman of the Senate Foreign Relations Committee from 1959 to 1974, the longest-serving chairman in the committee's history. He made his reputation as a tough and often critical voice in the conduct of US foreign relations.

In 1954 he was the only one of the 100 US senators to vote against an appropriation for the Senate Permanent Subcommittee on Investigations, the vehicle chaired by Senator Joseph R.

McCarthy, which launched a vicious witch-hunt in the US seeking out Communists. Fulbright also opposed the ill-fated Bay of Pigs invasion of Cuba, and was a powerful voice in the US Senate against the growing US involvement in Vietnam. In 1963, the distinguished US journalist and commentator Walter Lippmann wrote of Fulbright, 'The role he plays in Washington is an indispensable role. There is no one else who is so powerful and also so wise, and if there were any question of removing him from public life, it would be a national calamity.'

After leaving the Senate, Fulbright was attached to a Washington DC law firm. He was active in the promotion of international relations and took a lively role in the activities of Pembroke College's US members' group. *Inter alia*, he had also been the mentor of the Arkansas student Bill Clinton and had prepared the way for Clinton's presidency.

Fulbright lived until 1995. In 1987 he was aged 82, and though an old man, remained a powerful figure behind the scenes in the political world of Washington. What made him of immense potential assistance to me was that he had been one of the founders of the CIA under President Harry Truman in the 1940s.

Even more important, in the mid-1960s, as Chairman of the US Senate Foreign Relations Committee, Senator Fulbright had fought a bitter battle with President Lyndon B. Johnson over the Vietnam War. He had been provided with the detailed Intelligence analyses on the basis of which he could torment Johnson from within the CIA itself.

The CIA man who had been the link between Fulbright and the Agency was Dr William R. Corson. Either of the two Pembroke College men, Senator Lugar or Senator Fulbright, was in a strong position to help me, if he were so inclined, but Senator Fulbright was ideally positioned because he knew Corson well and because he retained huge influence within the CIA. I needed the CIA cover-up of Goodman's misconduct undone if I were to have any chance of rebuilding my life.

In June 1987 I told Dr Mackesy all of this in a long telephone call. He agreed with my analysis. He said he would himself approach Sir Roger Bannister and urge him to meet me so that I could explain to him what had happened and how he could help me. About ten days after my letter to Sir Roger had been sent to him, I received a terse reply scrawled on a blank sheet of paper without even so much as a college letterhead. It contained no expression of regret at the sudden death of my mother. Sir Roger said he was not minded to meet me but gave no reason. Then he wrote, 'There are some things in life we just have to accept.'

Of course there are things in life one just has to accept. However, illegality and immorality are two things one does not have to accept. Dr Mackesy told me he had tried very hard to convince the Master to help me, but the Master was adamant in his refusal.

Six months later, I received another letter from Sir Roger. This one was on the college's expensive, headed paper. He warmly invited me to contribute a substantial sum of money to the college for a building project. I threw the letter into the wastepaper basket and wrote to the college asking it to stop contacting me.

Had Sir Roger asked Senators Fulbright and Lugar to help me, those fellow-members of Pembroke would surely have taken steps within the US political establishment to have the damage to me undone.

11

Enter (and Exit) the KGB

'With the absorption of Europe by Russia, and of the British Empire by the United States, two of the three existing powers, Eurasia and Oceania, were already effectively in being.'

from *Nineteen Eighty-Four*, GEORGE ORWELL

Sir Roger Bannister and CNN between them had destroyed all the hope I had had since I had contacted Joe Trento from London in September 1986 hoping that my Kafkaesque nightmare was about to end. With hindsight the hope had been fragile, but at the time that is not how it had seemed to me.

Having spent a few short winter months in 1986/7 believing as well as hoping that all the misery was at an end and that I should soon be able to rebuild my life, by the summer I could see no hope. Once again, as I had done in 1985, I decided to go home to Ireland. This time, however, I had a plan. I had decided in July 1987 to research and write a new biography of the Irish political and military leader in the war of independence, General Michael Collins.

A few biographies of Collins had been written previously, the last in 1972 by a New Zealand schoolteacher, but none of them had been written by an author with an academic background in modern history who had gone through all the existing primary sources. I had that background and would have no difficulty doing the work and writing the book. The centenary of Collins's birth was coming up in 1990 and, if I worked really hard, I could have produced a book in time for publication on that anniversary.

I had no money. I approached various literary agents and publishers and the response was good. Most were interested in the idea. But, in return for any sort of advance, they wanted to see the first three chapters. So I had to complete all the research before I could get any money. That in turn meant that I must continue to live in the underclass until I could come up with three chapters that were acceptable to the publishers.

There is no major book-publishing industry in Ireland. Those publishers that do exist are too small to produce a big-selling book such as the one I was determined to write. So it boiled down to British publishers. I spent ten months working on Collins in the British Library in Bloomsbury. Then, in May 1988, I moved back to Ireland. I spent a few months in Cork City, and moved to Dublin in August 1988. I remained there until July 1994.

By the middle of 1989 I had done enough research to be able to write a draft of the first three chapters of the biography of Collins. I submitted the three chapters to the British literary agent who had been most keen on the book, and to four publishers. All rejected the material on the ground that it was too critical of Britain and her rule in Ireland.

Collins was a radical Irish nationalist who adhered to the physical-force tradition which held that Irish freedom would be won only by armed military insurrection against Britain. Collins had nothing but contempt for Britain and her Empire. That is the truth of the man. It is what I wrote. The British literary agents and publishers did not want such a Collins. The Collins they wanted was an emasculated version who had come to value and cherish Britain and her Empire. This was a perversion of the truth but, with hindsight, I can see that I was naïve in the extreme.

It was not enough to do the research and produce a book. I needed something else. I needed to produce a book that British publishers would be happy with. They weren't happy with the truth about General Collins.

I sent the three chapters that had been rejected to a prominent Irish politician, Senator Maurice Manning, who was then, as he is at the time of writing, the leader of the Fine Gael Party in the Irish Senate. Senator Manning is an academic at the National University of Ireland. He has written many books on modern Irish history. He was enthusiastic about my work on Collins. He offered to sponsor me for a Newman Scholarship at University College, Dublin, so that I could finish the book. The Newman Scholarship would have lasted for three years and I should have been paid £15,000 a year tax free.

At that time I was getting around £3,000 a year in unemployment benefit.

Senator Manning introduced me to Dr Tom Garvin, the Professor of Politics at UCD. He also was enthusiastic about my Collins research. Both these men had been glad that somebody with a background in modern history was at last tackling Collins. Easily the most valuable and most extensive records on Collins are to be found among the Mulcahy Papers in the UCD Archives.

Senator Manning believed that I should succeed in my application for the Newman Scholarship were I to be sponsored as well by an elderly, much-respected retired teacher of history, Maurice O'Connell, a descendant of Daniel O'Connell, the great Irish leader of the early nineteenth century. Daniel O'Connell had in 1829 secured full human rights for the mass of the Irish Catholic people – rights that had been denied them since 1691.

For this achievement Daniel O'Connell became known in his lifetime as 'the Liberator', a title that he retains today. His is one of the great names in Ireland's long pursuit of the return of her freedom from Britain. His statue towers above the country's main street, named after him. His tomb at the National Cemetery at Glasnevin is hugely impressive and greets the visitor just inside the gates.

After 1829 O'Connell strove for the repeal of the 1800 Act of Union, by which the independent Irish Parliament had been abolished when Ireland was formally joined to Great Britain to create the United Kingdom. In this he did not succeed. The reason for his failure is generally ascribed to his opposition to any form of armed military insurrection against Britain. This antipathy to physical force was a deeply-held conviction of O'Connell's. As a young man in the 1790s he had seen the French Revolution at first hand. He had been horrified by the violence.

From these early memories in France, when he became Ireland's political leader he refused to consider any form of violence as a means of freeing the Irish people from the union with Britain. Whether armed rebellion would have succeeded is open to question. All previous rebellions had been crushed with the sort of horrific violence to which O'Connell was totally opposed.

The subject of my proposed biography, General Michael Collins, did not share O'Connell's opposition to the use of physical force to free Ireland from British rule. On the contrary, his role in twentieth-century Irish history was as *de facto* commander-in-chief of the Irish forces which had fought the Crown in the war of independence. No such post as commander-in-chief existed in the Irish army, but British Intelligence, which was pitted against these forces, used this term to describe him.

However, Daniel O'Connell's descendant, the retired Professor Maurice O'Connell, unlike Senator Manning and Professor Garvin, was virulently opposed to my book proposal. He refused to sponsor me.

Professor O'Connell told me that I had got Irish history completely wrong, that the main thrust of that history was the constitutional activity of his ancestor and that the independence of Ireland in 1922 had nothing to do with the military activities which Collins had led against Britain in the war of independence.

Both Senator Manning and Professor Garvin were as appalled as I was by Professor O'Connell's actions. 'I suppose we should have expected him to take that line,' Senator Manning told me. 'He is completely wrong, but there is nothing that can be done.'

So it was that I did not get a Newman Scholarship and the £45,000 tax-free that would have lifted me out of penury.

In February 1988, while I had been still in London, I wrote to the new editor of the *Irish Times*, Conor Brady, at the newspaper's Dublin headquarters. It was a letter typical of those I had been writing week in, week out since the spring of 1984. I did not mention the CIA. I rarely did. I was well aware that to do so would be to provoke an instant rejection. I simply said that I should be moving to Ireland permanently in a few months' time and should be interested in working for the *Irish Times*. I enclosed a CV and some references. There was a big gap of almost four years in my CV for which I offered no explanation. I did get an acknowledgement from him saying that he would put my details on file and, should a vacancy arise for which I was suited, he might contact me again. I had had a number of such letters in the previous four years and I had never been contacted afterwards. In this instance, however, something happened. A book was published in the USA containing a series of articles about CIA scandals. I was told by somebody based in the USA that the book included an article by Joe Trento about me. Unfortunately, the information was not true.

In the belief, erroneous as it turned out, that what the CIA had done to me would soon be public knowledge, I wrote to Conor Brady again, explaining about the CIA and saying that I had not mentioned this to him because I had felt it would not be appropriate. News of the new book in the USA, I told him, had led me to conclude that I should now reveal all. Had I been called to an interview, I told him, I should have been frank with him. I got a courteous, hand-written letter back from Conor Brady, saying, 'I quite understand and agree with your position.'

When I learned that the book did not contain anything about me, I felt foolish. I wrote again to Conor Brady explaining what had happened. He did not reply. I had not expected him to do so.

In Dublin some 14 months later, in April 1989, I decided to approach the Soviet Union to ask it to restore my fundamental human rights. It was a purely pragmatic decision. Politics did not come into it. I was not a Communist or any sort of totalitarian. My conscious reasoning behind the decision to approach the Soviets was based on the ancient maxim: 'My enemy's enemy is my friend.'

My thinking was based on the Final Act of the 1975 Helsinki Treaty on human rights. I could approach any signatory of that Treaty if my human rights had been violated and my own government had either been the one who had violated them or had taken no appropriate action to remedy the violation by another state. If I were telling the truth, my human rights had been seriously violated by the US and British governments and the government of my own state, Ireland, had chosen to take no action. The Irish state had also had me unlawfully locked up and subjected to forcible injections of a powerful psychotropic mind-altering drug, and had then unlawfully deported me from my own country.

I thought it possible that the Russians might regard what had been done to me as something they could use for propaganda purposes. The US and Britain were constantly berating the Soviet Union for its routine human-rights abuses. My case would offer the Soviets the opportunity to counter with charges of their own.

I got it right. I wrote to the Soviet Ambassador to Dublin, Gennady Uranov, outlining what had been done to me, indicating that everything I had said could be verified via William Corson and Joe Trento in the USA and asking for help. The Ambassador turned the file over to the KGB station chief in Ireland, Sergei

Oleynick. Under the Soviet system, Oleynick was a more powerful figure than the Ambassador. He was a very personable young man in his early thirties who lived with his wife and small child in a big house in the southern Dublin suburb of Rathfarnham.

I spent about three hours with him one Sunday afternoon drinking tea and telling him what had been done to me. Oleynick was far from being the mindless Soviet apparatchik familiar to us in the West from propaganda and media spectacles like the James Bond films. He was suave, intelligent, worldly. He behaved like somebody born to privilege and power, who used the mechanisms of power as though he had been born to it.

Only a highly trusted officer would be able to take his wife and child to live in a Western country under the Soviet system. Oleynick clearly was such an officer. My guess is that his father was a senior figure in the KGB himself. Sergei Oleynick left me in no doubt that he was a member of a privileged elite. He was impressed with my account and I arranged to meet him one morning at 11 a.m. the next week at the Mont Clare Hotel, off Merrion Square, behind the Irish Parliament building.

When I arrived, Oleynick was not alone. He was in the company of a young Irishman of about the same age to whom he introduced me. Mark Brennock was then a political reporter for the *Irish Times*.

At one point during the morning I was left alone with Brennock. He told me that Oleynick's 'people' had given him the go-ahead to pursue my case. Brennock laughed. He was referring to KGB headquarters at the Lubianka in Moscow. Brennock found the idea of Oleynick's 'people' in Moscow amusing. Oleynick, on the other hand, was not foolish. He was clever and utterly ruthless. Brennock clearly did not see that. When Oleynick returned it became clear why Brennock had been summoned to meet me. Oleynick told me that he had to check out what I had told him at his home in Rathfarnham the previous Sunday, and he did not believe it would be a good idea for him to do it personally because of his Russian accent. So, if I would give to Brennock the names and telephone numbers of those I had said could verify my account, Brennock would make the calls. I gave him the names and numbers.

Among others, he spoke to Joe Trento in the USA. I know this because Joe Trento told me a few days later. He said that Brennock had told him he was working on a story about me for the *Irish Times*. I told Joe Trento that there was no question of the *Irish Times* running a story on me but that, instead, Brennock had been asked to make the calls on behalf of the KGB station chief in Ireland. William Corson had also been on the list and Brennock had briefly spoken to him. After Brennock had verified the truth of my account, I met him and Oleynick for a further morning conference at the Mont Clare Hotel. There Brennock told me, as though it were a joke, that he had gone to the editor of the *Irish Times*, Conor Brady, and offered him a story about me. Brady had dismissed the idea. Oleynick was busy at that time because the Soviet leader, Mikhail Gorbachev, was due to make a stop-off at Shannon Airport for a few hours as part of a world tour which had already taken in Communist China. Oleynick, as the KGB station chief in Ireland, was part of the reception committee. Yet he still made time to meet me the day before. He told me he had good news. Brennock, as I already knew, had verified all that I had told him.

This was important. If I had been an undercover CIA or MI6 operator seeking to penetrate the Soviet Union's Intelligence structure as a spoiler who could publicly embarrass the Soviets after duping them into accepting a bogus story as true, Oleynick's head would have been on the block. He might lose his licence to live an affluent and comfortable lifestyle in the West.

As it was, Oleynick was able to tell Moscow that my account checked out. Also, it would not have been difficult for the KGB via its network in Washington to check out the account on the ground there. Oleynick told me that these checks had indeed been made. He struck me as competent: a man of substance and stature within the Soviet Intelligence network. He told me that after seeing Gorbachev the next day at Shannon he would be flying at once to Moscow, having been summoned to give a first-hand account of my case.

Brennock found it all amusing and half-giggled at every reference to the KGB. It was very odd. Oleynick and I were cold, clear and businesslike in our dealings. Not so Brennock. He seemed to think that it was all a joke.

Oleynick explained to me that his people were very interested in my case but that nothing had been decided. As we shook hands, he said, 'The Ambassador has asked me to tell you that we will do everything we can to help. Denis, I hope we meet again. No, I am sure we will meet again.'

We never met again. When Oleynick came back from Moscow, he did not get in touch with me. It seemed that the Soviets had decided not to take up my case. These were momentous times. Nobody at the start of 1989 believed that the Soviet empire was on the point of collapse. All my life it had been part of the furniture – an apparently strong superpower. I had spent several months in the Soviet Union in 1979. I had learned that the Communist ideology had no popular base. But I had seen no signs that the apparatus of a totalitarian regime which had survived for three generations was weak and vulnerable.

Gorbachev was seen in the West as a moderate leader who would get rid of the worst excesses of the regime. This was wrong. Gorbachev was a figure similar to Oleg Kerensky, who had led Russia from the downfall of the Tsar in February 1917 to the Bolshevik *coup d'état* in October. Gorbachev was a transition figure who was not destined to last.

By the end of 1989 the Berlin Wall had been pulled down, the Eastern European countries of the former USSR were suddenly free and, within two years, Communism was abolished and the Communist Party made illegal in Russia herself. In that context, it did not surprise me that the KGB bosses in Moscow had not seen fit to take up my case. All that matters is that for a few months I had real hope that something good might happen in my life. That the hope of 'something good' by the middle of 1989 had driven me to approach the Soviet KGB was in itself testimony to how desperate I had become.

Shortly after the Soviets lost interest in me, I wrote to Douglas Gageby, a giant in Irish journalism, then in his early seventies. He had taken over the editorship of the *Irish Times* in the 1950s and had turned it from a peripheral Unionist newspaper into the main quality Irish daily newspaper. He had retired once in the 1970s but was brought back out of retirement when his successor as editor failed. He had recently retired again.

I wrote to him at the head office of the company, outlining how I had been introduced to Brennock by the KGB's Sergei Oleynick. A few days later, Gageby rang to tell me that my letter had just reached him that morning. He asked me if I could see him at 11 a.m. the next day. I went to his office. He thanked me for coming so soon and asked me to explain what had happened. After half an hour, he stopped me and said, 'Denis, why don't we go and have a drink?'

I was surprised and delighted. We walked to the nearby Burlington Hotel, where Gageby ordered a large brandy for himself and a large whiskey for me. I had told him he could verify everything by talking to Joe Trento and William Corson in the USA. I asked him to do so to make sure in his own mind that I was not 'a nutcase'. He replied, 'No, Denis, there is no need. There is nothing you have told me that I find in the least bit difficult to believe. These things happen.'

So simple: and yet so very many people had failed to reach the same conclusion. It was clear that Douglas Gageby had called me to his office to put a face to the letter. Having listened for an hour, he had come to the conclusion that my own GP and Dr O'Brady and Nurse Briggs at Guy's Hospital had reached: that my story was true.

Douglas Gageby, by the time he met me in 1989, had been at the helm of Ireland's premier newspaper for decades. He had lived through the start of the Northern Ireland troubles in 1968. He knew that terrible things had been done in the North of Ireland by nationalist and loyalist terrorists and by British forces. He also knew and admired my book *Political Murder in Northern Ireland*.

In that context, my account of what had occurred was not surprising or incredible. To Douglas Gageby, it was a personal tragedy for a man who had done nothing to deserve it. Douglas Gageby tried to persuade Conor Brady to give me a job. Brady was in two minds. It was difficult for him on a personal level. His was a human predicament. Nobody wants to be constantly reminded that has made a careless error of judgement. Some time after Gageby had spoken to Brady, I did, indeed, get a few months casual work as a sub-editor but it did not last long. In short, he chose not to give me a job. In the years that followed, Douglas Gageby would become a good and loyal friend, taking me out for a drink or to lunch every week, talking to me about my work on the Collins biography – which I continued notwithstanding the rejections of the British publishers. He could do nothing about getting me work, but I was proud that he had befriended me.

These years that I spent in Dublin from August 1988 onwards were tough. I had hoped that by writing and publishing my biography of Michael Collins I might claw my way out of my predicament. I spent my fortieth birthday in Dublin in September 1989. I had got some casual work as a sub-editor on the Irish television and wireless listings magazine. I worked there off and on, whenever they had need of casual journalists, for the next three years. There I met people who became my friends and I was glad and grateful for that.

But the work was mind-numbing for somebody with my background. Grateful though I was for it, it was at a level far below that at which I had started as a journalist. During these years, gradually, day by day, week by week, month by month, as I wrote off letter after letter seeking the sort of post for which I was qualified as well as low-paid casual work, I came to recognise that my life was passing by. When I had left Dulles Airport in April 1984 I had been 34 years and 7 months old. When CNN had cancelled Joe Trento's documentary at the end of 1986, I had been 36 years and three months old. When the Soviets had decided not to help me after all in June 1989, I had been 38 years and nine months old.

None of these defeats sapped my will or my determination to undo as much as possible of the damage that had been done to me. There were times when I knew great despair. Over the years, members of the Samaritans, founded by the Anglican minister, Chad Varah, in the 1950s to help those in despair, have been for long periods my only friends, complete strangers to whom I could, and did, go and say: 'Please help me. My life has been destroyed by the CIA. Nobody believes me. Everybody thinks I am mad. Nobody cares!' The Samaritans understood what I said to them because, like me, they are ordinary people and know what it is like to be an ordinary person. They listened and they talked to me. Every time I left them I felt there was still hope in a world run by a cruel, uncaring elite of hypocrites. Without the Samaritans, I should not have made it as far as I have.

Somewhere in my much-dispersed belongings I have their names – I used to write them down in my diary and send them Christmas cards at the end of the year; it was all I could do by way of thanks. One Samaritan in particular, Colette 4, a wonderful lady I used to go and see at the Marlborough Street Centre in Dublin in the late 1980s and early 1990s, stands out in my memory. Her birthday – 18 February 1948 – is the same as that of my elder sister, Mary Ann, who had died five days after being born. Colette 4 and all her colleagues gave me strength to keep going and hope in humanity when the world outside their building was so frightening to me.

By the summer of 1994 I had came to accept that my position was hopeless. I was then 44 years old. I was at that point living in a bedsit in Ranelagh, south Dublin. Problems arose with the land-lord. In his house there were six bedsits. One of his tenants had been there almost 20 years. Under Irish law, she would have security of tenure for life. The landlord did not want this. He circumvented the law by moving this lady into my bedsit. Instead of giving me hers, he moved me into another bedsit that was little more than a cupboard – a room he had great difficulty letting because it was so small, damp and unhealthy.

I had only two choices: accept the new arrangement or leave. I chose to leave. My father had written to me that he was having problems where he lived. He was by then in his seventies, living on a meagre British old-age pension, and he was being threatened by young hooligans who were picking on him because he was an old man living on his own. I packed a bag, picked up my dole one Monday morning and went to London.

When I had left London in May 1988, I had done so with hope in my heart that I could write the Collins biography and this would be my springboard back into a normal life. That hope had died. Six years had passed; I was no longer a young man. I had had some small hope – founded on Sir Douglas Wass and Mary Goldring – when I had made my way to London from Washington in 1984. That small hope had been swiftly dashed. Ten years later I had come to the end of the line in Dublin. Maybe things would be different in London. I had nothing to lose by trying.

12

'Death is better than this'

Essentia non sunt multiplicanda praeter necessitatem.

Occam's razor

Many young men of my generation in the 1970s married their girlfriends immediately after graduating from university. I was not one of them. So I started my career in journalism as a bachelor with a number of male friends whose weddings I had recently attended. When I met my married male friends for a pint after work, I used to ask how married life was treating them.

'Great. The best thing I have ever done!' would be the invariable reply. However, then my married friend, let's call him Mark, would confide: 'Mind you, Bob isn't enjoying things too much. He doesn't seem to be happy at all.'

Of course, I had had a few pints with Bob himself previously and he, too, had expressed great satisfaction with married life, adding only that things did not seem to be going too well with Mark. So, as I met my newly-married friends, I would get a picture of general discontent as each one assured me that they were blissfully happy but others of our group were far from it. Investigative journalism is like that. One collects pieces of a jigsaw, often, perhaps usually, from mendacious and hostile sources, and retains those pieces until one has enough to put them together to see a credible picture of what is there to be seen.

My view of *homo sapiens'* outlook on his world is that we are divided into two groups: those who believe in the conspiracy theory and those who believe in the cock-up theory.

I belong to the second category. Whatever success I may have achieved as a journalist has been founded on that view of life. Occam's razor is useful, because it makes sense of life to me.

William of Occam or Ockham (1284–1347) was an English Catholic priest, philosopher and theologian. His work on knowledge, logic and scientific enquiry played a major role in the transition from medieval to modern thought.

Occam, like a good journalist of today, held that knowledge is rooted first in axiomatic or self-evident truths, formal proofs and theoretical demonstrations, secondly in empirical verification of hypotheses, and in logical propositions flowing from those two sources. In his writings Occam stressed Aristotle's principle that 'entities must not be multiplied beyond what is necessary'. It is this principle that came to be known as 'Occam's razor', or 'the law of parsimony', which holds that the simplest of two or more competing theories is usually preferable, wherefore an explanation for unknown phenomena should first be sought in terms of what is already known.

A real-life application of Occam's razor would be in the evaluation of the so-called crop circles in farmers' fields, which began to be reported in Britain in the 1970s and which caused much controversy in the British press. There were two competing explanations as to the origins of these crop circles. The first was that flying saucers from far distant galaxies were creating them. Many people believed this theory. The second explanation was that pranksters were using simple implements to flatten the crops into circles.

Occam's razor, applied to the known fact of unexplained crop circles appearing all over Britain, would lead a scientifically-minded observer to conclude that, given the lack of evidence for alien beings in distant galaxies with the technology to come to earth, the second and simpler explanation was more likely to be true. For we know that humans can create the phenomena known as crop circles.

As things turned out, two *homines sapientes*, and not alien beings from a galaxy far, far away, admitted in the 1990s that they had started the crop-circle phenomena. For good measure, they demonstrated that it involved nothing more complicated than planks, rakes and baler-twine. Nevertheless, many people continue to believe that aliens were really responsible and that the two men who confessed to starting things off (their initial prank led to copy-cat crop-circles all over the place) are part of an elaborate plot to hide 'the truth'.

Such true-believers belong to the 'conspiracy theory' category. On the basis of Occam's razor, I believe in the 'cock-up theory'. Occam teaches that the simplest answer is more likely to be correct, especially when we are working with unusual phenomena.

In the early 1970s, when I was faced with two conflicting interpretations of the state of my friends' new marriages, I could apply Occam's razor. All my male friends told me that they were very happy to be newly married. Yet they all confided to me that our other married friends were not happy. The simplest explanation was that my male friends were not ideally happy to be newly married but, because I alone was unmarried, they would not individually tell me the truth about their own marriages.

Perhaps the most famous modern disciple of Occam is Arthur Conan Doyle's fictional gentleman detective, Sherlock Holmes. In the quotation often attributed to him, but which Conan Doyle never wrote, Holmes explained to Dr Watson: 'When once the impossible has been eliminated, whatever remains, however improbable, must be the truth.'

Truth is the end and object of good journalists, and we serve that end with utter devotion. Conspiracies do exist, but they are to be identified by applying Occam's and Holmes's principles. At Oxford, I was taught to use my mind this way. It was called *a priori* deductive reasoning: a step-by-step approach to the truth on the basis of established first principles.

If an interviewee could talk coherently for two hours or more without contradicting himself or revealing anything incredible – e.g. flying saucers or messages from beyond the grave – then, like any good journalist, I tended to give him the benefit of the doubt.

I start, as a journalist, with a completely open mind, but not an empty one, and I stand on the fundamental principle that life is a series of cock-ups, not a series of conspiracies, and that the simplest explanation of any phenomenon – the explanation founded solely upon known facts – is likely to be the correct one, no matter how incredible it may seem to be.

Solving a jigsaw puzzle is a good analogy for what an investigative journalist does: he collects pieces of information which often seem unimportant in themselves but when placed alongside other seemingly unimportant pieces of information present a part of a picture. One has to be disciplined enough to be able to say, even if one has a huge amount of jigsaw pieces, many of which fit together, that one does not have enough to make a decision. This often happens. One is left facing the reality that, unless something turns up, one is never going to see a clear picture.

That is the way I worked. Since it all began in 1984, I have never made any claims that could not be independently corroborated. On one occasion a serving British officer who worked under cover as a feature writer for the *Belfast Telegraph* asked me about loyalist murder gangs and, in particular, about the murder of the Ulster Defence Association/Ulster Freedom Fighters' commander, Thomas Herron. I told him some people believed that the British army had murdered Herron. The officer/reporter looked at me in disbelief and replied, 'Surely you don't believe that, Denis?'

I replied, 'I didn't say I believe it. I said that I had heard people say this.'

I knew perfectly well who had murdered Herron. The murder had been ordered by the UDA/UFF boss in the Shankill Road. The British army knew it, too. What the British undercover officer was trying to do was to get me on board. I didn't want to get on board. Later, at a party one night I met a young Provisional volunteer from the Upper Falls Road whom I knew vaguely. He told me that he played rugby in a team with the British officer, who had said he was very interested in Gaelic sports because he was Welsh, and had asked the young Provo to sponsor his membership of the Gaelic Athletic Association in the Upper Falls. What, the Provo asked me, should he do?

'If I were you,' I replied, 'I should not do it.'

The young Provo thanked me. He had come to much the same notion himself. The Gaelic Athletic Association had been founded in the nineteenth century as part of the national revival. It was a profoundly radical, nationalist body. At that time members of the British forces, including the police, were formally banned from membership. The very idea of a *soi-disant* 'fellow Celt' with a toffee-nosed English accent, whose usual attire was a dark-blue three-piece pinstriped suit with club tie, being admitted to a branch of the Gaelic Athletic Association in the ultra-nationalist Falls area of Belfast was absurd. Had the young Provo been foolish enough to try, he would have got a bullet in the back of his head.

Several months later, the Provos missed killing the British officer by ten minutes. He got a telephone warning from British army HQ at Thiepval Barracks and drove straight to Aldergrove Military Airport. From there he was flown straight back to England. Some years later, I bumped into the British officer in Fleet Street. He was working for a major international news agency: no doubt for Queen and country as usual.

Such were the absurdities of 'secret service' operations on the ground in Belfast in my time there. Charlie Chaplin could not have devised a more laughable script. At the time people, even if they had no connection with 'the Troubles', were constantly worrying about whether the British were tapping their phones. Why? What difference could it make? As a journalist described by his MI5 file as 'politically unreliable', according to Martin Dillon, I might have been a suitable subject for phone-tapping. It never bothered me: my telephone calls were dull.

Between August and November 1973, for example, they would have listened to scores of telephone calls from Fiona Macdonald Hull in Britain, pleading with me in tears to give up my career and move back to Britain and marry her. These conversations had no value for British Intelligence. If the tapes still exist, they will disprove the lies that Ms Macdonald Hull told the following January to the British Special Branch to the effect that I was a top Provo officer and had indicated that I planned to bomb her sister's wedding.

In that context, it would be very much to my advantage if the British secret service had bugged my telephones. From their point of view, though, it would have been a complete waste of time and money. Everything they knew about my activities, all of them legitimate, they had obtained already from Dillon.

My flat was searched to my knowledge once by the Provos. At the time I had noticed nothing. Being told that people had gone through my belongings did not affect me, but I can see how such things could affect others. A young trainee British journalist, Rob Watson, for example, lived a few avenues away from me in the same upper-class area between the Malone and Lisburn Roads in south Belfast. I knew Watson quite well. He had graduated from a British university in the summer, had won one of the coveted places on the Thomson Newspapers Graduate Journalism Trainee scheme and had been sent to the *Belfast Telegraph* by the Thomson Organisation. The scheme was designed by the company to produce journalists to be sent to its major Fleet Street titles, *The Times* or the *Sunday Times*.

Watson had visited me at my flat a few times for a drink and a chat. He had been in Belfast for only six weeks when he returned from work one early evening to find the large house where he had been living cordoned off by armed police and British soldiers. When he presented himself to the police there as a resident of the building, and provided proof that this was so, he was let in.

He learned that the smart, sober-suited young 20-something businessman whom he had passed on the stairs for the previous six weeks was one Gerard Adams. Adams had been arrested at the house earlier that day and sent to Long Kesh internment camp. Rob Watson was stunned. It preyed on his mind that for six weeks he had been sharing a house with the man believed to be the Provo commander in Belfast. He could not cope with this knowledge.

Adams has always denied being a member of the Provisional IRA, stating that he has always been a non-violent member of the Provos' *soi-disant* political wing, Provisional Sinn Fein. Although locked up for long periods, he has never been convicted of a terrorist offence.

Watson went in to see the Editor of the *Belfast Telegraph*, an elderly, upper-class Englishman called Eugene Wason, the next day and told him that he could not cope with living and working in Belfast. Wason told him to take a few weeks leave to visit his family in Britain and reconsider his decision. Rob Watson went to Britain and never returned, his career in journalism over. As a result of his departure, the journalists at the *Belfast Telegraph* held a meeting and voted never again to accept graduate trainees from Britain. Thomson Newspapers never again sent non-Northern Ireland residents to the newspaper.

Rob Watson had experienced what in the First World War came to be called shell shock, now known as post-traumatic stress disorder. Belfast was a war zone. Rob Watson, who had no roots in Ireland at all, could not cope with the knowledge that Gerard Adams, the man he had passed on the stairs and exchanged polite small talk with for six weeks, was the most wanted alleged Provo terrorist in Belfast.

On two different occasions Provo officers, Martin Meehan and one of his associates, tried to have me murdered.

For whatever reason, Meehan's associate reported to his local

Provo company in the Oldpark that I, his new journalistic colleague, was an officer in the elite Special Air Services Regiment of the British forces. The SAS – pronounced with a bitter hiss as 'Sass' by all Northern Catholics – is a crack British army special-forces regiment, based in Hereford, which specialises in undercover and counter-terrorism operations behind enemy lines. It is rightly feared by its enemies. It rarely takes prisoners and only then if it needs information from them. At the time, Catholics in the North believed that it was engaged in assassinations of republicans.

At that time, though, the regiment was not committed to Northern Ireland, although individual members were seconded there on special duties. The false identification of me as an under-cover SAS officer was calculated to precipitate a process which would lead to my death. On one level, it was flattering to be identified as no less than an officer of this elite regiment whose well-known physical standards were so high that I could not realistically have hoped to pass them. In reality, though, Meehan's associate was cold-bloodedly seeking to have me killed.

The Provos, believing themselves to be a gallant guerrilla army, processed his information through their usual channels. At the level of the 'battalion', my apartment was raided while I was not there. Dillon told me that they found nothing there except my passport, which they examined carefully. The enquiry, he said, came to the official conclusion: 'This man is a frequent visitor to Communist countries and we conclude because of this that he is an officer in the SAS.'

That the highest level of the Provisional IRA would base a life-or-death decision on the assumption that British SAS officers would take their passports with them, and have them stamped each time, when they went on operations in Communist countries says all that needs to be said about the level of general intelligence of this 'Army of Privates'.

Public perception of the SAS had them parachuting at night into enemy-infested territory or abseiling down cliffs or buildings, their faces blackened, their weapons at the ready, not politely lining up at Immigration to get their passports stamped. But what do I know compared to the Provos? At the time they examined the stamps in my passport, I had visited Canada and the USA in 1967 and 1970 respectively. And in 1969 I had travelled overland from

London to Istanbul and back in a bus when a student in the summer. My companions in the bus were mainly students. That trip had taken us through Belgium, Germany, Austria, Italy, Yugoslavia, Bulgaria, Greece and Turkey.

Of these countries, Yugoslavia and Bulgaria were Communist, but only the latter was in the Moscow-controlled Warsaw Pact. However, Greece, a Western democracy, did use a suspiciously Cyrillic-type alphabet for its passport stamps. So the reality of this 'SAS officer's' 'frequent visits' to 'Communist countries' had been confined to brief excursions to two Communist countries in the summer of 1969 at the end of his first year at university.

It was with such catastrophic stupidity that the Provos operated. They killed people on the basis of such 'reasoning' on a regular basis and thought themselves to be not just right to do so but also humane and fair to 'investigate' before they condemned and murdered their victims.

Any attempt to get me killed had to be approved by the senior command of the Provos. It was then that Old Andy heard about it and immediately quashed it. Dillon told me that a squad was sent to pick up Meehan's associate. He was hooded and taken to a safe house where, in the garden, a handgun was put to the side of his head and the trigger pulled; no bullet was in the chamber because the gun was empty. 'If you ever f***ing try anything like that again, the gun won't be empty,' he was told.

Old Andy sent for me when it was all over and told me what had happened. He told me he had also had to stop Martin Meehan in Ardoyne from killing me. Meehan was a far more important Provo than his associate. 'You know I will always give you total protection,' Old Andy said to me, 'but it would be better if you stayed out of Ardoyne.'

Nobody, myself included, was safe for a moment at any time in any part of Belfast. I was covering a war. I was seeing people killed and buildings blown to smithereens. The most painful of these experiences was talking to victims' relatives. A dead body is a dead body, even if it is in bits and pieces and barely recognisable. Talking the next day to the wife and children of the man that dead body had once been was something else. But they coped, and so did I. In August 1969, when I had thought the Irish army was about to liberate the North and that a call to arms would be issued which I should respond to, I had a very great fear that I should not be able to cope with battle conditions. In Belfast three years later I experienced such conditions. I could and did cope.

I suppose that part of this coping mechanism was my utter contempt for the absurdities of the ham-fisted British attempt to infiltrate the Provisional command structure. Had I responded to the overtures from the British secret service, I have no doubt that they would have wanted me to bring them along to one of my regular meetings with my friend on the Provo Army Council, Old Andy. The mind boggles at the thought of such an event!

For many of these years, my contemporary at Pembroke College, Michael Bettaney, was the boss of MI5's operations in Belfast. I learned this a decade later, when he was put on trial in Britain while I was in the USA. Bettaney was straight out of Charlie Chaplin's film *The Great Dictator*. At Pembroke he was in the University Officer Training Corps. He was attracted to far-right politics and weird ultramontane religion. Dressed in his full British army uniform as a lieutenant – the Officer Training Corps was a branch of the British regular army, and in the summer vacations Bettaney and his comrades would be sent to Belfast and Derry and go out on patrol with real soldiers under their command.

This is the man who was recruited by MI5 and rose to be its top man in Belfast, overseeing the dirty war against the Provisional IRA terrorists. Then he tried to defect to the Soviet Union. He just walked into its London Embassy, which as everyone knows is under total MI5 surveillance by CCTV cameras. Spotted by his colleagues on the CCTV, he was arrested, tried *in camera* and spent some 15 years in more or less solitary confinement in a category A prison.

I know a Provo bomber serving life for terrorist murder who was approached by MI5 and asked if he would be willing to be Bettaney's friend in jail. The deal was that Bettaney, who was not allowed to mix with the other prisoners because he knew too much, was lonely and, if the Provo agreed to be his friend and keep his mouth shut about whatever Bettaney told him, the Provo would be released early. The Provo refused.

Bettaney was let out on licence in 2000. He was given a house and a live-in girlfriend, somebody who had written to him the year before his release. Women often write letters to notorious prisoners, and Bettaney's trial was a sensation, mostly because almost all of it was held *in camera*. Perhaps the woman was a lonely, attractive 30-something who needed a friend and was lucky enough to find that Michael Bettaney needed one too. Perhaps.

Anyway, Bettaney lives, as far as I know, in a nice modern detached house with a comely wench for company. Provided he keeps silent, he will remain there in comfort. If he tries to reveal the masses of information he has about MI5 and the British army's dirty war in Northern Ireland in the 1970s and 1980s, his licence will be revoked and he will go back to solitary confinement in his category A jail cell.

The CIA had seen potential in me. Why did I not ask for a job analysing raw field data from agents in the field? I could have tried to negotiate a deal, and maybe the CIA would have done one. The truth is that I never for one moment considered doing a deal. I am a free man and I intended to stay that way. I feel sorry for Bettaney. He is not a free man and he knows it. I do not regret not trying to do a deal with the CIA or MI5.

By the end of 1995 I had come to the conclusion that there was no hope of a better tomorrow. In the preceding months I had approached Lord Rees-Mogg, a former editor of *The Times,* and Melvyn (now Lord) Bragg. The former is on the traditional conservative wing of the Establishment. The latter is a millionaire on the traditional liberal wing who had bankrolled Tony Blair's successful campaign for the leadership of the British Labour Party.

Both agreed to see me. Both expressed sympathy and a desire to help me, but it seemed there was no way they could. When it became clear that even two such powerful leaders of the British Establishment could do nothing for me, I wanted to die, because death was better than what faced me. But there was always an insuperable barrier: a man who commits suicide goes straight to Hell to burn there for all eternity. That is what I had been taught as a child in a pre-Vatican-II world. In fact, since at least the Middle Ages the Church has taught that the suicide can be forgiven, for he may have repented *inter pontem et fontem* – between the bridge and the water below. But I was not taught that. I could not commit suicide. Eventually, I decided to let the CIA kill me. I found a way that, it seemed to me, could provoke them to do so while absolving me from responsibility.

In November 1992 Sean McPhilemy had told me, 'William Corson is very worried about you. He told me to tell you that the CIA does not like you trying to clear your name and that if you don't stop making trouble for the CIA it will kill you.' I saw this not as a threat but as a promise. All right, then, let them kill me. It was time to bring matters to a head. If the CIA were going to kill me, let them do it now, at this time of my choosing. My ordeal would at last be at an end.

I decided to write to the CIA and copy that letter to various others. On 3 March 1996 I wrote a letter to Bill Taylor at the Center for Strategic and International Studies. I had also written a longer letter to Mark Brennock, which I copied to Taylor, to Lord Bragg's secretary and to a dozen journalists and a lawyer. In the letters, I wrote, 'I want my life back. If the CIA does not undo the damage it has done to my life, at the end of October I will travel to Okinawa, Japan, and kill twelve white US soldiers.'

Of course, I had neither the intention nor the means to do any such thing. I could scarcely afford the bus fare to the airport, let alone the airfare to Okinawa. I was desperate, and I wanted someone to take notice. The letter to Taylor was intended to provoke the CIA into paying attention.

I copied the letter to various people in the hope that they might assist me. Instead, as a result of those letters I was arrested, charged and convicted of a trumped-up offence in a Soviet-style show-trial, held in a category A jail and then tortured for several months in a secure lunatic asylum.

I had had enough of the misery and humiliation. With hindsight, of course, I should not have written the letters. But, after all that I had endured, for once I had been pushed beyond the boundary, and I was not thinking rationally. The letters were a mistake, but they finally brought matters to a head by forcing the CIA and its MI5 puppets into out the open. They arranged for me to be prosecuted. However, they faced a difficulty. It was quite clear to everyone that I did not actually intend to travel to Okinawa, still less to kill anyone there. I had neither the means nor the know-how.

At no point did I contemplate the possibility that I was committing a criminal act. Nor had I committed one. By the time the public authorities managed to drag the case to trial, all I faced were four separate charges of wilfully seeking to convince four recipients of the letter that I intended, with seven months notice, to travel to Okinawa to kill twelve white soldiers at the US base there.

The British authorities had approached all four recipients named in the charges and had asked them to make a complaint against me. None of the recipients had thought to make any complaint before the authorities had put them up to it. The authorities were unable to charge me with threatening to kill anybody, because in law I had not done so. They had to comb through a redundant piece of Victorian legislation passed in 1861 to find a long-extinct offence that they could resurrect to charge me with.

If I had intended to go to Okinawa and kill a dozen servicemen, it would not have made a whole lot of sense to give anybody notice. The odds that one untrained, middle-aged man without even the means to raise the airfare could take on 27,000 US trained soldiers at the heavily defended Okinawa base were scarcely great.

All four complainants, like the dozen recipients who made no complaint even when the British authorities pressed them, knew perfectly well that my copying to them my letter to Bill Taylor would have been self-evidently counter-productive if I had actually intended to carry out the threat that the letter contained. Therefore, no one had any intention of making a complaint against me until someone talked them into it. Scotland Yard approached everyone to whom I had sent my package at the start of March. All but the four rightly refused to cooperate, realising that the case against me was baseless. No evidence was put before the judge and jury at my trial late the following year on which a conviction could be founded. A conviction could only be justified were it to be proven beyond reasonable doubt that it had been my intention that these four persons should believe what Scotland Yard coached them to say they believed.

Bill Taylor, the recipient of the letter of which the others merely got copies, made no complaint. Not one US citizen played any official part in the case against me. Yet the barristers for the Crown, during idle chit-chat with my defence lawyers, told my then barrister that the Crown Prosecution Service was 'coming under really enormous pressure from the American authorities to convict your client'.

Lieutenant-Colonel Taylor, a distinguished US career soldier, had seen no reason to complain. Yet the judge was told that all US military bases around the world had been put on alert: therefore, I had to serve almost a year locked up.

Taylor ought to have been the star witness, but he played no part in the case. The response of the CIA at Langley upon receipt of the letter I sent in March 1996 was to put an end to me and 'the trouble' I had caused once and for all. To do this it did not decide to kill me, as William Corson had feared and I had hoped, but to have me locked up for life in a criminal-lunatic asylum. And that is what the authorities thought they had succeeded in achieving. They did not think this book would ever appear.

I had never thought the authorities would try to lock me up in a lunatic asylum yet again. I had thought their choice would be between killing me and undoing the damage they had done to me. That they would use the legal system against me had not occurred to me. Nobody suffered, nobody died. Even had the letters been a criminal offence, at worst all I should have got was a police caution.

The CIA at last had something definite against me that it could inveigle its puppets in British Intelligence to use in the criminal courts, with their puppet judges and lawyers. Certainly, the quality of my life was affected by being put in prison. While I was on remand in custody in various British prisons, my standard of living actually improved.

When I was convicted and kept in solitary confinement before I was shipped to the lunatic asylum, that improved quality of life deteriorated. But at no time was I ever tempted to exchange what I then had and what lay ahead of me for being returned to the horror that my life had been for the twelve years before my arrest.

13

Dawn Raid

It was at night that they came for you, always at night.
The proper thing was to kill yourself before they got you.
from *Nineteen Eighty-Four*, GEORGE ORWELL

On 2 May 1996, London was in the grip of a ferocious campaign of bombings by terrorists of the Provisional IRA, pursuing this bloody policy as what they termed the 'economic war' against Britain.

In February the Provos had killed two innocent civilians with a massive bomb at the Canary Wharf office complex in London's Docklands. In April one of their terrorist operatives had blown himself up on a London bus at the Aldwych in central London. I was then living with my father in south-east London. The dead Provo terrorist from the Aldwych bomb came from Catford in south-east London, about a mile and a half from my father's house.

On that May day two Detective Constables from Scotland Yard's Organised Crime Squad (I do not recall their names, but I shall call them John Smith and James Edwards) appeared in secret before a London magistrate, William Pendle, and applied for arrest and search warrants against me, stating that they had evidence that I was a Provisional IRA terrorist engaged in the current bombing campaign in London and that they believed my father's house in Deptford was being used to store large quantities of weapons, ammunition and explosives.

Pendle granted both warrants. This is routine. The law of England and Wales says that a magistrate must satisfy himself that there are *prima facie* grounds that a crime has been committed, or is reasonably likely to be committed on the basis of evidence, before any warrants can be issued. However, as a matter of course, and contrary to their legal duty, nearly all magistrates tend to take the word of a police officer that this is the case without troubling to ascertain whether any evidence exists to justify the warrants. The magistrates' courts of Britain were not called 'police courts' for nothing – that is exactly what they were.

The Bench may (and certainly should) have paused before granting the warrants, for two reasons. First, terrorist crime in London does not come within the purview of the Organised Crime Squad. All terrorist crime is dealt with by Scotland Yard's Anti-Terrorism Squad, a quite separate unit of the London Metropolitan Police which concentrates solely on dealing with terrorism. It was very strange that two policemen from a quite different squad should seek warrants to deal with 'a dangerous terrorist', as I was described to Pendle. It was something that should have alerted him. Theoretically, any constable may apply for any warrant, but an alert magistrate, particularly in the highly-charged atmosphere of the time, ought to have been particularly vigilant in matters where the police were alleging terrorism. The Provisional IRA's terror campaign was, indeed, organised crime in the general sense: but the particular offences of the Provisionals were manifestly terrorist offences first and foremost.

Secondly, the application for warrants was made on the normal routine basis for everyday crime. This is not the way the London police dealt with the Provisional IRA threat. It was and is much more convenient for terrorist suspects to be arrested and detained under the 1975 Prevention of Terrorism Act. This law, which had been passed as a temporary short-term measure to deal with a significant Provisional IRA bombing campaign in Britain in 1975, had been renewed every year since.

Tens of thousands of innocent Irish people had been arrested in that time. The Labour Home Secretary who had introduced it, Roy Jenkins, had described it as 'draconian' and had justified it as only a short-term measure. This law gave the police far greater powers than those given to Smith and Edwards by the magistrate Pendle. Had the Act been used, I could have been arrested and held incommunicado for a minimum of seven days and, at the end of those seven days, the police could have applied to a magistrate for an extension. Throughout that period of incarceration I should not have had access to any visitors or to any lawyer, and I could have been subjected to intense interrogation with no witnesses present. But Smith and Edwards did not use the Act to deal with the alleged dangerous terrorist, inferentially because they knew perfectly well I was not a terrorist. They used a procedure never used for dealing with terrorists. But Pendle granted the two warrants.

The 'dawn raid' took place the next morning, 3 May. Smith and Edwards did not see any reason to get up too early. They arrived at my father's house at 7.30 a.m. They had missed me by an hour and a half. I was at that point driving a minicab – a legal but unlicensed taxi – and had left at 6 a.m. as usual. My father told me what happened.

The policemen rousted him out of bed and cursorily flashed the warrants at him. He admitted the three policemen who wanted to come in. A fourth sat outside in the car throughout. The policemen did not physically harm him, but subjected him to their usual personal abuse and insults. In that part of south-east London the police are universally referred to as 'the filth', and with very good reason.

Although they had a warrant to search the entire house for 'weapons, ammunition and explosives', the policemen did not search for any such things. The house was an Edwardian semi-detached with three floors: ground floor with basement, first floor and second floor. In total there were nine rooms in the house. The policemen did not at any time enter the basement. They checked the rooms on the first and second floor to see if I were there but, finding that I was not, made no attempt to look for weapons, ammunition or explosives.

The three rooms in the basement they did not enter could have contained a huge amount of Semtex, machine guns and thousands of rounds of ammunition. The rooms did not contain anything at all, but the four policemen did not know that, and they were not in the least interested in checking.

In the 1970s in Belfast I had frequently visited the homes of ordinary people that had been searched for weapons by the British army or Royal Ulster Constabulary. Invariably, floorboards would have been torn up and walls stripped. The house would have been reduced to a building-site and the security forces would have left the residents to carry out the repairs to their homes themselves.

No such damage was done at my father's house this May morning. Not a single floorboard was torn up. Had I been a Provisional IRA terrorist, a huge cache of weapons could have been hidden under the floorboards and these policemen would have not found them. They did not look.

My father and I had redecorated one of the rooms and there were twelve large black plastic bags containing debris in the hall and one of the rooms, waiting to be dumped on a skip. The police stepped around these black plastic bags and saw no reason to open even one of them. They could have been filled with Semtex. They were not, but they could have been for all the policemen knew.

As well as this, my father was in the middle of laying a lawn in the rear garden. The ground had been turned over with a rotary cultivator, and half of it had a freshly-laid lawn, while the other half was rank weeds. Where better to hide a huge amount of weapons, ammunition and explosives than under a newly-laid lawn? The policemen had no interest in the garden. To get to it they would have had to go into the basement. They did not bother.

All they did was insult and abuse my father. They also took away two computer disks from my room, even though their warrant did not permit them to take away computer disks. It specified only weapons, ammunition and explosives. Of some 50 computer disks there, two had labels which indicated that I had used them in 1996. So the policemen took those two. Three others had also been used by me that year but did not have labels indicating this. So they missed them.

It was not much of a search, and it was plainly not a search for the purposes authorised by Pendle. No weapons, no ammunition, no explosives. Just two out of the five computer disks I had used in 1996. Neither of the disks contained a 'master-plan' for a Provisional IRA bombing campaign in London. They knew that. It was not what they were looking for.

My father was a proud Irishman. All his life in London since 1941 he had been the victim of personal abuse and insults from the likes of those policemen. He later told me that one of the constables, a man in his fifties, leafing through some of my papers and said, 'Your son must be a very clever man. Detective Smith is a very clever man, too. He has four GCSEs.'

Smith was a relatively young man in his late twenties or early thirties. The General Certificate of Secondary Education was an examination taken in schools of England and Wales by students between the ages of fifteen and eighteen. In Ireland the equivalent was the Leaving Certificate. In the USA it was High School Graduation. The British police force was then a wholly proletarian organisation, where educational qualifications played no significant role in recruitment.

The British police were largely drawn from the uneducated working class. In any professional sphere, the possession of no higher qualification than GCSEs would not equip somebody so much as to start on the bottom rung of the ladder. In the police force, however, anybody with even the barest qualification stands out because the overwhelming mass of policemen are insufficiently educated to have gained qualifications of any kind. My father was not impressed by Detective Smith's great educational achievements. To the 50-something copper's remark, he replied dryly, 'My son is a graduate of the University of Oxford.'

That shut them up. Had the policemen not felt the need to abuse and insult my father, they could have been in and out in ten minutes. As it happened, they stayed for half an hour and then left, taking only the two computer disks. As I was not around, they had obtained all they had come for.

If the police had truly been searching for explosives, the Anti-Terrorist Squad would have mounted the raid. They would have come late at night or much earlier in the morning, they would have had coppers stationed at the rear of the house to prevent escape, there would have been more than four and, most crucial of all, they would have been armed.

Some two months later, at Hammersmith, west London, the Anti-Terrorist Squad did raid a private house in the belief that it contained Provisional IRA terrorists. A score of heavily-armed policemen surrounded the house in the early hours of the morning. When one of the Provisional terrorists appeared in the front doorway, he was shot dead on sight. That is the way things would have panned out had there ever been any suspicion that my father's house was a base for the Provisional IRA and contained a huge terrorist arsenal.

I was to meet Winston Paisley in the autumn of 1997 when we were both prisoners in Her Majesty's Prison, Belmarsh, London's only top-security jail. He had been convicted of murder and had been given the mandatory life sentence. He was determined to appeal the conviction because he was innocent. He told me his story and it was clear to me, on the basis of my knowledge of the workings of the legal system, that he should have been acquitted of the charge.

He was a young black man in his early twenties with no previous criminal record. He had been in a nightclub one night when a man he had never met broke an empty beer bottle over the back of his head as he stood drinking at the bar. In a reflex action, Winston Paisley had turned around and struck his assailant in the neck with the glass of beer from which he had been drinking. The blow severed the assailant's jugular vein and he died within minutes from loss of blood.

Winston Paisley wanted to appeal the conviction on the ground that he had acted in self-defence. No lawyer would act for him, so he would spend hours each day in the prison library poring over law books in an effort to master the procedures necessary for him to appeal the conviction without representation.

I realised at once that his endeavours were doomed to failure. This was why no lawyer would represent him. He needed the permission of the courts to launch an appeal and that permission would not be forthcoming because of the way the British legal system operated. Winston Paisley's grounds for appeal were that two independent witnesses had, before the trial, told his then lawyers that they had seen what had happened, that he had been the innocent victim of a serious unprovoked assault and that he had reacted instinctively in self-defence.

Self-defence is a defence in law to a charge of murder. The two witnesses had not been called to give evidence for Winston Paisley's defence at the trial. He had been puzzled by this. After his conviction he became convinced that if the court had heard these two independent witnesses – two men whom he did not know any more than the man who had attacked him – he would have been found not guilty by the jury.

He may have been right but it did not matter. All that mattered was that the defence he had put to the court had not included these two witnesses, though they had been willing to give evidence at the trial. The English Court of Appeal rules *a priori* that each and every defence put at a trial by an accused's lawyers is the best possible defence that the accused can offer. It does not allow convicted persons 'a second go' so that they can put an alternative defence to see if that works. The accused has one chance, and once chance only.

Once convicted, a person can only appeal on a point of law. In the absence of new evidence that had not been available to the defence at the time of the original hearing, the decision of a jury in a criminal case is irreversibly definitive as to fact and is not appealable.

Among the few grounds of appeal are the emergence of new exculpatory evidence or a defect in the procedure of the trial – for instance, that the judge, who makes the decisions on points of law and presents that law to the jurors, had acted improperly in some way.

Winston Paisley wanted to appeal the convictions not on a point of law but on the basis that had the jury heard the evidence of self-defence from the two independent witnesses they would not have found him guilty of murder. The reply of the Court of Appeal to such an application for an appeal is always to say to the convicted man, in effect, 'It is your own fault for not presenting the witnesses to the court at the trial; you knew of the evidence but chose not to present it.'

Although I had no personal experience of the British criminal justice system before my arrest, I had known for as long as I had been a journalist that the Court of Appeal applied a strict definition to the word 'instruct' when applied to an accused and his lawyers – that 'instruct' means to give orders. However, Winston Paisley's tragic situation, and that of countless thousands of others like him, was caused by the reality that at criminal trials a quite different interpretation of the word 'instruct' applies.

The dictionary gives three definitions: to order someone to do something; to teach someone how to do something; or to brief a lawyer.

It is this third definition which applies to all defendants on Legal Aid in criminal trials in England and Wales. What does that third definition mean? It clearly means something distinct from the first two meanings. What it makes clear is that the principle applied by the Court of Appeal – that 'instruct' means that a defendant in a criminal trial orders his lawyers to present whatever defence they actually present, and that the responsibility for the defence they present rests entirely upon his shoulders and has nothing to do with the actual lawyers and the advice they gave him – does not apply when somebody 'instructs' his lawyers.

The reality is that legally-untutored defendants do not 'instruct' – i.e. give orders to – their Legal Aid lawyers. Winston Paisley's lawyers decided for themselves what defence to present at his trial. If he had objected, they would have withdrawn from the case, leaving him defenceless. Legal Aid lawyers will not present a defence on the instruction of a defendant as it is defined by the Court of Appeal.

The Appeal Court's principle is a monstrous hypocrisy in urgent need of reform. *Inter alia,* it deprives all defendants of the right to appeal on the ground that their lawyers were incompetent. Imagine a situation where all doctors were considered incapable of committing any mistake at any time. Think of all the terrible tragedies that some people undergo as a result of incompetent doctors and think of the world as it would be if it were legally impossible to challenge such mistakes on the grounds that no doctor can ever be negligent. Yet that is the way the criminal justice system works in Britain.

Winston Paisley did not have hundreds of thousands of pounds to pay for lawyers, so he had to accept Legal Aid lawyers. Legal Aid is granted by the courts. It is tightly restricted on grounds of cost. All Legal Aid lawyers know how much money is available for each defendant. They work to that sum and will not work beyond it, however much their clients may need additional effort.

Winston Paisley did not know why the two key witnesses were not called by his Legal Aid lawyers. They did not tell him. They did not seek his permission before presenting his manifestly incomplete defence at the trial. They proceeded on the basis that beggars can't be choosers and that he had to accept their view or they would not continue with his case.

Like me, he had no previous experience in the criminal courts. As a result, he had no understanding of what was going on. An 'old lag' would have spotted the danger at once and would have had the nous to intervene, even if it meant a terminal row with the lawyers. But Winston Paisley was not an old lag. He made the mistake of trusting his lawyers. He was wrong to do so. By the time he realised that, it was too late.

The Court of Appeal told him that it had been his decision not to present the two eye-witnesses at the trial and because of this 'decision' he had no grounds for appeal. Lawyers in the British legal system cannot, by law, be incompetent, wherefore their alleged incompetence cannot be grounds for an appeal against conviction.

I knew this. As a journalist I had witnessed the most appalling injustices in trials because of the incompetence of defence lawyers. Even though everything that happened to me was a new experience and I was surprised over and over again by my previous naivety, of one thing I was never in any doubt: the Court of Appeal would regard the defence presented at my trial by my lawyers as a defence which I had conceived myself – the best of all possible defences in the best of all possible worlds.

By the time I met Winston Paisley in Belmarsh, I had been convicted on the bogus charges that the British authorities had taken pleasure in bringing against me. I had been determined never to find myself in the tragic position of Winston Paisley, convicted on the basis of a defence that was not his own and in which he did not believe but which, in law, had at all times been his chosen and best possible defence. As far as I was concerned, any lawyer who worked in my name would proceed on the basis of my orders – my instructions – or he would not represent me. As a matter of course, Legal Aid lawyers expected an accused to knuckle under and accept the threat – blackmail really – that unless he went along with them they would leave him to appear in court with no representation, something that would inevitably lead to a conviction.

I knew from my experience as a journalist that no lawyers are better than bad lawyers. I was not frightened by the threat of lawyers refusing to work for me. I was frightened of what was being planned for me, but I was not going to cooperate by accepting lawyers who would not present the best possible defence. That best possible defence cost a lot of money. I did not have it. No lawyer would apply to the court that such money be made available from Legal Aid funds. It was a stalemate. I should, therefore be convicted, but my conviction would provide no fig-leaf allowing those who had brought those charges to maintain that I had agreed in any way with the process that had led to my conviction. I had seen too much injustice in the courts in my years as a journalist to make that mistake.

I learned of the unexpected 'dawn raid' later that morning when I spoke to my father on the telephone. He told me *inter alia* that, amidst all the insults and abuse he had taken from the coppers, they had told him that I had written letters threatening to kill American soldiers in Japan. I finished work at once. From the telephone book I got the name of a firm of solicitors, Mackesy's of New Cross in south-east London.

I spoke to one of the partners, John Lownes, on the telephone and explained briefly that police had come to my father's house in my absence with arrest and search warrants. Lownes told me to come in at once. When I got there, Lownes told me not to go back to my father's house in case the police were watching it. I told him what I had done two months earlier and why. He was astonished. He had never dealt with anything like it.

Lownes, a small, stocky man with a thick Scottish accent, was in his early sixties at the time I met him. He is one of those hard-as-nails, no-nonsense, working-class Scots who are almost a self-caricature. I signed a 'green form' for Legal Aid so that he would be paid for seeing me, together with an application form for further legal services.

Lownes telephoned Scotland Yard and spoke to Smith, who had apparently been in charge of the raid on my father's house. He arranged for me to present myself at a local police station in Catford at 3 p.m. to surrender to the arrest warrant. Another solicitor, William Brundell, an Englishman about the same age as Lownes, joined us after about half an hour. Lownes made me repeat word for word what I had told him.

The job of Lownes and Brundell at that point was very simple. Smith had told Lownes on the telephone that he had an arrest warrant for me. The solicitors' bread-and-butter business was in dealing with clients who have been arrested and charged with criminal offences. They were experienced. Not having seen the letters I had written, they could not give a definitive opinion. But on the basis of what I had told them – namely that I had sent various letters two months earlier, the main one to the CIA, and in them I had given seven months' notice of my supposed intention to go to Japan and kill American soldiers – they said that I seemed not to have broken the law against threatening to kill people.

William Brundell and I duly arrived at 3 p.m. at Catford Police

Station. We were kept waiting half an hour for the two men from the Yard. When they arrived, they surprised Brundell and me by swaggering. I remembered what my father had told me about 'the very clever' Constable Smith, with his 'four GCSEs' and I saw at once exactly what he meant. These were two boy-wonder coppers who thought they were the bee's knees.

One of the things that intrigued me was that they were from Scotland's Yard's Organised Crime Squad. Whatever the legality of my letters, I hadn't written them as a member of a criminal gang; I wasn't in the Mafia. Why would I be allocated to Organised Crime? At that stage it was all baffling.

Before leaving the offices of Mackesy's I had discussed what I should do after being arrested. The lawyers' advice had been that I should agree to be interviewed so as to put on the record that I had never at any time intended to travel to Japan and kill any American soldiers. As far as they were concerned, the only possible charges I faced were those of threatening to kill American soldiers. The law said that for such an offence to have taken place I had to have had the intention of actually killing American soldiers.

When we reached the police station, I was formally arrested and escorted to an interview room. There, as discussed with my solicitors, I told the policemen that I had never had any intention to murder anyone, and that it ought to have been blindingly obvious that I had no such intention, or I should scarcely have written to a dozen people giving advance notice.

Smith started by giving me part of the letter I had sent to Mark Brennock. At no time was I shown the letter I had sent to Lieutenant-Colonel Taylor in the USA. I was asked if I had written the page I was shown. As it was one of the three or four pages of the letter, I had to read it carefully to be sure that it was my work. I said it was.

What, Smith asked, had I expected Mark Brennock to do when he received that letter? What had been in my mind when I sent him that letter? I restated what the lawyers had told me to say: I had never at any time intended to travel to Japan and kill American soldiers.

Smith showed me another piece of paper. I looked at it and agreed that I had written it. Again he started on at me. He got the same answer. Edwards burst in. How could I send letters to people saying that I was going to murder American soldiers? I never said I intended to murder American soldiers, I replied. They both burst out laughing.

Curiously, at no point did either of the two policemen put to me formally any allegation of criminal conduct. In passing, I wondered just how mediocre must the police force of London be for two such intellectually limited and emotionally immature young men to be the superstars they thought themselves to be.

At the end of the interview, I was brought before the station sergeant and bailed on my own recognisance. Nobody paid any money and nobody was liable to pay any money should I abscond or, indeed, should I use my passport, which they did not seek to take from me, to fly to Japan later that afternoon and kill any number of American soldiers there on my arrival. I was asked to return to the police station in three weeks' time. As I left the police station with Brundell, Smith called after me, 'Goodbye, Denis!' I ignored him. The ordinary uniformed copper who opened the door to let me out of the station, said to me, 'Are you not going to say goodbye to the constable?' I replied that I was going to do no such thing.

Outside the police station, I had a chat with Brundell before we parted. He told me that the two arrogant coppers were the juniors of Scotland Yard's Organised Crime Squad. 'The real detectives,' he said, 'would not have been bothered with something as trivial as this. They are not going to press charges because they haven't got a case against you. I can't see it getting to court. What would be the point?'

Almost two years later, another solicitor, James Nichol, wrote me a letter in which he said, 'In my opinion, you should not have been charged with any offence and had you been charged and been able to put your defence to the court, my view is that you would have been acquitted.'

But putting my defence to the court would be the problem. I was to be denied that. But this May day in 1996 I did not know that. I was on a learning curve. When I got home, I was able to read for myself the arrest and search warrants the police had obtained from the too-incurious magistrate Pendle the previous day. There I saw the allegations that I was a terrorist and that they had been given search warrants, not to take away two computer disks, but to locate weapons, explosives and ammunition.

Clearly the coppers had lied to the magistrate, who had granted the warrants unlawfully because there had been no *prima facie* evidence of terrorism on my part. So I tried to speak to Lownes on the telephone the following day. He was away at court, so I wrote to him. I asked him to go to court and have the arrest and search warrants quashed because the coppers had lied to get them. Nothing happened. I called again. Again Lownes was out at court. So I wrote again. This produced a telephone call from Lownes. He said, grumpily: 'Mr Lehane, I have read your letters and I think you are probably right. But who is to pay for me to go to court to challenge the validity of the warrants?'

I was taken aback. I had signed two forms for Legal Aid in his office the day I met him. I had thought that he and Brundell were my lawyers. There were, he told me, but what I wanted would require thousands of pounds to pay a barrister to spend time before a High Court judge.

'But won't Legal Aid pay for that, if I have a case?'

'No. The Legal Aid Certificate only covers attendance at the police station: nothing else.'

14

Defenceless

'You don't think the Party would arrest an innocent man, do you?'

from *Nineteen Eighty-Four*, GEORGE ORWELL

By the second week of May 1996, after my solicitor had told me that I had grounds but not funds to challenge the arrest and search warrants, I knew I had problems. If I could have challenged the warrants, the complications would probably have wrecked any prosecution of me, stopping the process dead in its tracks and leading to serious charges against the boy-wonder policemen Smith and Edwards

The letter I had sent to Lieutenant-Colonel Bill Taylor in March 1996 was, as I had expected it to be, sent immediately to CIA headquarters in Langley, Virginia. At the foot of the Taylor letter, less than one A4 page in length, I had appended the names and addresses of all the people I had copied the letter to, plus a copy of the separate letter I had sent to Brennock.

I had been arrested as a potential Provisional IRA terrorist, but I had not been questioned about terrorism. I had instead been questioned about my proposal to travel to Japan to kill American soldiers there. My solicitor told me that, in due course, the Crown would decide to drop the case. All I had to do was wait and I should be told that the police would take no action against me: 'You know, these detectives can have quite an enjoyable time, flying all over the world on cases like this one. They know it will never come to court but they will milk it for all it's worth in trips and expenses before the case is dropped. It is a perk for them. They do it all the time.'

The decision whether to prosecute was the responsibility of the Crown Prosecution Service. The police would have to submit a report to the CPS, which would decide whether any law had been broken, whether it was in the public interest to prosecute me and whether they would be likely to get a conviction. In the weeks that followed, Lownes or Brundell called the two policemen regularly.

At first the solicitors were told that it was too soon to say whether there would be a prosecution. In July Lownes was told that the Crown Prosecution Service had decided to send the file 'to a much higher level'.

I had learned from a different source that, as a matter of routine, the initial complaint against me, which had come from the CIA following the main letter which I had sent to Bill Taylor in Washington, had been channelled through MI5, which had in turn handed the matter over to Scotland Yard. The Yard had not been too impressed by what had been passed on, which was why the two inexperienced boy-wonders in the Organised Crime Squad were assigned to deal with it. They in turn had sent back their findings to the Crown Prosecution Service.

The Crown Prosecution Service had not dropped the case, as Lownes and Brundell had believed they would. Instead – perhaps to please the security services on both sides of the Atlantic – they had dredged up the Offences against the Person Act 1861, a defunct and little-used piece of Victorian legislation.

Under the heading *Letters Threatening to Murder,* Section 16 of the Act, entitled *Threats to Kill* says, 'A person who without lawful excuse makes to another a threat, intending that the other would fear it would be carried out, to kill that other or a third person shall be guilty of an offence and liable on conviction on indictment to imprisonment for a term not exceeding ten years.'

In August 1996, more than three months after my arrest, Lownes told me over the telephone that when I next appeared at the police station I should be charged. He was surprised. The charge was an obscure one. I was not charged under the usual law on threats to kill, which dated from just ten years previously. The authorities could not use that law because it obliged them to prove that I had actually intended, at seven months' written notice, to travel to Japan and kill American soldiers. That this claim was ridiculous was self-evident. Otherwise, why had I been bailed on my own recognisance and released, with no restrictions on my movements and no confiscation of my passport?

With Brundell accompanying me, in August 1996 I attended Catford Police Station, where I was formally charged with one count under Section 16 of the Offences Against the Person Act 1861 of intending Vincent Browne, a resident of Dublin, to understand by a letter I had sent him in March 1996 that I intended to travel to Japan later that year to kill US soldiers there.

I was asked if I had anything to say. I was about to say a great deal when Brundell told me to say nothing. I was once again given unconditional bail and ordered to report to Bow Street Magistrates' Court the following month. The policeman said to me, 'If you do not appear in court, you will be guilty of *another* offence.'

I had committed no offence. Even if I had, in law I was legally innocent until proven guilty but here was this ignorant copper giving me a warning about committing *another* offence. I wanted to say something but Brundell told me to shut up.

I was so angry at this – and now it seems silly to have been angry, given what I now know of the administration of so-called justice in England and Wales – that I wrote a letter of complaint to the head of the legal system, the Lord Chancellor. The bureaucrats in his office sent my complaint to the Police Complaints Authority, which wrote many months later quoting a British High Court ruling to the effect that 'Accordingly, the caution remains valid even if the precise words required are not followed by the police officer.'

There you go, then. The police can make it up as they go along and the High Court of England and Wales will rubber-stamp it. Today, I am astonished at my naivety and innocence. At that time, despite all the serious acts of injustice I had witnessed, I still believed that the system was essentially sound, that there was a hard core of fair play and justice and that injustice that I had witnessed was an exception to a fair and just rule. I was wrong. Injustice is systemic in the British courts.

I presented myself at 10.30 a.m. on 17 September 1996 at Bow Street Magistrates' Court. I was not legally represented. I met the inspector, Paul Stodge, who was in charge of the boy-wonders at the entrance to the court. It was almost funny. He was just leaving as I was coming in. The security men at the entrance were absent. I had a briefcase with me. I made Inspector Stodge search my briefcase. He said there was no need to.

I replied: 'You are quite wrong. After all, your men have told a magistrate that I am a Provisional IRA terrorist with huge amounts of weapons and explosives. I could have a bomb.'

I compelled Inspector Stodge to search my briefcase and then have me walk through the metal detector. My keys set off the alarm, so I had to empty my pockets and walk through again. The inspector was not amused. As I was waiting outside the court to be called, the Crown Prosecution Service solicitor, Andrew Faers approached me.

'I understand you don't have legal representation, Mr Lehane.'

I grunted in reply.

'I wonder, then, if I could have a word with you?'

This time I replied emphatically, 'No, you can't.'

Faers was taken aback. What he wanted to do was run through the procedure with me, as he would have done with the solicitors if I had wanted them there with me. I was not inclined to play the 'all chums together' game.

When I was called before the magistrate, as I stood in the dock, Faers said to the magistrate: 'I regret that I have not had the opportunity to speak to Mr Lehane before the case was called, your worship.'

True and not true. He had been denied that opportunity because I wouldn't speak to him. The magistrate did not know that. Who cares? It was all an elaborate charade. Had I let Faers speak to me, or had Lownes or Brundell been there and he spoken to them, as they would have let him do, before going into court, he would have disclosed that a second charge was about to be levied on me. This was identical to that naming Vincent Browne, but this time naming Mark Brennock. It had taken five months for Brennock to make his complaint.

As well as Faers, there was a barrister hired for the Crown Prosecution Service. He told the court that there was no objection to continuing bail – this had gone on now for four months – except that they wanted an order forbidding me to contact prosecution witnesses. I was allowed to respond to this application. I told the magistrate that I had received a letter from the only complainant of whom I was aware before that morning, Vincent Browne, in which he had said, 'It is not my view that you should be charged with any offence and I will do all I can to help you.'

If the order forbidding me to approach prosecution witnesses were made, I told the magistrate, how could I take up Browne's offer of help? The magistrate asked me if I had the letter from Browne with me. No, I said, I had had no idea that it would be needed. In that case, the magistrate said, he would grant the prosecution's application.

Early in 1997 I had a cup of coffee after an appearance at Bow Street Magistrates' Court in the company of the solicitor Stephen Hewitt and the barrister John Gordon. Gordon was a large, stout, typical 'G'day, mate!' Australian. Aged 53 to my 47 that day, Gordon had married late in life. His wife, Pauline, was 40 and they had two children aged 6 and 4.

Gordon was still a junior barrister in spite of his age. He had lived and worked in London since he had been at university there as a teenager. Given that the maximum jail term for the charges I faced was ten years, I was entitled to both a QC and a junior barrister. Hewitt, the solicitor, told me, when he engaged Gordon, that he 'should be a QC but is not because he makes judges angry'. Making judges angry, Hewitt explained to me, was a sort of badge of honour. It meant that Gordon had forgone a glittering and lucrative career on behalf of his clients. I never saw any evidence of it, though.

At the end of 1996 I applied for a job selling Monckton shirts in London's trendy King's Road. I didn't get the job. I got something else – an offer of the hand of friendship from an old acquaintance. The Honourable Christopher Monckton (as he then was) is now the Third Viscount Monckton of Brenchley. This pillar of the British Establishment is the grandson of Sir Walter Monckton, who became the 1st Viscount in 1957.

Sir Walter Monckton had been lawyer to King Edward VIII and had drafted his Instrument of Abdication. He remained the lawyer of the Duke of Windsor (as the former king then became) until his death. During Sir Winston Churchill's 'Wilderness Years' in the 1930s, when Churchill was an almost lone voice on the Conservative backbenches in the House of Commons warning of the threat of Nazi Germany, Sir Walter Monckton MP was one of the very few to support Churchill and probably the closest of those few confidants.

He served under Churchill in the coalition government during the Second World War and after Churchill's return to power in 1951. He was Minister of Defence in Anthony Eden's Cabinet in 1956 when Nasser nationalised the Suez Canal, but resigned two weeks before the military operation to retake the Canal on the grounds that it was wrong in principle and unworkable in practice.

I had first met Walter Monckton's grandson, Christopher, in 1975 when we had both been journalistic colleagues in Leeds on the *Yorkshire Post*. His family originated in Yorkshire, where they were landowners at the time of the Norman Conquest. The senior branch moved to Ireland four hundred years ago and became the Earls of Galwey (that was how they spelt it). Christopher, though, is descended from the junior branch that settled in Kent. He lives in the Highlands of Scotland, being descended on his mother's side from the Colyer-Fergussons of Spittalhaugh in the Borders. On his mother's side he also has Yorkshire, Irish and Maltese blood and is, therefore, typically British. His wife, Juliet, is of Danish and Irish descent.

We spent a lot of time together when we first met, as colleagues do on such newspapers. Christopher remembers those times as 'ones where I drank a lot of beer'. We all did. Christopher remembers drinking pint after pint with Arthur Scargill, then the leader of the National Union of Mineworkers, in Whitelocks, a fine sixteenth-century pub in the centre of Leeds. Christopher kept a clear head by eating not one but two massive portions of the pub's famous ham, eggs and chips by way of blotting-paper.

He eventually succeeded me as deputy leader-writer of the *Yorkshire Post*. By 1978 – the 'year of the three Popes' – Christopher had become the editor of the Catholic weekly newspaper *The Universe* and I was based at the Houses of Parliament as a lobby correspondent for the US news magazine *Newsweek*. I telephoned Christopher a number of times because of articles I was writing for *Newsweek*, whose bosses in New York were very keen to get information on the then Archbishop of Westminster, the late Cardinal Basil Hume, who was one of the favourites for the Papacy in each Papal election that year.

Christopher, in a celebrated editorial in the *Yorkshire Post* in 1977, had tipped Hume for the job as Archbishop of Westminster, and had then made sure his horse won by arranging for powerful friends in Yorkshire to send copies of the editorial to the Papal Secretariat of State at the Vatican. If you are getting the impression of a calculated and effective shamelessness, you are right.

Christopher told me that he had known the late cardinal on

the Yorkshire country-house circuit, and had heard him preach at Ampleforth, where he had been abbot until the Pope had translated him to Westminster. At one point I told Christopher that my own Catholic faith had lapsed. He promised me that, were Cardinal Hume to end up as the next Pope, he would arrange an early lunch between the three of us where their expert attentions would be exerted to bring me back to the faith. As the world knows, the late Cardinal Hume was not chosen by either Papal Conclave in 1978.

Christopher later worked in Margaret Thatcher's policy unit at 10 Downing Street for four years. His career has been dogged by a severe and rare form of Graves' Disease, which eventually left him unable to work full-time. His wife had kept things going by founding a shirt-manufacturing business, and her gentlemen's striped business shirts were sold in the King's Road under the name 'Monckton Shirts'.

An article in the Londoner's Diary column in the *Evening Standard*, published in late 1996, said that the then Leader of the Opposition, Tony Blair, bought his shirts at Moncktons. I happened to read this piece and wrote to Christopher to see if he would give me a job selling shirts in his shop. I told him what had happened to me in the USA and that I was unexpectedly facing criminal charges.

Christopher contacted me when he heard that I had applied for the job. He said he was very sorry to hear of my troubles and that, unfortunately, the shop had been sold, so a job was out of the question. Nevertheless, he invited me to meet him for dinner. He also invited me to spend Christmas with him and his wife at their neo-Classical palace in north-east Scotland. It was very kind, but I just wasn't in the festive mood.

Anyway, we met the following week at the library of the Middle Temple, of which Christopher is a long-standing student member. We went to an old journalists' haunt in Fleet Street, El Vino's, where we had a rather good bottle of champagne, followed by dinner at a restaurant. I was dressed respectably in a grey suit and black raincoat. Christopher remembers me at this meeting, because it became important later. I was clean-shaven and my hair was black.

Over dinner, Christopher listened to my account of events, including the letter I had written in March to Lieutenant-Colonel Taylor and the people I had copied it to. He was sympathetic, but said he thought the letter had been a mistake. At that point, I was facing two charges: of seeking to get Browne and Brennock respectively to believe that I intended at seven months' notice to travel to Japan and kill American soldiers. At the time Christopher and I had dinner that November evening, my 'seven months' notice' had run out, I had made no attempt to travel to Japan and nobody had made any attempt to stop me.

Nothing that I told Christopher surprised him. He said that he had had to deal with similar cases for Margaret Thatcher when officialdom had acted wrongly against innocent individuals. He told me that unless something was done I was heading for disaster. He said it was clear to him that the purpose of the charges, absurd though they seemed, was to have me locked up in a mental home. He was not dismayed, however. He said he would appear on my behalf at the next routine court hearing. To get the show on the road, Christopher asked me to have my lawyers contact him. He said he could not intervene unless he heard from them, because he did not want to interfere with their conduct of my case unless they approved of what he proposed.

Christopher was not in the least bit overawed by the situation. We were together for several hours and it was a convivial, social meeting of old friends and former colleagues. It enabled Christopher to get the measure of me. He said at one point: 'Denis, I feel strongly that you still have a strong contribution to make as a journalist.'

That was not my view, but I was flattered and gladdened. But where we both were in agreement was that it was imperative that the legal charges should be got out of the way and the CIA should agree to undo the damage it had done to my life. Towards the end of the evening, I said to Christopher: 'When you met me, you had no reason to believe that I should be in any state to go to El Vino's and then to a restaurant for dinner. What would you have done if you had found a down-and-out smelling of urine?'

Christopher replied, 'Had I found you like that, I should have dealt with you as I found you and helped you on that basis.'

It was a great relief, after hearing people for so many years tell me that what had happened to me was no big deal, to find somebody who understood exactly what I had been through. Christopher and I parted on friendly terms.

All that needed to be done was for my solicitor to meet

Christopher and Christopher would arrange for the CPS to drop all charges against me and then approach the CIA to get it to undo all the damage it had done to me since April 1984. Thank God for Christopher Monckton! If only my lawyers had contacted him as he had asked!

I had hired Hewitt in October 1996. At that time, it had never entered my mind not to defend the charges vigorously. The only question was how. For a while I had decided to do without legal representation and act for myself. I knew well the old adage that 'a man who represents himself in court has a fool for a client'. So I approached the firm of Fisher Meredith, which I plucked out of the *Yellow Pages*, because I realised, after my brief experience as a defendant in person, that I had to have lawyers behind me, even when representing myself.

I asked if they would act for me under Legal Aid by providing legal advice while I acted for myself. No, they would not. Fair enough. I should do without a solicitor. However, after I was ambushed with the second complainant, Brennock, and was ordered not to contact prosecution witnesses, even though I had a letter from one of them telling me he would like to help me and did not want me charged with any criminal offence, I concluded that I should not be treated fairly if I acted on my own.

I needed lawyers to deal with the CPS's tricks. By hiring Hewitt, my reasoning was that I could put the best possible defence to the charges. Hewitt was a pear-shaped, fresh-faced Englishman in his thirties. He described himself to me as 'a plumber'. His meaning was that he was a technician of the legal system, an artisan who repaired damaged lives by use of his expertise.

I had employed plumbers when I owned a house. They invariably underestimated the cost of a job, rarely turned up when they said they would, misrepresented what was wrong and what needed to be done, and left me with no clear idea at all of what they were doing to my property. After I decided to hire Hewitt, we had a long meeting of some two hours where I outlined what had happened and why. I asked Hewitt to speak to Christopher Monckton, William Corson and Joe Trento.

Later John Lovesey, a former Managing Editor of the *Sunday Times* under whom I had worked, spoke to Corson and Trento himself and told me that both would appear at the trial and speak in my defence. I told Hewitt this immediately and also gave him Lovesey's number. My personal doctor for the previous eleven years, Dr D. A. Parsons, told me he would give evidence at the trial that I had no history of mental illness. I asked Hewitt to contact him. At the end of my first meeting with Hewitt, I was pleased. I had told him what had happened and why I had written the letter. I had told him who was available to give evidence on my behalf (including Alex Coxen, who could describe his encounters with Mary Goldring and Sir Douglas Wass in 1984). I had told him I wanted Wass and Goldring subpoenaed for the defence. When I left Hewitt, I had thought the defence was well in hand.

I knew the two charges that I then faced had no *prima facie* evidence to support them. Because of this, before I had engaged Hewitt, I had already opted to take the unusual step of having a full committal hearing before a magistrate at Bow Street Court. At this hearing, the prosecution would present its case before a magistrate and I could cross-examine the witnesses and argue that no grounds existed to support the charges. On my own, I had made the application for such a hearing (which could not be refused in law), and I had been granted a two-week hearing for February 1997.

In the view of senior lawyers who have looked at the charges, that ought to have been the end of the case against me. When I appointed Hewitt of Fisher Meredith to represent me, that committal hearing was more than four months away. 'There is plenty of time,' Hewitt had told me when I had appointed him.

John Gordon had his chambers in the Middle Temple. Hewitt, Gordon and myself had a number of three-hour sessions there. These sessions involved every aspect of my past life except the defence to the charges.

'What has any of this to do with the charges? Why don't we just cut to the chase?' I asked Hewitt at the start of the second long session with Gordon. Hewitt replied, with great sincerity, talking as a parent to a child: 'We'll get to that. We need to know the background to the case. There is plenty of time. When we understand the full picture we can then give you the best legal advice.'

So, we went through a second conference with counsel. After thinking about things afterwards, given that the next session was three to four weeks away, I decided that, to save time, I should write down my 'life history' up to the start of the case against me.

I did so and sent it to Hewitt. Problem solved? Oh, no. Now, he had pages and pages of typed narrative, Hewitt insisted on going through what I had sent him, page by page. We started, at that third meeting, from the beginning. Hewitt took me through it line by line. It would have taken years at the rate we were going.

When I had first met Gordon in Hewitt's company, he had given me a photocopy of the relevant part of the 1861 Offences against the Person Act under which I had been charged. He asked me to read it. I did. He asked whether I understood it. I said I did. Had I intended Browne and Brennock to believe I should go to Japan to attack US soldiers there? No, I replied. Then my plea was not guilty and the onus of proof was on the prosecution. My view is that we should have gone straight from there to the next stage, which was to explain why I wrote the letters and what I expected the two complainants to believe when they got them. This did not happen. At no time did we get to that second stage.

We were always on the point of reaching the heart of the matter, but never quite got there, except for at one meeting where I got exasperated with all the biographical guff Hewitt insisted in going over with a fine-tooth comb.

'Look,' I said, 'I don't see the relevance of any of this. What is important is why I wrote the letters. I want to deal with that.'

Gordon paused and said to me, 'Why did you write the letters?'

'I wrote them,' I said, 'because I had had enough and I wanted to provoke the CIA into either killing me or undoing all the damage it had done to me.'

Without a pause, Gordon replied, 'It is not a defence in law that one intended that another party should commit a criminal offence.'

'But that is the truth!'

'And it is not a defence in law to the charges,' Gordon said. He was right, of course.

The date for the two-week-long committal hearing at Bow Street Court came. The MI5 witnesses, Browne and Brennock, were flown over from Dublin and put up in London hotels for the duration. I arrived at the court that morning to find Gordon and a junior solicitor I had never before seen from Hewitt's firm awaiting me. I was told Hewitt was out of the country on holiday, and would be away for the entire committal hearing. Gordon, the barrister, said,

'Never mind, we'll go ahead anyway.' I told him, 'No way!' He tried to persuade me to proceed.

'I'd like to have a look at the prosecution witnesses before the trial,' he said.

However, I instructed the junior solicitor to tell the presiding magistrate that I was waiving the committal hearing. That done, we all trooped into the court. The magistrate asked me if it was my wish to waive the committal hearing. I said it was. He then remanded me on unconditional bail and set a date in March for my next appearance. The case was referred to Southwark Crown Court for trial. As I left the dock, the magistrate said, 'Thank you, Mr Lehane, for your decision.'

The meeting in the pub for coffee with Gordon and Hewitt had been on the previous visit to Bow Street. The next court appearance was the first in the Crown Court where I should later be tried and where for the first time the judge who would preside at the trial appeared. It was what is called 'the pleas and directions hearing'. This is where the defendant has the charges formally put to him and, for the first time, can plead guilty or not guilty.

Judge Peter Fingret was not an MI5 officer, but I wondered whether he had been hand-picked by MI5 for the case. Among the fifteen judges available for a criminal trial at that court, Judge Fingret was the one they assigned when it was expected that an insanity defence was likely to be used. They knew whether or not this was likely because, on a routine basis, prosecution and defence lawyers – the 'learned friends' – communicated on such matters and with the judge.

I had no intention of using an insanity defence, nor had I any intention, if convicted, of seeking to use insanity as a mitigating factor. In theory, it was impossible for my sanity, or lack of it, to be a factor, before or after the conviction, without my permission. The theory would be shown to be wrong in due course. What can be said is that when Judge Fingret was assigned to my case I had given no indication to anybody that I intended to plead insanity at any point in the proceedings. Had the choice of Judge Fingret been wholly random, the odds against him being chosen for my case were long. But perhaps it was not random. Two different people who knew what they were talking about had filled me in on what was taking place. When I first appeared before Judge Fingret, his lightly educated cockney female clerk said to me, 'Lehane, you are charged with [etc., etc.]. How do you plead?'

I responded, 'I am in law an innocent man until proven guilty. Why am I not addressed as "Mr Lehane"?'

I looked straight into Judge Fingret's eyes as I said these words. He was enthroned maybe ten yards directly in front of me, on a raised dais, the cockney female immediately below him. There was silence. My question had been directed to Judge Fingret. He knew it. I knew it. Everybody there knew it. He chose to say nothing. Gordon and Hewitt rushed from their seats between me and the cockney clerk and started talking to me in loud whispers.

'Don't worry about it. Just plead not guilty and we can leave. It doesn't matter.' Yes, it did matter. 'Mr Lehane' is what I had been all my adult life. It is what I was till that clerk addressed me otherwise. It did not matter to Hewitt and Gordon. It mattered to me. The operatives of the legal system are firmly bound by strict codes on how to address each other and the judges. It is all 'Your honour' this and 'My learned friend' that. It matters. The formality dictates the status of each. Dispensing with the 'Mr' before my name mattered in the same way. This clerk would not dream of addressing me as anything other than 'Mr Lehane' were we to encounter each other in the ordinary course of events outside the court. She addressed me as she did because as far as she was concerned I was already a convicted criminal.

I was not a convicted criminal. I was innocent in law until proven guilty. But this did not matter to her. In her ignorance she revealed the instinctive corruption of the system: it is a mechanism for locking people up under the pretence that fair play and justice are at the heart of the procedure.

I don't know how long the silence lasted. I told Gordon and Hewitt that I had no intention of saying anything. They told me I had made my point and now to reply. I told them no. It seemed a long silence.

Then the clerk spoke. She said: 'Denis Lehane, how do you plead to the charges?'

I could live with that. I replied, 'Not guilty!'

My plea was, and is, the truth. But, as Gordon had told me, the truth does not matter. It plays no role in the British legal system.

15

Banged Up

Power is power over human beings. Over the body –
but, above all, over the mind.
from Nineteen Eighty-Four, GEORGE ORWELL

The only part of the legal system that I know personally is the law
of defamation and specifically libel. I know it very well. It was part
of my job to know it and I had worked very closely with the best
libel lawyers in the land during my professional life. The lawyers
did what I told them to do. I was never a supplicant. The former
Managing Editor of the *Sunday Times* under whom I had worked,
John Lovesey, unknown to me at the time, wrote a letter to my old
colleague Christopher Monckton early in 1997 saying: 'What
impressed me more than anything about Denis Lehane were the
fierce arguments he would have with the *Sunday Times* lawyers.
The thing was that Denis always won.'

In all my career as an investigative journalist in a state (Great
Britain) where there is no legal freedom of the press and the laws
of libel are such that they could have been written by rich and
powerful crooks for the purpose of preventing journalists from
writing the truth, I received many legal notices of action for libel
arising from articles I had written. I never lost a case. As Lovesey
told Lord Monckton, I always won.

In April 1997, when I wanted a new lawyer, I wrote to the richest
and most successful libel lawyer in Britain, Peter Carter Ruck. I
explained my situation and asked if Carter Ruck could recommend
to me a firm of good criminal defence lawyers who would work for
me on Legal Aid to put my defence to the court. He was kind
enough to write back with the name of the blue-chip firm of Claude,
Hornby & Cox of Great Marlborough Street.

I contacted them and arranged to meet a solicitor, Janet Dalton, on the 'green form' scheme that enables anybody at all to walk in off the street and see a solicitor for an hour. Legal Aid will automatically pay the lawyers for two hours' work, provided the person walking in off the street signs a green form. On that basis, I went into central London, signed the green form and told Ms Dalton how things were with me. Ms Dalton, then in her late twenties, was a Cambridge graduate from Northern Ireland. She struck me as able and businesslike. It did not surprise me that she, a comparatively junior solicitor just starting out on her career, would be assigned to me by such as firm as Claude, Hornby & Cox. Their senior, expensive lawyers would be dealing with the high-cost private cases.

Ms Dalton would be on salary as a junior solicitor gaining experience and it didn't matter to the firm that she worked on Legal Aid cases because she was getting valuable experience. I had had and sacked two hard-bitten, dyed-in-the-wool working-class-hero types of lawyer who did only Legal Aid. Janet Dalton and Claude, Hornby & Cox came as a welcome blast of fresh air. At that 'green-form' meeting I told her exactly what I wanted from her. When I got home I wrote to her setting out in writing what I wanted and telling her that, if she could not or would not, do that, I did not want to hire Claude, Hornby & Cox.

In the letter I told her: 'Before you address the charges themselves, I wish you to do the following:

1 Contact by telephone in the USA Dr William Corson of the CIA and his friend the journalist Joseph J. Trento, and obtain from them all details of what the CIA did to me in the spring of 1984 and after;

2 Obtain from my GP, Dr Parsons, a report on my health with particular reference to my mental health in the light of what William Corson and Joe Trento tell you;

3 On the basis of the responses to item 1, provide me with a legal opinion as to what the British authorities should have done when I reported to them on my return from the USA in 1984 what had been done to me and recommend what action in law I can take against them.

Only after the first 'green-form' meeting with Ms Dalton and after she had received and read my subsequent letter to her reiterating my needs, did I sign the white Legal Aid form agreeing that Claude, Hornby & Cox should represent me in place of the previous firm. At our 'green form' meeting, I had told Ms Dalton that Christopher Monckton, an old colleague from the *Yorkshire Post* who had worked for Margaret Thatcher when she was Prime Minister and had excellent government connections, had offered to intervene, but that Hewitt had refused to contact him as I had requested. I had told her that I wanted her to contact Christopher Monckton as a matter of urgency, by telephone, so that he could swing into action.

The next day I telephoned Ms Dalton. I asked her if she had read my letter. She said she had. I asked her if she was able to act for me on the basis of that letter. She said she was. I told her I was delighted to engage Claude, Hornby & Cox as my solicitors. This did not turn out to be as easy to do as I had thought. I had to appear at Southwark Crown Court with both Ms Dalton and Stephen Hewitt to obtain Judge Fingret's permission to change my representatives. He consented, but the very procedure itself was to be a presentiment of terrible things up ahead.

When I had first met Ms Dalton the trial was four months away. No longer was there 'plenty of time.' To save time, she asked me if she could keep whoever Hewitt had instructed as the barrister because a new barrister would take time to master the case. I had agreed. Moreover, I had made clear to Ms Dalton that Gordon himself had told Hewitt that he needed a QC to lead him and that, as a result, I wanted her to appoint one. She said she had no problem with that but that it would help were Gordon to remain as the junior. What she asked was reasonable.

Claude, Hornby & Cox remained my solicitors for precisely four weeks. Then I sacked them because in those four weeks they had done none of the three things I had told them to do before they addressed the charges. Nor, worst of all, had Ms Dalton spoken to Christopher Monckton.

As an interesting postscript to this, I had occasion to telephone Ms Dalton from my Dublin apartment on the afternoon of 21 October 2008 because I wanted to verify a fact about her and it seemed to me that the best way was to contact her directly. I Googled her. I found she had become the senior partner in the moderately sized and well-located firm of solicitors, Dalton, Holmes Gray of D'Arblay Street in central London. It did not surprise me. She was clearly extremely bright and competent, with a brilliant future ahead of her. I was sure that, had she been in charge of a properly prepared and funded defence, she would have secured my acquittal.

From the time I had surrendered to Catford Police Station on the afternoon of 3 May 1996 I had been on unconditional bail. I had had to turn up at a police station every three to four weeks to sign a book. Early in 1997 I wrote to the editor of the *Sunday Times Magazine*, Robin Morgan, whom I had known on the *Sunday Times* almost two decades before. He had agreed to publish a long investigative piece by me on the murder by Royal Navy officers of a young student, Sean Harper, two years before. The Ministry of Defence had covered up the murder. My piece was to be put in the magazine due to run on Sunday, 23 March. The issue would be printed at the start of the month.

Once I had finished that piece for Morgan, he sent me to Dublin to look into the unsolved disappearance and probable murder of an American student. I needed to speak to the murder-squad detectives. I was told by the Garda Siochana (Irish police) press office that a formal letter needed to be sent from Morgan to the Commissioner. In response to my request, Morgan faxed the letter and I spent most of February in Dublin talking to the murder-squad detectives on the case and others involved. It was a successful trip. I had a good piece to write.

However, on Sunday 2 March I learned that Vincent Browne had gone to Morgan's bosses at Times Newspapers and had spoken to them about me.

On 3 March Morgan told me he had no choice but to sack me. The issue dated 23 March was due to be printed within the following 48 hours. Morgan took the piece on the murder of Sean Harper and its cover-up by the British Ministry of Defence from that issue. The casualties were the grieving parents and family of Sean Harper. Nothing could have brought him back, but that article – which his mother Judy Harper, who had seen the galleys I had sent to her, had told me 'is exactly what we have been looking for, thank you so much, Denis' – would have helped those left behind to cope with their loss because the truth had at last been published.

I had broken no condition of my bail by working for Morgan, for my bail was unconditional. I had not been forbidden from seeking to earn my living, or from travelling to Ireland or elsewhere. At the next court appearance, the CPS would apply for such restrictions, but they had not been there when I had gone to Dublin in February.

Before I had made the Dublin trip, I had written to Brendan Keenan, Group Financial Editor of the Independent News and Media group. I wanted him to be a defence witness at the trial. One year earlier, he had received the same copy letter from me as Browne and Brennock. I wanted him to say why he had not felt any need to make a complaint to Scotland Yard about me. My intention was to call every single person who had received the letter and had not made a complaint. By February 1997, almost a year after the letters went out, only two complaints had been registered.

I did not get Keenan on the phone when I was in Dublin. Upon my return to London, my energies were devoted to trying to persuade Morgan to run the Harper article and let me continue with the one I had researched in Dublin and then, when it was all in vain, I had to break the news to the Harpers. At the next court appearance I learned that Keenan had now made a complaint and I was forbidden from leaving the country.

In the first week of May, I received a letter from the office which dealt with my unemployment benefit (as it happened, because of devolution of the British bureaucracy, it was in Belfast) instructing me to return my payment book and advising me that all further payments had been cancelled. I phoned up the dole office in Belfast to ask what had happened. A functionary replied, 'We have been told by your son that you died on 3 March and that somebody has been impersonating you to collect your unemployment payments ever since.'

I do not have a son and I was certainly not dead. The dole office may not have been sure whether I was alive, but their records would show that I did not have a son. The official I spoke to believed that I was dead and that the man who was talking to him was a fraudster. In passing, I noted that 3 March was the day I had officially stopped working for Morgan. It is just not possible for somebody to telephone any branch of the British bureaucracy with a claim that somebody else has died. If it were, all hell would break loose because it would be a good way of doing damage to an ex-spouse or ex-significant other. How was it possible for somebody to claim he was my non-existent son and get my dole cut off at once on the grounds that I was dead?

'The man who telephoned us saying he was your son had all your details – National Insurance number, date of birth, every-thing,' the official said. He added: 'He said he was sending your death certificate in the post, but it hasn't arrived yet.'

In 1997, there was not one person who could have had so much personal hatred for me as to get my dole cut off by lying to the dole office. At that time there was nobody in my life. No family. No friends. My only preoccupation, once Morgan had sacked me, was the bogus charges.

MI5, however, had all the bureaucratic details the dole officer told me my alleged son had provided. What mattered was that my sole source of income had been cut off. I wrote to Southwark Crown Court telling it that I should be surrendering to the court within two days. I put my affairs, such as they were, in order and turned up as promised. I was surprised to find Hewitt and Gordon awaiting me.

'What do you want?' I asked. 'I sacked you.'

'The court asked us to help you,' Hewitt replied.

I spent a night in Brixton Prison and was brought back to the court the following day. From there I was sent to a bail hostel at Tulse Hill, south-west London. The boss there, Sean Caldwell, was a diminutive, shaven-headed bachelor in his thirties. I did not take to him. Before retraining as a probation officer, he had been a schoolteacher.

The day after my arrival at the bail hostel I had a meeting with Bill Leeburn, a probation officer. The meeting was routine, because Leeburn had been assigned as my personal probation officer. Leeburn, also in his thirties, told me that he had qualified as an architect and worked for one of the largest architectural practices in Britain. In an economic downturn he had been made redundant and had been out of work for a year before coming to the conclusion that his career as an architect was at an end.

The year of unemployment had affected him deeply, as it does all people who find themselves on the scrap-heap. Being dumped by an employer, however it is explained in terms of economic downturns, deeply affects one's self-esteem. I knew this. When he had realised that he was not going to get a job as an architect, he had decided to retrain as a probation officer. It was a brave decision to write off years of his life and start again from the beginning but Bill Leeburn did not regret it. On the contrary, he told me, he enjoyed his new job very much: 'I now wake up in the morning feeling it is great to be alive.'

Bill Leeburn had told me about his abortive career as an architect, his period of unemployment and his black depression for a purpose. He told me that I should follow his example, that my career as a journalist was over and that I had to start again as he had done. He seemed to be suggesting that I should become a librarian and that, if I decided to pursue this new career, I could get a job in a nearby council library. I have to say that I have never harboured ambitions to be a librarian in a British public library.

'I am arranging for you to get a council flat when the case is all over and I don't expect to have any difficulty,' Bill Leeburn informed me. That would come in handy for the assistant librarian's job. My future, he was saying to me, was assured. That, of course, was his job. And that is how I viewed the things he said to me. I concluded that he was a young man who was all fired up by his new career and was doing his very, very best to help me.

His boss, Caldwell, was another thing altogether. He would tell me, during an interview a few days later, that I was guilty of all the charges. When I told him that I was innocent and cited the obscure provision of an 1861 Act of Parliament, he smiled derisively and said, 'That is nonsense. That is the Act that they use all the time for people like you.'

From the moment I arrived at the bail hostel in May 1997, Caldwell knew I was going to be convicted at the trial in September. So, too, it seemed, did Bill Leeburn. All of his arrangements were predicated on my being found guilty. Indeed, had I wanted a flat in Lambeth and an assistant librarian's job in the same London borough, it would have been very much to my disadvantage to have been acquitted.

There is no legal obligation on local authorities to house all the homeless. Women with children have to be housed, even if the only accommodation is bed-and-breakfast hotels. Men often have to sleep rough in the streets. However, probation officers can sometimes place released criminals at the top of the waiting list for council flats, because finding permanent accommodation for released criminals is regarded as a paramount requirement if they are not to re-offend.

Thus, by committing a criminal offence a man can jump to the head of the waiting list for permanent accommodation at the tax-payer's expense. Leeburn thought I should be found guilty and sent away somewhere for nine months: plenty of time for him to arrange a council flat for me on my release.

In the few weeks I spent at the bail hostel I attended several interviews about my future. At each interview, though, I was a passive spectator. I just listened. On one level it was fascinating to watch the wheels turn. There were flaws in their procedures, how-ever. In the first place, I had no historical connection with Lambeth. The bail hostel was the one and only time I spent there outside Brixton Prison. I had not applied anywhere for housing. I was not on the Lambeth housing list. I had previously been living in my father's house in Lewisham. Had the dole office in Belfast not cut off my dole because 'my son' had informed them that I had died at the start of March, I should probably still have been there, so I had not applied to be on the housing list there either.

Technically, being sent to a bail hostel was not classified as custody. I therefore had to pay rent. As I was unemployed, I should be entitled to unemployment assistance and the local authority, Lambeth Council, would pay my rent.

The day after my arrival at the bail hostel I attended, as instructed, Lambeth Town Hall to apply for housing funds to pay the rent at the hostel. I filled out the form truthfully. I gave my father's house as my permanent address and described the bail hostel as a temporary residence. No matter how long one spends in jail – 20 or 30 years even – the jail does not become a permanent address.

My father's house was not in Lambeth, so the bureaucrats at the Town Hall rejected my application for housing funds on the grounds that I was not a resident of their borough. The boss of the bail hostel, Sean Caldwell, called me in to see him when he received the rejection. He told me to reapply and, this time, to give the address of the bail hostel as my permanent address. All the other prisoners there had done so, and if I did not do so, he would send me back to the court on the grounds that I had breached the conditions of my bail.

There were about 30 other prisoners in the bail hostel. Most, perhaps all, had no connection with the Borough of Lambeth, which was nevertheless paying their rent because they had done what Caldwell had told them to do: they had given the bail hostel as their permanent address. Caldwell warned me that unless I did the same, he would call the police and I should be sent to jail. I told him to go ahead.

Caldwell picked up the telephone, called Brixton Police Station and declared me to be in breach of my bail conditions. He required me to be arrested. I had seen this happen to other prisoners in my time at the bail hostel. On each occasion, the prisoner would be given the option of waiting for the coppers or making his escape before they arrived. All the prisoners I had seen previously in this situation had opted to make a run for it.

But I had nowhere to run to. I told Caldwell I would wait for the coppers. He was surprised. He did not understand. The coppers, two of them, arrived after about half an hour and I was taken to Tower Bridge Magistrates' Court. In the cells I was approached by the duty solicitor but declined his services. When I appeared in court, the magistrate asked me why I had no solicitor. I told him I did not want one. He said there was a duty solicitor who would act for me on Legal Aid. I told him I knew all that but still didn't want one.

Disconcerted, the magistrate paused and thought for a few seconds. Perhaps, in those few seconds he searched back in his memory for the rules of the legal system and recognised that he could not refuse to deal with a prisoner because that prisoner refused to use a lawyer.

Why, the magistrate asked me, had I breached the conditions of my bail? I told him I had not breached them. I had merely refused to give the bail hostel as my permanent address because it was not my permanent address. The magistrate decided I should be admitted to a different bail hostel. I went back into the cells while somebody rang around the London bail hostels to see if there were any vacancies.

The magistrate and I each foresaw days and days of fruitless endeavour as I spent the night in jail and was then brought to the court and put in the cells while somebody telephoned bail hostel after bail hostel to see if any of them would take me on my terms.

I told the puzzled magistrate as he rambled on about bail hostels, 'I have made no application for bail.'

Puzzled, he said, 'I don't understand.'

'I don't want bail. I told the judge that when I surrendered to the court at the beginning of the month. I never wanted to go into the bail hostel. I was put there.'

'Are you sure you don't want to talk about this to the duty solicitor?'

'Yes. Quite sure.'

'But if you don't want to go into a bail hostel, you will have to spend your remand in jail.'

'Yes. I know that. It is what I told the judge at the start of the month.'

The court sent me to Belmarsh, London's only top-security prison. I hadn't liked the bail hostel but, bad as it was, I had assumed that 'real prison' must be worse. I was wrong. Had I known the truth, I should have refused police bail when I had been arrested on 3 May 1996 and spent the next two and a half years in jail, instead of just the year I served.

It strikes me as laughable today, but I had thought prisons contained only 'hardened criminals' and that I should be in danger of serious assault from them. I was wrong. Completely. In the year that I spent behind bars, the only attacks I suffered – apart from one by a disturbed prisoner, which was triggered by warders – came from warders themselves. After one such unprovoked attack in Brixton, I spoke to a black Methodist bishop who was on the Prison Board of Governors, which in theory, though not in practice, had the authority to ensure that the warders did not give prisoners a good kicking. I told him that, in my view, 25 per cent of the warders were violent psychopaths. He replied, 'You are wrong. It is only five per cent.'

It is a cliché that jail is full of innocent people who should not be there. It is also the truth. As an innocent man put there on trumped-up charges, I had thought I should be exceptional. I found I was not. I found jail the most honest place I had ever been in. There were no hardened criminals (except among the warders). Only men like myself. I fitted in there because I was like everybody else, innocent or guilty. I made friends. It happens when one is locked up for many hours a day with two other prisoners in a cramped cell. You have to get on. You talk, you laugh, you share histories, you make the best of what you've got.

The quality of my life improved in the period I spent in various prisons up to the political show-trial. Then, when I was put in solitary confinement (or sometimes in the hospital wing as a deranged lunatic), the quality plummeted.

The explanation is simple. When I turned up in jail I had lost the support of all but a tiny handful of people. Her Majesty, in her wisdom, chose to put me in an environment where making friends was a way of life. It killed the boredom and it distracted one's mind from dwelling on the loss of one's freedom.

Being locked up bothered most of my colleagues because, as I learned from the visiting days, on the odd occasion somebody came to see me, these 'hardened criminals' had family, friends, wives, girlfriends and children. Apart from my father, and Michael Fitzpatrick and Neil Middleton (who lived in Paris and Dublin respectively), I was on my own.

To me the so-called 'loss of liberty' did not exist. I had lost nothing. My liberty had been taken away long before. The heavy steel doors and iron bars provoked no sense of loss in me. I had nowhere to go. Iron bars do not a prison make. I was already in prison long before the steel doors shut behind me. What I did not lose was my self-respect. They can capture you physically, but they cannot capture your spirit unless you let them. I was not going to let them.

In the first few weeks I spent at Belmarsh in the late spring of 1997, one of the warders tried to get my new colleagues to kill me. Why he did it I never knew, but it happened.

Prisoners are required to work or be educated as part of what is called their 'rehabilitation'. A small amount of money is credited to the prisoner's account at the tuck-shop, where once a week he can buy anything from radio batteries to chocolate bars. Work at Belmarsh consisted of putting together three-pin plugs for electrical appliances. The worker got one penny for each plug assembled. I opted for education.

One of my classes was art. The warders locked us in during the classes, and they carefully searched us when they unlocked the doors to let us out. This was because there were knives in the art-room, which could cut throats just as well as paper. All knives had to be accounted for before we were allowed to leave. A middle-class lady teacher took the sessions. All of the teachers were ladies from outside the prison service. They were very good. They tried to make their classes interesting and largely succeeded.

One morning not long after my arrival at Belmarsh I was contentedly at play painting a flower when one of the other prisoners, Tommy, approached me. Tommy was short and wiry with the mien of an old lag, though I doubt if he had seen his 35th birthday.

'What you in for?' he asked me.

'What's it to you?' I replied.

'What it is to me is that we believe you are here for noncing a twelve-year-old girl. If that's true, we're going to cut your throat.'

That got my attention. 'Noncing' is prison argot for unlawful sexual intercourse with a minor. To fellow prisoners, it is the worst offence that a prisoner can commit. Nonces never did time in the ordinary prison wings because they would not survive. A prisoner could apply under Rule 43 to be lodged in a special unit among fellow paedophiles.

When we left the prison for appearances in court, we were all processed, given a change of clothes, searched and then held in a large wired-glass cage in a locked reception area. The nonces appearing in court that day were always processed before the rest of us arrived; then they were locked into single cells in the holding area. There they would have to wait while the rest of us were processed.

Then, once we were all in the main holding cage (at Belmarsh there were two, side by side) the nonces would be taken out of their cells and led to the armoured paddy-wagons, where they would be locked into tiny, individual cubicles. There they would stay until they were let out at the court.

The transfer of the nonces from their holding cells to the prisoners' paddy-wagon would be accomplished swiftly. But there was always time for the ordinary prisoners to voice their detestation with threats and abuse. Nonces were the lowest of the lowest of the low.

I was not a nonce. I told my colleague, Tommy, that day in the art-room that I had been charged with threatening to go to Japan to kill American soldiers. He told me that they needed proof – a copy of my charge-sheet from my lawyers. I told Tommy I had no lawyers. He said I could still get the charge-sheet from the court. I was going there for an appearance later in the week. That would do, he told me. If I were a nonce, he made clear, they would cut my throat.

The day came for the trip to court. By then I knew that all my fellow prisoners believed that I was a nonce. I was puzzled by this. Rumours like this did not just arise. This was serious. In the holding cage, I asked one of the other prisoners, Tony, where the rumour came from. Tony pointed at the warders: 'They are the ones who are saying it,' he said.

That puzzled me even more. I told Tony what I had told Tommy, that I was not a nonce. He replied, 'The only thing that has kept you alive till now is that you haven't made an application under Rule 43. If it weren't for that, you'd be dead.'

This was all said in a matter-of-fact way. The warders all around us would not have known the subject of the conversation. We could have been talking about greyhounds for all they knew.

I appeared alone in the dock before Judge Fingret. I told him: 'The warders at Belmarsh are telling the other prisoners that I have been charged with sexually abusing a 12-year-old girl. I have been told that if I return this evening without details of the true charges against me, my throat will be cut.'

I asked for a copy of the charge sheet and formally requested that an investigation be undertaken by the police against the warders at Belmarsh to discover why they were telling lies to the other prisoners knowing that, if their lies were believed, I should be murdered.

What the warders had done was light-years worse than the bogus charges I faced. The warders had been trying to engineer my murder. Judge Fingret was unmoved. He told the court clerk to give me a copy of the charge-sheet. He refused to order an investigation against the warders. One law for us, one for them.

As luck would have it, I met Tony in the holding cage on the way back into Belmarsh. I gave him the rap-sheet. He looked at it and then gave it back to me. 'That's OK,' he said. 'Sorry if you've had a hard time, but we had to make sure.'

I told him I understood. Prison society is conservative. Nonces are pariahs in prison society. There is honour even among thieves. Noncing broke the rules and prison society dealt with offenders according to those rules. The rule of law inside prison has nothing to do with the warders, lawyers and judges. The prisoners themselves run things.

I had at no time feared for my life after Tommy had told me what the warders were saying about me. I was not charged with being a nonce and I knew I could prove it. I was comfortable that the other prisoners would treat me fairly and appropriately. The next art class I attended, the other prisoners greeted me warmly. At one point, Billy, who was doing six years for burglary, interrupted some exchange with the words, 'Nah, leave him alone. He's had a bad enough time already!' What Billy meant was that he wanted to make a statement that I had had a rough time but now it was over.

Tommy told me in great detail where the rumours had come from. One of the warders on duty in the education department had made sure that all the right prisoners knew that I was a nonce. I did not know who the warder was, and he had to be pointed out to me. I had no recollection of ever having encountered him in any routine activity where I might inadvertently have aroused his displeasure. I could see no reason why he would do what he had done.

My life had been saved by the routine justice of the society in which I lived. Real justice. My colleagues had not taken the warder's word alone. They had given me the opportunity to clear my name. I had done so. As a bonding exercise between me and my fellow prisoners, it was a great plus for me. The same people who would have cut my throat had I indeed been a nonce now became good friends.

We attended the same classes together. There were plenty of discussions and debates. The teachers from outside were really motivated to help us and they were great. It was valuable and fun. Whatever had been the objective behind the warder's behaviour or behind Judge Fingret's reluctance to order an investigation, it had failed.

One day, when I was at Her Majesty's pleasure in the bail hostel, a little red dot appeared on the wall of my cell. It then started wiggling about in various patterns. I thought it was a laser sight on a rifle, but I did not immediately hide under the bed. Instead, I watched the little red dot, fascinated, and waited for the show to start.

Curious, I climbed up to the window to see if I could locate where the red light was coming from. Not a sensible course of action had it been somebody's intention to shoot me right between the eyes with a rifle. But in the minutes I had spent watching the little red dot tracing its crazy patterns on the cell wall, I had not felt that my life was in danger. Whatever else was happening, I was not in the middle of a MI5/CIA 'hit'.

So I looked out of the window. My cell was on the second floor at the back of the building. From the window, 25 yards away in direct line of sight along an alleyway, I saw two men parked in a non-descript car – an ageing Ford or Vauxhall 'economy/family' vehicle. The car was parked at right-angles to my cell. The men, both balding with cropped hair and in their late thirties or early forties, had had to drive off the main road into a side road and then turn into the alley. They were wearing leather bomber jackets.

The men were a certain type that I had encountered in Belfast in the early 1970s. If I were to speak to either of them, I should expect a working-class accent, probably Estuary English.

The red light disappeared when I put my head to the window. I knew this because when I saw the men I looked back to the cell wall and the light was no longer there. I saw no rifle. The two men were sitting talking. I looked at them for a minute or so. Their ages, descriptions and clothing suggested a couple of plain-clothes NCOs in the special forces.

I climbed down from the window and waited to see whether the red light would come back and play more games on the cell wall. It didn't. After about ten minutes I climbed back to the window. The car and the two men had gone.

Another odd thing happened not long after I arrived at Belmarsh. A young black man tried to make friends with me. He was tall, lean, aged about 30, with an educated American accent. In my year in Her Majesty's custody, I met many nationalities, but he was the only American.

My colleagues in the prison population were overwhelmingly working-class Afro-Caribbeans. They comprised four per cent of the general population, maybe 40 per cent of the prison population. Many were from Brixton. The tall American sought me out and tried to engage me in conversation. He said he would lend me some books that were intellectually stimulating. He said he had thought about me when he had received these books. But this was a man who did not know me. He had no reason to believe that I was in need of intellectual stimulation

He tried to engage me in conversation on two or three other occasions, always apparently by chance. He wanted to get to know me. I did not want him to do so. After a while he gave up. Not long after, he left my part of the jail, and perhaps left Belmarsh altogether.

On the whole I had no problems with being locked up by Her Majesty until I was officially classified insane. Things were fine. I enjoyed being in jail. It was interesting. I should not have missed it for the world. The warder's failed attempt at murder-by-proxy merely ensured my total acceptance by the prisoner society in Belmarsh. That was a massive boost for me. It meant that in the five months I spent in jail before trial, I had a good time. I got three squares a day and plenty of cups of tea. I spent some mornings in the education wing. When I was banged up with two cell-mates, I chatted, laughed and joked with them.

We all did what needed to be done to accept our lives and not go mad. That is how we got through prison. We knew the rules. Not the ones in the big fat book (which I once spent a fascinating day reading when a copy arrived in the cell) but the real rules by which we all lived.

When I had first entered Belmarsh, the new prisoners like myself went through what was called an 'induction programme'. This grand-sounding title meant a not unintelligent senior warder sitting on a table swinging his legs to and fro as he said, 'Basically, if you f*** with us, we'll f*** with you. If you don't f*** with us, we won't f*** with you.'

The first thing every prisoner had to accept in jail was that he had no rights. Period. In the official rule-book, there were pages upon pages about prisoners' rights. A prisoner was entitled, for example, to have a manual typewriter in his cell for his personal use, but in a small cell designed for two with three bunks it was difficult to see where this typewriter could have been put.

Though warders were strictly forbidden to strike prisoners, the 'good kicking' was a regular and routine response to misbehaviour, real or imagined. Prisoners brought up before a governor, on whatever charge, would inevitably be found guilty irrespective of the truth.

Needless to say, the fine Legal Aid lawyers who were being paid to represent prisoners in court would never dream of investigating the 'good kickings' their clients received from warders.

After my release, to be sure, there was a highly-publicised case of violence by warders at Wormwood Scrubs and Wandsworth. I had done time in both, and I knew them to be the worst prisons in London because of the warders' culture of violence.

Any prisoner who tried to live his life in prison according to the rules in the rule-book would, if he were lucky, go mad. If he were unlucky, he would end up like 'Charles Bronson', who was in solitary confinement in the same block at Belmarsh when I was there. He was what the papers call – because that is what they call all of us – 'a common criminal'. He had been arrested and sentenced a quarter of a century before. He had challenged the system and the system had crushed him.

Long after he should have been released at the end of his sentence, he remained there because prison governors had routinely added periods of custody to the original sentence. I had some experience of this myself during my brief prison career. On one occasion, in Wandsworth, I appeared before one of the governors to face some spurious charge or other. The governor started by saying, 'Have you had enough time to prepare your defence to the charge?'

I replied, 'No.'

The governor promptly cited a judgment of the House of Lords, the highest court in Britain on all questions of law. The mischief of this judgment was that two hours were sufficient from the time a prisoner was served notice of a charge (which was in writing and was usually shoved under the cell door by one of the warders at night) to the time when he was brought before the governor for summary trial. Not enough time – in any view – to contact one's lawyer and have him attend, let alone for him to listen to the prisoner's side of things and prepare a defence.

That is how the *soi-disant* Charles Bronson found himself in jail long after he had served the time for his original offence. I never knew his real name. He changed it by deed poll to the name of the

American film actor of the 1970s, apparently because he admired his macho image.

We other prisoners in Belmarsh regarded Charles Bronson with awe. He was our hero. It would be nothing to him to take on half a dozen warders and really hurt two or three before the numbers told and he received another good kicking.

We all had the same distaste and disdain for the system and those who staffed it. We all accepted the reality and worked around it as best we could. Not so Charles Bronson. He attacked the lies and hypocrisy of the system head on. It destroyed him, but his courage and his persistence won our admiration for his spirit, for his refusal to accept he was an unperson with no rights at all. We all felt like Charles Bronson but none of us dared to emulate him. As his prison life showed, in any fight with the system there would be only one winner.

In July 2002 the European Court of Human Rights in Strasbourg ruled that this British custom of prison governors adding on additional time to prisoners sentences after summary hearings was illegal under international human-rights law. Tens of thousands of prisoners who, like Charles Bronson, had been dealt with in this way in British jails over the years, reports said, would be getting substantial compensation from Her Majesty. I hoped Charles Bronson took Her Majesty to the cleaners for damages for all the extra time he had spent banged up.

16

The Baron and the Baroness

In our society, those who have the best knowledge of what is happening are also those who are furthest from seeing the world as it is.

from *Nineteen Eighty-Four*, GEORGE ORWELL

By August 1997 I was faced with four identical charges under the same section of the 1861 Offences against the Person Act. The first three were made by three Dublin-based persons who had been individually persuaded to lodge a complaint against me by Scotland Yard's wonder-boys during their expense-account visits to the Irish capital. The fourth and last charge was a strange one. It arrived in the summer of 1997 and was in the name of 'Ms Sarah Jane Whalley'.

Ms Whalley was, and may still be for all I know, the secretary to the then Melvyn, now Baron, Bragg, at his offices at the now-defunct London Weekend Television. If I had ever met her, it would have been when Lord Bragg had me in those offices at his request late in 1995. The baron is a well-meaning peer. He met me because I had asked him for help getting work. He wrote some letters which came to nothing. I think he concluded that I was 'a never-ending story': that he had tried his best but could not spare me any more time. As a result, he did not reply to my last letter to him. Instead, Ms Whalley was delegated to deal with me.

Thus it was, and for no other reason, that I directed the copy of the letter to Taylor in March 1996 to this lady in the belief that it would be forwarded to Lord Bragg.

Ms Whalley's statement outlining her complaint against me said that nobody had read the letter from me when it had arrived in March 1996. In accordance with Lord Bragg's instructions, she had filed it. There it had remained for more than a year until the boy wonders had gone to see her.

Her statement to the Dynamic Duo said she very much enjoyed her job as Lord Bragg's secretary. How nice. I was glad to read it. Perhaps good lawyers would have had the charge related to Ms Whalley struck out on the ground that Batman and Robin had put her up to it: for otherwise my letter to Lord Bragg would never have been read at all.

Late in the day, I decided not to present a defence to the charges, and not even to attend the trial. At first I had strongly wished to prepare a full and proper defence. Central to this was the need to bring William Corson and Joe Trento over from the USA. Her Majesty's taxpayers had paid for the Caped Crusaders to visit Ireland, had paid for Browne and Brennock to fly over in February for the aborted committal hearing, and would fly them and Keenan from Dublin for the trial.

The CIA and MI5 had been active as well as the Yard's super-heroes. The amount of public funds spent in the USA and Great Britain to bring me to court was huge. One glimpse of that huge operation came nine days before the start of the trial, when a bulky package from the prosecution was delivered to my cell.

This package contained statements by seven residents of the USA, CIA and other US service personnel, who, I was informed, would be called by the prosecution at trial. Most of these witness statements had been made at least a year before and should have been given to me then. It is not acceptable for the Crown to with-hold the bulk of its case against a defendant until a few days before the trial begins. The defendant is entitled to know what charges he faces at trial and on what evidence the Crown will rely.

When I had asked Judge Fingret in open court six months earlier to name the Crown witnesses I had been forbidden to contact, he had refused to name them. Instead, he said, 'You know who they are.'

No, I didn't. The Crown's delivery to me of seven witness statements from US nationals only one of whom was known to me, just nine days before trial, proved that Judge Fingret had been wrong. I presume the seven witnesses all gave evidence at the trial. However, I was in the cells and had no legal representation, so I do not know.

Given the Crown's ambush with the very late witness statements from several people I had never heard of, I should really have applied at once to Judge Fingret to rule that the statements and the witnesses were inadmissible.

If he had refused this request, an application for an adjournment of several months so that I could consider this new evidence should have been made. I made no such applications. Why? Because I had no confidence in Judge Fingret's impartiality. He had already failed to order an investigation into the potentially lethal decision of one of the warders to tell my colleagues in prison that I was a nonce. I knew he was determined that the trial would start on Monday 15 September 1997. Nothing I or anyone said could change that.

The seven witness statements were evidence that it had long been the intention of MI5 and the CIA that three Irish nationals would be flown from Dublin and seven US nationals from the USA. In response to that, my wish that William Corson and Joe Trento be brought over on Legal Aid to give evidence on my behalf seemed proportionate. However, no lawyer that I approached would make the application to the Legal Aid Board. So there was not a level playing field.

I got the idea of just refusing to participate in the Crown's pantomime from George Bernard Shaw, the Irish playwright. After the 1916 Easter Rising in Dublin, the British executed 13 leaders of the Irish army by firing-squad. A fourteenth, Roger Casement, was taken from Ireland to London and tried at the Old Bailey for high treason.

If convicted, Casement would be hanged, a horrible way to die. Casement decided to defend himself. Shaw asked him why. Shaw's view was that the trial was a charade, and that there was no chance of an acquittal. By mounting a defence, Shaw said, Casement would endorse the process itself. Better by far to take no part in what was planned as a political show-trial and judicial murder.

Casement understood Shaw's point. He knew he was going to be hanged and that nothing he could say or do at the show-trial would affect that. The British wanted their pound of flesh and they were going to get it. But Casement believed that he could publicise Ireland's cause and counter the British black propaganda by a final address from the dock before being sentenced.

Thus he turned Shaw down. He went through with the charade and made his speech from the dock. It was immensely powerful. But I had always believed that Shaw's was the correct analysis of the situation.

It was that long-held belief which led me to take the action I took. Since the 'dawn raid' of 3 May 1996, I had persistently sought Legal Aid lawyers to present my defence and I held the strong conviction that in a fair courtroom that best defence would have succeeded. But I did not find any lawyer who would accept my instructions, even when I gave them in writing. So I opted for George Bernard Shaw's advice. If I could not present the best possible defence to the court, I should take no part.

About a week before I had surrendered my bail in May 1997, I had met the solicitor James Nichol in the company of his business partner Carolyn Taylor, a niece of the then Lord Chief Justice of England and Wales.

Nichol, then aged 52, was a working-class hero from the tough north-east mining country. He had been a solicitor for 11 years. Ms Taylor, he told me, would sit in on the interview because he valued her opinion. She sat without making any comment during the entire interview. She did not make a good impression on me.

Nichol's naivety was the making of him. He saw no inconsistency between his brand of radical, revolutionary socialism and the fact that his mentor and business partner was a member of the traditional elite.

I met this odd couple at their offices close by Finsbury Park Underground Station in North London. Nichol had been recommended to me by John Hendy QC, a barrister from the London working class who had studied law at Queen's University, Belfast, in the early 1970s when I was there. A long-time girlfriend of mine, Claire O'Driscoll, remembers him from that time, but I did not meet him until I returned to London.

Hendy had made a big name for himself defending people claiming unfair dismissal. A lifelong socialist, he had been dismayed by the arrival of Tony Blair with his self-styled 'New Labour' Party, which had dumped its working-class socialist guiding principles. Not long before I met him, Hendy had left the Labour Party. With Nichol and the leader of the National Union of Mineworkers, Arthur Scargill, Hendy had founded the Socialist Labour

Party. The three men were the *politburo* of the new party.

However, Blair and 'New Labour' swept to a landslide victory on 1 May 1997. The newly-created Socialist Labour Party received derisory support. The Socialist Labour Party has now ceased to exist. I mention this because Nichol was, when I met him in that general-election month, widely regarded as the most radical of Britain's senior lawyers working on Legal Aid.

Nichol had two huge scalps to his name. The first was the successful defence of Clive Ponting, a senior civil servant under Margaret Thatcher, who had leaked state papers to a newspaper showing that the government had misled Parliament and the people. Ponting was prosecuted under the draconian Official Secrets Act, a law all civil servants have to sign. The Act made leaking confidential information an imprisonable offence.

The significance of the Ponting acquittal was that Nichol's defence accepted that the prosecution case was correct as to fact. Clive Ponting had been caught red-handed. He had done what the prosecution said he had done. What he had done was a serious criminal offence. How, then, did Nichol get Ponting off? By simply inviting the jury not to convict him. Nichol accepted that his client had committed the crime. He asked the jury to rule that Ponting was innocent notwithstanding. Nichol won. It was a sensation. That was when he became known as 'Famous Jim'.

However, what Nichol had done was not new. The strategy of telling a jury that the defendant had committed the crime but that nevertheless it should not convict him is well established in history. In the 1830s, Sir John Peel, as Home Secretary, had reformed the British legal system, eliminating some 200 offences which had carried the death penalty. Juries had become accustomed to acquitting defendants charged with, for example, stealing a sheep, because conviction would lead to hanging, a disproportionate punishment. Juries no longer believed that in these 200 categories the punishment fitted the crime.

Unlike Clive Ponting, I had not committed the offences of which I was charged, and Nichol had told me at that first meeting in May 1997 that I should thus not be convicted of them, His advice, as he was going on holiday and could not take the case, had been that I didn't need a lawyer. I should be acquitted simply by representing myself.

Nichol seemed precisely the lawyer for me if I were to put my defence to the jury. Had I, indeed, been guilty of crimes, Nichol could have offered the same defence which had been successful with Clive Ponting: that I did not deserve to be punished because much worse crimes had been committed against me and had gone unpunished.

Nichol's second claim to fame had arisen from another high-profile case, the murder of Carl Bridgewater, a twelve-year-old boy, on a Staffordshire farm some nineteen years before. Four innocent men had been convicted. The police had framed them. When I met Nichol in May 1997, he was awaiting the verdict of the Court of Appeal on his latest attempt to get the convictions of the 'Bridgewater Four' overturned.

By the early summer of 1997 the Bridgewater Four had become Three because one of the innocent men had died in jail. Nichol won that appeal. Just like the acquittal of Clive Ponting, it was a ground-breaking decision. 'Famous Jim' had struck again.

I was in jail myself when I saw the television news reports of Nichol's latest stunning defeat of the legal Establishment. There was great jubilation on the steps of the Royal Courts of Justice in the Strand. Nichol's interview after the decision inspired me to contact him after my own trial. What riveted my attention was his statement: 'The legal system is completely unfair. It is inherently flawed. It is rubbish.'

Before the Anglo-Normans came to Ireland the Irish people had lived under their own laws, known to us as Brehon Laws. These are an ancient and sophisticated series of codes and oral traditions which were superior to those in Britain, being of greater longevity. According to the Brehon Law, fasting in protest at injustice was an appropriate response in cases where overwhelming wrong was imposed by superior force. It brought shame and responsibility for the outcome of the fast upon the wrongdoer.

The greatest hero of Irish mythology, Cuchulain, was known not only for his victories against foreign invaders, his bravery, his good deeds done for the underdog and his sacrifices for his fellow warriors, but also for his fasts in support of causes he believed in but could not fight for. Cuchulain's protest fasts were comprehensible to the traditional Irish people down through the centuries. They made sense to the generation which fought and won the war of independence against Britain between 1916 and 1921. They make no sense to the British. To them, starving oneself to death is an absurd, ridiculous gesture.

Anglo-Saxons regard protest fasts as proving their own racial superiority to those who use them. Mohandas K. Gandhi used a comparable tradition of fast in Hinduism against the British as part of his successful campaign to gain independence for India.

I had written again to Judge Fingret and asked him to appoint 'any solicitor except Hewitt and Fisher Meredith' to represent me, and to seek an adjournment. The judge did not reply.

I decided that the time had come to stop eating. On the evening of Friday 5, September 1997, I handed a brief letter to one of the warders on my wing. It said that I should take no more food of any kind. The warder read it and then said to me, 'Oh, I can't deal with this.'

He went away. Five minutes later, a senior warder, one with two stars on his shoulder, came to my cell. He asked me to confirm what I had written. Was I 'going on hunger strike'? he asked me.

'If you like,' I replied.

'Any particular reason?'

'Because I don't have lawyers and the judge won't appoint any,' I replied.

He went away. I had had nothing to eat since supper three days previously. I had not taken food at any of the following mealtimes but I had taken mugs of tea with no milk or sugar. Nobody had noticed what I had been doing. I had waited for more than 48 hours to tell the warders because I had never gone without food for any period of time before. I feared that I might make a fool of myself in front of the warders if I were to start a fast only to find I could not maintain it.

I could maintain it. Almost a week into my hunger-strike, I was summoned before a group of senior warders and a governor in a room off the wing. Did I know where I was? Yes, I replied, I was in jail. Did I know what I was doing? Yes, I was refusing all food in protest at the way the legal system had been treating me. I wanted to defend myself against the charges because I was innocent but no lawyer would defend me on Legal Aid.

The governor told me that the prison service knew nothing about the charges and were not involved in the legal procedures.

Had I made use of the facilities available to contact Legal Aid lawyers? Yes, but I had had no replies.

It was clear that their primary concern was that I had not stopped eating in protest at them or anything they had done. I reassured them that I had no complaints about the prison regime, and that the focus of my fast was the legal system and the judge.

Did I have any requests? Yes, I should like some additional tea bags so that I could drink more tea. Not a problem. The two-star senior warder went to the kitchen and gave me a big bunch of tea bags. He said that when they ran out I must ask for more and he would make sure I got them. They did run out and I did get some more when I asked. There was no attempt to persuade me to resume eating food.

At each meal call, when my two cell-mates were summoned to collect their food, an officer would bring me a dinner-tray. I was getting room service. It occurred to me that by going on hunger-strike a prisoner could avoid ever leaving his cell: the warders would wait on him with food at each mealtime. Alas, I had to forgo that luxury. On arrival, each plate of food was offered to my cell-mates and, if they did not want it, flushed down the toilet.

A day or so later, I was moved to the padded cell on the ground floor. This is a single cell where they put people who are thought to be in danger of killing themselves. Everything is made of softish plastic and there are no sharp or hard edges. It was by far the best accommodation I had in my year as a guest of Her Majesty.

Sunday, 14 September 1997 was my 48th birthday. The warders on my wing at Belmarsh celebrated by not delivering any food to me all day. But in the afternoon I did get a surprise visitor to my cell. The door was unlocked and one of the prison governors stepped in. He came with a hand-delivered letter to me from Baroness Shirley Williams of Crosby. The letter pleaded with me to engage Hewitt and Fisher Meredith to represent me at the show-trial which would begin the next day. The baroness wrote: 'We have spoken to Mr Hewitt a lot and we like him very much.'

This was the fourth letter on the subject that I had received in 24 hours. I had had one from Hewitt himself and one each from John Lovesey and Alex Coxen. If one counted two previous letters from Hewitt in the previous week, this came to six letters that I had received pleading with me to engage Hewitt. Though I had sacked him after six months because I did not think he had done enough to prepare my defence, now I was bombarded with letters like confetti from people I had not contacted and who had not, certainly for a year, sought to contact me.

Each one was telling me that they had spoken to Hewitt and liked him very much. The logic of their letters, individually and collectively, was that only my bizarre refusal to let Hewitt represent me was standing in my way of an acquittal. I should learn that the gravamen of Hewitt's approaches to Williams, Lovesey and Coxen was that I had become mentally ill and this mental illness was preventing me from seeing that he would be able to secure an acquittal on all charges. Coxen had been a friend at university. I had worked for Lovesey at the *Sunday Times*. Neither had made any attempt to visit me in jail since I had been there the previous May. Why should I pay attention to any of these people? I didn't. I threw all their letters away.

On the 11th day of my hunger strike I was driven in the paddy-wagon from my luxurious cell in Belmarsh to Southwark Crown Court for the start of Her Britannic Majesty's political show-trial.

Each weekday morning in every jail in London the same routine begins. The prison warders change from the night to the day shift at 7 a.m. The drivers and guards of the armoured paddy-wagons have been on the go for maybe an hour before that. At the various courts scattered through the metropolis, private security guards are checking in and making ready to receive that day's prisoners.

In their palatial stockbroker-belt mansions, the learned judges are still snuggled up in bed while all the lesser actors in each day's drama are getting themselves ready. It is a complex system, perhaps not unlike running a railway.

At Belmarsh on the morning of Monday, 15 September 1997 the routine went as usual. Along with all the other prisoners, I got up at around seven. The previous night, the warder on his rounds reminded me I would be going to court next day and should take all my things with me. After washing and dressing in the cell, I packed my very meagre belongings into a large black plastic bag.

Prisoners going to court are taken out of the cells early and moved to the holding cage. There I was searched, exchanged my prison uniform for my own clothes, and was given breakfast. At about 7.45 a.m., we all were loaded on to the paddy-wagon. Different prisoners were headed to different courts. I was going to Southwark Crown Court, the first stop, which from Belmarsh is a straight run down the M2/A2 until one hits the London commuter traffic at Greenwich. Then one crawls.

I was decanted with the others for Southwark at around 8.30 a.m. I was on first-name terms with all the Securicor guards, almost all of them black, many from Africa, who were laid-back and, not being part of the prison-warder service, were in no way threatening or hostile, unlike the warders we had left behind at the jail.

The courts themselves would not start until 10 a.m. Prisoners spent the intervening time in the cells. Sometimes a prisoner from a category B jail – Belmarsh is category A – would bring in reading material, a book of some kind, or one of the Securicor men would give us a daily newspaper. Otherwise we just sat and talked, about ten to each cell, and drank tea.

As soon as we were lodged in the cells the Securicor guards went to each spy-flap and took our orders for tea, which was brought to us within a few minutes. As soon as they had served the tea, they came back with notebooks to take our orders for lunch, a packaged meal heated up in a microwave and eaten with plastic cutlery. There was always the same choice: chicken curry, vegetable curry or beef curry. The chicken and beef curries went fast. Not so the vegetable curry.

We got our teas and gave our orders for lunch to our friends the Securicor guards, just like getting on a commercial airliner. The difference between the public sector (the warders) and the private sector (Securicor) was stark. There was not the heavy atmosphere of implicit violence which marked our relationships with prison warders. Here in the bowels of the court we were accorded a certain inherent dignity as fellow men, which was not how we were treated in jail.

Those who smoked were able to light up at these times of peace and reflection at the start of the court's day. Rules said that prisoners could only have ten cigarettes each. In theory this was to stop 'baroning', where spivs cornered the black market in 'salmon and trout' (rhyming slang for 'snout', which, in turn, is slang for cigarettes) and became 'barons' of contraband.

Those prisoners who were heavy smokers had already learned to moderate their habits. Ten fags would not last a chain-smoker long in the cells. At just after 9.30 a.m. there was the usual commotion when the lawyers turned up. The half hour between 9.30 and 10 a.m. was when prisoners met their lawyers, perhaps for the first time.

Often the barrister would arrive at the court having never heard of the client until that morning when he had been given the details of the case. Legal Aid, after all, is limited. A lawyer cannot make a good living unless he takes on a certain number of clients each week. To study the case notes, let alone prepare the best possible defence, could not be accommodated in the money-making machine that is the working day of the busy lawyer.

As the Securicor men unlocked the cell doors, one of them, a young African called Michael, told me that my brief had arrived. I told him that I did not have a brief, that it must be a mistake. Michael went away. He came back and said, 'Denis, there is no mistake. There is a solicitor here who says you are his client.'

I went to the series of rooms where prisoners met the lawyers. To refuse to do so would have given Michael problems, and I did not want to do that. And there was Hewitt, sitting there. When this week was over, I wrote a letter of complaint to the Law Society, the body which regulated solicitors, accusing Hewitt of professional misconduct. The letter would be ignored. This Monday morning, I did not want to see Hewitt.

'What are you doing here?' was my greeting.

'I have come to help you, Denis . . . '

'I don't want your help.'

'Your friends John Lovesey and Alex Coxen have come. They are willing to speak on your behalf. What shall I tell them?'

'Tell them no.'

'Shirley Williams is here, too. What shall I tell her?'

'You can tell her no as well.'

I did not use the word 'no'. I spoke more bluntly than that. It is one of those times when one is so angry that one counts to ten over and over again in one's head. Then, later, when the anger has gone one reflects on what has happened and one regrets very much counting to ten rather than hitting someone hard.

I just left Hewitt and went to Michael and asked to be locked up. I said that I would not see that solicitor again. At 10.25 Michael came to the cell and told me that the trial was about to start. I told him that I was not going to attend. He knew this already. All the other prisoners had left the cells by 10.30 and I was the only one there.

At Belmarsh the searches on leaving for court were thorough and they would not allow prisoners to take magazines or books to read. So a day in the court cells from 8.30 a.m., when the paddy-wagons dropped one off, and 4.30 p.m., when they arrived for the return journey would be boring. Happily, however, one was allowed to carry a Bible which the warders would not confiscate. I passed the time by reading it. As I always do, I found the Gospels powerful and comforting. The Old Testament did not impress me so much. After about half an hour, alone in my cell, I was reading the Gospels when the door was unlocked and Margaret, the Securicor boss at Southwark Crown Court, was there alongside Michael. This had never happened before.

'Baroness Shirley Williams wants to meet you,' Margaret said.

In the legal system of England and Wales, only lawyers could visit prisoners in the court cells. It was a rule they adhered to strictly. Whatever else she was, Baroness Williams was not a lawyer. She was a veteran politician who was then in semi-retirement. I had many years before written to her – as I had written to thousands of others – seeking her help. She was in a position to help because she had gone to school in Hollywood with Senator Edward Kennedy and they had been friends ever since.

In my letter, I had told her what the CIA had done, and I had asked her to approach Kennedy to help me. She had replied in Bannisterish mode telling me to accept what had been done and get on with my life. In May, Lovesey had written to me in the bail hostel with the 'wonderful news' that the baroness had told him she would contact Senator Kennedy to take up my case. The letter struck me at the time as bizarre. It began with the words: 'Your life is about to change completely for the good!' Sounded like a newspaper horoscope. As things turned out, that is about what the prediction was worth.

Now in September the baroness turned up uninvited. I had read and thrown away her letter delivered to me by the governor at Belmarsh the previous day. It had never occurred to me that she would turn up at the Court. She had, in fact, been recruited by Hewitt.

Hewitt had on file a list of names and addresses of people I had told him to contact to prepare my defence back in the autumn of the previous year. He had failed to contact any of them when I had given him instructions to do so. Baroness Williams was not among those names. William Corson, Joe Trento, Christopher Monckton, Dr Parsons and Sean McPhilemy were the people I needed to help me with my defence, but if Hewitt had contacted any of them he had not told me. Christopher Monckton has confirmed to me that no lawyer acting for me contacted him at all: yet I had asked all of them to contact him.

Baroness Williams of Crosby had been a major public figure in Britain from the late 1960s to the middle of the 1980s. The child of immensely wealthy British parents, she has variously been a socialist, a social democrat and a liberal democrat. At the time she came to Southwark Crown Court she was President of the Liberal Democrat Party.

She had once been touted as a possible first woman Labour prime minister. That morning I met a well-dressed, slightly dotty, well-meaning, elderly matron of the British upper classes. She did not need to tell me Hewitt had told her I was insane. There is a certain manner of speaking to people labelled insane which I had long ago learned to recognise at once. The person speaking to the lunatic talks slowly and clearly in short sentences with short words clearly enunciated. There is nothing the lunatic can say to dispel the attitude being used towards him. This is because the person is not listening.

The distinguished baroness was forewarned and forearmed when she came to the cells of Southwark Crown Court to see me that morning. Nothing I could say would have dispelled the view she had of me. She was not there to listen.

Why did I agree to see her at all? Two reasons. First, her connection to Senator Kennedy. Just as Senators Lugar and Fulbright could have helped me in 1987, in 1997 Senator Kennedy could have done so. But, just as ten years earlier it was vital that somebody known and trusted by those senators made the approach, so it was now. The baroness could get to Kennedy and make him take up my case.

Secondly, I was curious. I was hunkered down in one of the cells with my Bible, while several floors above me the show-trial was proceeding without me. The other prisoners would join me for lunch at one and I should have people to talk to, but until then I was on my own. I was curious, and I certainly had time on my hands. I believed that I had nothing to lose.

'I have spoken to Judge Fingret,' she began. 'He is a very good judge and he is worried about you. He wants to help you. We all do. Your friends are in the court taking notes of the evidence. They are very worried about you, too. They are going to stay all day in case you change your mind about seeing them. I am afraid I can only stay till 2.30. I have a long-standing appointment at 3 o'clock.'

'There is no need for you or them to stay. I am happy as I am. I got all the letters and I am not interested in what they said. As far as I am concerned, none of you should ever have come here and I don't want you to stay. You are all wasting your time as far I am concerned.'

I wondered, in passing, about the technicalities involved in Baroness Williams being granted an interview by a Crown Court judge first thing Monday morning at the start of a trial. Had it been only when Judge Fingret turned up for work that day that he had learned that the baroness was there to see him? Or had it all been set up over the weekend? Some sort of strings had to have been pulled, for the duty governor himself had hand-delivered the baroness' letter to me in my cell at Belmarsh. On balance, I concluded that Judge Fingret had been expecting the baroness that morning.

Shirley Williams paid absolutely no attention to what I told her. She had not come there to listen. She had come to 'help' me. Listening to my lunacy would not help me, she was convinced. I watched her subtly, gently but firmly, trying to circumvent what she regarded as my insanity to get me to help myself.

I saw that there was no point in my seeking to convince her that my account of what the CIA had done to me was true and that I was not insane. I knew that nothing I could say to her would change her mind. But, just as she portrayed everything that she said to me in terms of sweet reasonableness, I had a crack at turning it around on her. She wanted me to see a psychiatrist and, if I agreed, she would arrange for one to come and see me in the cells. Just for a conversation, she said. Nothing more. For her benefit as much as for mine.

'Baroness, I have no problem with that.'

'Please don't call me Baroness . . . ' That got my attention. There was just a slight pause before she said, 'Call me Mrs Williams.'

Well, that put me in my place. When I had been a lobby correspondent at Westminster, politicians of all degrees regarded journalists with fear. We decided what we called them. In the baroness' case, she was known as 'Shirley', if not 'Shirl'. How times had changed, I thought. I smiled. One of those small things which can break a tension. 'Call me Mrs Williams!' Doubtless, to her my sudden smile was the inexplicable rictus of the chronically insane.

'Mrs Williams, I have no problem speaking to your psychiatrist but I'll only do so if, before I do, you talk to Christopher Monckton and ask him whether what I say about the CIA is true or not. Nobody claims that he is insane. He spent four years in Margaret Thatcher's private office. His grandfather, Sir Walter Monckton, was Churchill's friend. Christopher is the heir to the viscountcy. If you ring him up, he will come to the court. He told me last year that he would be willing to ask the CPS to drop all charges against me but Hewitt did not contact him. It is one of the reasons why I sacked him. If you speak to Christopher Monckton, you will know the truth. He may still be able to get the CPS to stop the trial. Please ask him to come here. And you should then speak to William Corson of the CIA and Joe Trento of CNN. They will also tell you that my account of what the CIA did to me is true. They were willing to fly to London to give evidence on my behalf and Hewitt did not contact them. That is another reason why I sacked him. Just over a week ago, I got notice from the prosecution that it intends to fly in seven new witnesses from the USA for the trial. I read their witness statements. The statements are a year old. They had kept them until just before the trial was due to start.'

As I spoke, I became more and more angry. But Shirley Williams was unconcerned. She had secured my agreement to speak to her psychiatrist. She had not been expecting me to give in so easily. She had come prepared for a fight and I had given in without one. All that mattered to her was that I had agreed to see a psychiatrist and tell him my account.

I had agreed. Good. I was mad. I needed 'help'. That is all that mattered to her. So she humoured me. She did not know Christopher Monckton. How could she contact him? How could she ask him to come to the court at such short notice? Insane, of course,

I did not believe that these were insuperable obstacles. If she had a pen and paper, I told her, I would write down his telephone numbers, including his mobile number, plus numbers for both William Corson and Joe Trento in the USA. I told her that *Who's Who*, the directory of Britain's elite, contained a full biography of Christopher Monckton. Unlike 'Mrs' Williams' title, Christopher's title is a real one which will be passed on to future generations *ad infinitum*. Baroness Williams is only a life-peer. Her title is one that cannot be passed on.

The baroness found a piece of paper in her handbag and gave me a ballpoint pen to use. I wrote out the telephone numbers of all three men. I gave the paper to her with the pen. There was nothing remarkable about the pen. It was not a disposable pen but a 'proper' pen for which one would obtain refills. Such a pen could cost anything from £10 to £100. It was a ballpoint pen. But the baroness did not want to take it back.

'It's all right. You keep it, Denis. I have another one.'

'No. I can't. They'll take it off me when I leave tonight.'

She didn't understand. What she understood was that she had made a small gesture of kindness to me and I, in my lunacy, had refused it. What I had said to her was the truth. It was a nice ballpoint pen and I did not have one in jail. I should have been happy to have accepted it from her but it would have been a waste of time, because it would have been confiscated before I got on the paddy-wagon. What is to a baroness a writing implement is to a prison warder potentially a very dangerous weapon. In the hands of a violent criminal lunatic like myself, the baroness's ballpoint pen could have been used to could poke out a warder's eye.

But Mrs Williams did not want to be told. In her position one avoids at all costs arousing the anger of a lunatic who can erupt over trivial matters, such as ballpoint pens. Refusing her pen was to her an ungracious act which served only to underline just how insane I was. All of this I observed. There was nothing I could have said to her that day which would have made her treat me any other way than as a lunatic who had to be humoured.

She said Judge Fingret was deeply upset that I had stopped eating 12 days beforehand (though not so upset that he had delayed the start of the trial that was grinding on somewhere above us). So, would I resume eating? And, because everybody wanted to help me so very much, even though I refused to countenance the idea of Hewitt being re-engaged as my solicitor, would I at least appear in court to tell that nice Judge Fingret why I had written the letters?

If I would only do these two things, plus agree to nothing more sinister than have a conversation that the baroness would arrange for me, Mrs Williams would speak to Christopher Monckton. If, after speaking to him, she felt it appropriate, she might also speak to William Corson and Joe Trento in the USA. If she then believed there was a *prima facie* case for the CIA to answer, she would get Senator Kennedy to bring it up before the United States Senate Sub-Committee on Intelligence.

I agreed. I also asked for two things to enable me to do what she wanted: one, that I later be provided with writing paper and a pen so that I could draft overnight a statement to be made in court the next day, and two, that Judge Fingret order the prison authorities at whichever jail I was taken to at the end of the day to put me in a single cell where I could prepare the statement in peace and quiet.

For all that it had been for me deeply humiliating and dis-tressing to be patronised by the baroness, she and I had agreed a deal. The deal was simple. It could not be misunderstood by any-body who had been in that small interview room in the Southwark Crown Court cells.

The baroness wanted three things from me:

1 That I should resume eating normally;
2 That I should appear in court and tell the judge why I had written the letters;
3 That I should have a conversation with a psychiatrist.

I agreed, provided that the baroness did the following:

1 That she would speak to Christopher Monckton and convey to him that I wished him to attend the court as she had done that day;
2 That, once she had ascertained from Christopher Monckton that my charges against the CIA were true, she would contact William Corson and Joe Trento in the USA;

3 That, should she discover from these telephone calls that the
CIA had a *prima facie* case to answer and as long as I kept to my
side of the bargain, she would ensure that Senator Kennedy
take up my case in the US Senate's Sub-Committee on
Intelligence.

Interestingly, there was no talk of her 'asking' Senator Kennedy
to help me. She spoke as though it were a done deal: as though she
knew he would take up my case. I believe she said what she said
because she did not envisage being required to deliver. I do not
think it occurred to her that I could be telling the truth. Indeed,
that had been my problem all along: most people are not willing to
believe anyone who says the CIA is out to get him. She had been
told I was insane and everything that I had said to her during this
meeting seems to have served only to confirm to her that this label
was well merited.

This strange but short meeting ended at around 11 a.m. About
an hour after I had left the baroness in the interview room,
Margaret again came to my cell. She handed me a letter which
she said had been sent down to the cells on behalf of Baroness
Williams. It was a written statement of how she understood our
meeting to have finished.

The letter contained no reference to my request that the baroness
should speak to Christopher Monckton. Nor did she refer to my
request that she speak to William Corson and Joe Trento in the
USA. Maybe the baroness writes to everybody in the same way, but
the letter was the sort of thing an elderly maiden aunt would write
to a ten-year-old child. The main points were: 'You agreed to end
your hunger strike, to tell the judge why you wrote the letters and
to have a conversation with a psychiatrist. In return, I will ask
Senator Kennedy to put your case before the United States Senate
Committee on Intelligence.'

Notwithstanding that she had left out Messrs Monckton, Corson
and Trento, I was happy enough with that. Telling the judge in front
of the jury why I wrote the letters would not affect the conviction: I
had long known that was a foregone conclusion. Having a conversation with a psychiatrist, unless we discussed cricket (and even
then I am not sure that that would have saved me), would lead
inevitably to my being found insane on the basis of my charges

against the CIA. What mattered to me was that the baroness had put in writing the promise to ask Senator Kennedy to take up my case. That is why I sent the letter to Neil Middleton in Ireland as soon as I had the opportunity to do so. I wanted a third party to witness the written undertaking the baroness had given.

In fulfilment of my promise to start eating, I had the chef's special in the court cells that day. Chicken curry. In fact, I had two of them. My friend Michael, the African Securicor guard, gave me a second one. He knew I hadn't eaten for eleven days. It tasted like manure. But then it always tasted like manure.

It was already a day of surprises, so I should not have been surprised when at two o'clock Michael came and told me that the baroness was once more in the interview room. I should say that Margaret, Michael and the other Securicor guards at the court had known me for months. This flurry of to them hitherto unheard-of activity, with a famous politician they had only seen on television turning up in all her glory twice in the interview room to speak to a common criminal such as myself, did not pass unnoted.

The baroness was not alone. She was attended in the interview room by the barrister John Gordon. I had not seen him since I had surrendered to the court in May. I should have realised that he would be there once Hewitt had turned up. By way of introduction, the baroness said to me: 'I have spoken to the judge and he said that he had no power to order that you be given a cell on your own and paper and a pen so that you could write your statement. So I have asked Mr Gordon to come here to see if he can help. He has been here all morning listening to the trial and he thinks he can help.'

Of course the judge had 'no power' to give orders to HM Prison Service. But no prison governor would ignore a request from a Crown Court judge that a prisoner be given a cell and paper and pen. If there was nowhere else to put me, they could have put me in the punishment block. Those are single cells. They have a mattress on the floor to sleep on. It would not have been beyond my wit and ability to sit on the floor with a pencil and paper writing my statement in a block cell.

But there were other cells. I should spend much of the rest of my jail career in solitary confinement. There are plenty of such cells in Her Majesty's prisons. While the general wings, where prisoners were two or three to a cell, were full to bursting, there was always room to put a prisoner in solitary confinement or in a block cell.

Gordon said, 'I've spent all morning in court listening to the prosecution witnesses. The case against you is very weak. The chief witness, Vincent Browne, is unconvincing and I could easily destroy him in cross-examination. I have been very frustrated sitting there and being unable to do anything to help you.'

Then the baroness took up the theme, like his partner in a music-hall double act: 'Can I make a suggestion? As you may not be able to write your statement tonight, why don't you let Mr Gordon represent you?'

How would that be better for me than going into the witness box and making a statement without notes? Gordon said, 'I can get you off, if you trust me. I know their case. It is weak. On the basis of the evidence of Browne, the witnesses aren't convincing. If you let me have a go at them, I can get you off.'

All right. Not an offer to refuse. I agreed.

'There is just one problem,' Gordon said. 'Legally, I have to be instructed by a solicitor.'

'Well, get one.'

'Well, the easiest thing would be to get Steve Hewitt to be the solicitor.'

I did not have confidence in Hewitt, but in the end I agreed. It would have been perverse not to do so. After all, all these fine people wanted to do was to 'help' me. Only a madman would have refused their kind offer.

At 2.30 that afternoon I was taken up in the prisoners' lift from the underground cells to the second-floor courtroom. My escort was my Securicor friend Robert – a young man of West Indian origin who read soft-porn magazines while waiting for his charges to emerge from the court. Judge Fingret was expecting us. In his robe and his wig, Gordon was brief and to the point: 'Mr Lehane wishes me to represent him in this trial. He understands that he must have an instructing solicitor and, given the circumstances, he applies that the firm of Fisher Meredith (Solicitors) be so engaged for the purpose of my representing him.'

Judge Fingret was ever so kind. As the baroness had told me, he was 'a very good judge' and he, too, wanted to help me. When he walked into the court and sat on his bench, he looked at me standing in the dock before him and told me that a man who had not eaten for eleven days should not have to stand in his court. I had his permission to sit down. I was happy enough standing up. I did not expect to be there very long. Having listened to Gordon, Judge Fingret asked whether I wanted to instruct Fisher Meredith. I consented, but only to the extent that they were needed to legitimise Gordon's appearance in court.

I had watched my share of American television series about courts and lawyers in the USA, starting way back in the early 1960s with Perry Mason. There, accused men did not sit in the dock, looking guilty of the most heinous crime. They sat in the well of the court with all the lawyers. There was always an official stenographer taking full notes of every court appearance as well as of the trial itself.

Before my trial I had written to Judge Fingret asking for a copy of the official transcript of the trial to be provided to me when I arrived each day at the court. Though all my other letters of request to Judge Fingret were not answered, this letter was answered. There is no official stenographer at Southwark Crown Court, but an outside firm would do transcripts for me at £700 a day, payable in advance. I did not have that money. I did, however, feel that it was contrary to natural justice that a man accused of a crime, who had no funds to pay for a transcript of the proceedings of his trial on a daily basis, should be denied access to the record of the evidence against him because he was too poor to pay for the transcript.

Judge Fingret formally noted that Hewitt was re-engaged as my solicitor. Gordon then asked for, and got, an adjournment until 10 a.m. the next day. I was taken back to the cells. I never saw the baroness again. Nor, as far as I know, did she contact those whom she had said she would contact.

17

A Monstrous Catch 22

'You are prepared to lose your identity and live out the rest of your life as a waiter or dock-worker?'
'Yes.'

from *Nineteen Eighty-Four*, GEORGE ORWELL

The paddy-wagon collected me and the other prisoners from Southwark Crown Court and took us to Brixton Prison, which had vacancies that evening. As luck would have it, I was put in a two-bunk cell with a Libyan called Rajeeb who had a number of university degrees and spoke English fluently. His clothing was expensive and impeccable. He stood out clearly among his cell-mates. That week the London tabloid newspapers were describing him as 'the bogus Arab prince'.

Rajeeb's trial, like mine, had been scheduled to start that Monday. We had met that day in the cells of the court. I remained in the cells when called to attend the show-trial. Rajeeb joined me later that morning after his year-long bail had been revoked and his lawyers were arguing before the judge without the jury. We talked. We had plenty of time for more talk after we were put in the cell at Brixton and the door was locked that night.

Rajeeb, one of the security staff of Colonel Mu'ammar Gaddafi, President of Libya, had been charged with a complex fraud, which he denied vehemently and indignantly. The charges against him concerned a massive promotional exercise in the UK that he had commissioned from his base of operations in Rome. He was charged with deceiving a British company, which he had hired to mount the operation in London, into spending some £100,000 that he had no intention of paying.

At that time President Gaddafi was public enemy number one in the West, much as Osama bin Laden is today. Rajeeb was convinced that he had been tricked. His defence was that he had paid the British company for its initial services but that he had cancelled the contract with them when his company in Rome had decided not to proceed with the promotional operation.

The Crown Prosecution Service had leaked to journalists that Rajeeb had posed as an Arab prince, which he was not, in order to defraud the company. Rajeeb was incensed at this. Libya's royal family had been abolished by the revolutionary government of Gaddafi when he had overthrown King Idris in 1969. To Rajeeb, a member of the Libyan Revolutionary upper-class elite, to be accused of passing himself off as an Arab prince was an insult which he disdained.

Yet the leaks were taken up by the London tabloids and they sent reporters to the trial of the bogus Arab prince who had defrauded an innocent British company of £100,000. Rajeeb believed that the adverse publicity campaign and the trial itself were all a put-up job by MI5. He had been on bail which had required him to live in London for almost a year. He was forbidden to return to Rome and his passport had been taken from him.

The reason why Rajeeb was in the cells was that, with no warning, at the very start of his trial the prosecution had asked the judge to cancel his bail on the ground that he was likely to flee the country, notwithstanding that he had surrendered his passport and had remained in London awaiting trial for almost a year. Through his experience of British justice, Rajeeb had acquired the same mixture of contempt and distaste that I had. The difference between him and me was that my only access to lawyers was via Legal Aid, which made my supposed lawyers answerable not so much to me as to the legal system in general and to the trial judge in particular. Rajeeb, however, was wealthy and his company paid for the best lawyers.

Rajeeb and I spent several hours that first day in the cells in the bowels of the court together. At Brixton we shared a cell for the night of Monday, 15 September 1997. When prisoners are banged up in their cells, they talk. Rajeeb told me his story. I told him mine. We were at the same intellectual and educational level and shared a common enemy in British Intelligence. One of the many differences between inside a British jail and outside is that inside claims by prisoners that they are innocent of all charges and are the victims of put-up jobs, whether by the police or by the secret services, are not automatically rejected. Rajeeb returned over and over again to the reputation of 'British justice' throughout the world and how false it was.

He told me: 'The British have been telling us for centuries that British justice is the best in the world and that every man gets a fair trial, but it is just not true. In Italy, lawyers work for the client and they do what they are told and they spend a long time working on the case; but here, people like you, Denis, you cannot even get a lawyer to work for you. In Italy that could not happen. And yet the British have been telling all the world for hundreds of years that their system is the best in the world. It is not. It is the worst.'

In that week of September 1997, I saw Rajeeb more than once try to help prisoners whose Legal Aid lawyers had refused to defend them as they had wanted to be defended and rather than do as they were asked had told the judge they were abandoning the case. These lawyers would have been paid for all the meetings they had had with the defendant, court appearances before the trial and for the whole day, even though they had left the prisoner in the lurch at 11 in the morning.

I saw Rajeeb try to explain to these people how to present their own defence; with the huge amount of paperwork their quondam lawyers had accumulated dumped on the poor souls to sort out in the crowded cells, it was virtually an impossible task. What Rajeeb succeeded in doing with these prisoners was to instil in them a sense of self-worth and dignity.

Rajeeb was acquitted on all charges. He had brilliant lawyers who tore to shreds the prosecution's 'bogus Arab prince' case. Upon acquittal, in British justice, an innocent man is not allowed to walk from the dock out of the court and go back to his life – or, in Rajeeb's case, get the first plane to Rome. No, he is sent back to the cells to be locked up until the judge gets around to signing the paperwork.

Thus it was that after his acquittal Rajeeb was once again my companion in the cell. It was there he made me his offer. We knew that I should be convicted and sent to a secure lunatic asylum where I should be tortured with the objective of getting me formally to withdraw all my allegations against the CIA and admit that I had been insane since 1983.

We knew that I should never be released until or unless I agreed to abandon the truth. Rajeeb told me to agree to their terms. I had been led to believe that if I agreed I should spend a limited period in the secure lunatic asylum by way of a cure and then be released on licence to a council flat on a sink estate in the London Borough of Lambeth, where I should be given a menial job as a librarian in a council library.

So, when Rajeeb and I talked, we knew everything but the length of time for which I was likely to be held. Rajeeb said that I should agree to everything they wanted and that, when they released me, he would fly me to Rome that same day where a job would be waiting for me in Gaddafi's service. He was confident that they would not hold me for very long if I agreed to admit that I was insane.

He knew this from experience. He told me: 'A friend of mine was charged with killing three Israelis in London and he pretended to be insane. When his family visited him in jail, he pretended not to know them. His wife insisted that he must know her and he had to tell her quickly that he was acting this way deliberately and that she should shut her mouth or else they might realise he was not insane. He spent six months in custody and then they freed him. Halfway between London and Rome on the aircraft, he suddenly became sane again. He left London insane and he arrived in Rome sane. That is what I am asking you to do, Denis.'

Rajeeb asked me to think about the offer. If I accepted it, he said he would arrange for me to receive money on a regular basis while I was in the secure lunatic asylum.

The incident of his friend who had been convicted of killing three Israelis in London seemed to refer to a series of bomb attacks a few years earlier where soft Israeli targets had been attacked. I knew what such bomb attacks looked liked because of my years in Belfast. I did not take Rajeeb up on his offer. To have done so would have been absurd. Why on earth would a man who had refused to compromise his journalistic integrity and independence for the CIA want to throw in his lot with Gaddafi?

When we arrived at court the next morning, I had expected John Gordon, my barrister, to continue where he had left off the previous day. There was no need for Hewitt to be there: he had no role to play except as the solicitor of record to permit Gordon to strut his stuff.

I was not sent for at 9.30 a.m. with the rest of the prisoners to see the briefs in the interview room. I found this surprising, but I got a message not long afterwards via Margaret, the Securicor boss. My solicitor had telephoned to say he would be in at lunchtime. This could only mean that the trial had been further adjourned until the afternoon.

I had assumed that Hewitt had had a conversation with Judge Fingret on the telephone. In fact, he had been ensconced with the judge at the court that morning, discussing behind my back how they were going to proceed with me.

After all the toings and froings of the previous day, I spent a relaxed morning in the cells reading my King James Bible until the other prisoners came back down for lunch. Once again I had the chicken curry.

I was called into the interview room at 12.30 p.m. There I found Hewitt and Gordon awaiting me. The previous afternoon I had asked the baroness and Gordon to ask Christopher Monckton and Sean McPhilemy to attend the court the following day if possible. Christopher lived in the far north of Scotland but spent a few days most weeks in London on business. I knew he would have flown down from Scotland had he been asked. Sean lived in Oxford, 56 miles from London. He would have no difficulty in attending the court. I had given Gordon details of how each man could be contacted.

The first thing I asked when I was brought in to see Hewitt and Gordon was whether or not Christopher and Sean had come to the court. I was told that neither man was 'available'. In fact, yet again they had not been contacted as I had requested. Instead, Hewitt told me he had arranged for me to meet the baroness's psychiatrist that afternoon.

This surprised me. The baroness had not asked that I should have my 'conversation' with a psychiatrist during the trial. My expectation when I had left the court in the paddy-wagon the previous evening had been that I should meet Gordon at 9.30 the next morning at the court, we would review the case, and the trial should resume at 10 a.m.

I had no confidence in Gordon's certainty that he could demolish the prosecution case. I believed I should be convicted because no proper defence, let alone the best defence, had been prepared.

Never mind, I thought. There is always the Court of Appeal after a wrong conviction. Later four different solicitors, two in Britain and two in Ireland, reviewed the case. All concluded that I had grounds for appeal and that the appeal had in law to be granted. I expected Judge Fingret to convict me and then to send me to a secure lunatic asylum. It was there that I had intended to fulfil my promise to the baroness to have a conversation with a psychiatrist. I expected that, as usual, the psychiatrist would conclude that I was insane on the ground that my account of what the CIA had done to me was self-evidently delusional. I had been down that road before.

But I had hoped the baroness would fulfil her side of the bargain by ascertaining via Christopher Monckton, William Corson and Joe Trento that my account was not delusional but true in every respect. I had to proceed on the basis that she would keep her word. So, when Hewitt told me that a psychiatrist would be arriving at 2 p.m. to see me, I agreed to see him.

I assumed, but no one told me, that the trial could not resume until I had had my 'conversation' with the baroness's psychiatrist. Either way, I wanted to discuss with Gordon what we had agreed in open court the previous afternoon he would do. He did not want to discuss it: he said he had a lunchtime appointment outside the court. We parted, having agreed to meet again after I had seen the baroness's psychiatrist. My final words to Hewitt were, 'No more surprises, right?'

He nodded with a sort of world-weary look as if to say, 'How can you still doubt me at this stage after all I have done for you?'

At 2 p.m. the baroness's shrink was waiting for me in the interview room. Dr Anthony Maden was a dishevelled, diminutive 30-year-old in a crumpled grey suit, sitting in a sort of heap. He quickly came to life on my entry into the room. He was a registrar, a lower form of life than the consultant I had expected. The first thing I did was to put the baroness's letter before him on the table between us.

'My understanding of this meeting is that you are here at the request of Baroness Williams and that this will be not a consultation or an evaluation but a conversation. She has written this down so that there can be no misunderstandings later. Are you clear about that?'

Maden glanced at the letter but did not read it. He nodded and said, 'OK, of course, of course.'

He then took out a large notebook and pen, took the cap off the pen and opened the notebook, which was empty.

I said at once: 'What are you doing?'

'I am taking notes.'

'Do people having conversations with each other normally take notes?'

Dr Maden looked at me briefly. Then he put away his pen and notebook and said, 'If you don't want me to take notes, that is fine by me.'

So we began. It was clear that Dr Maden knew my CIA account in some detail. He let me speak but, when he did interject with questions, they were always based not on what I had said to him so far in the meeting but on information which he had obtained before meeting me. Like all his breed, he had accepted the conclusions in the paperwork, and was drawing his questions from that, and not from his conversation with the patient.

Time passed. I soon realised that there had never been any intention of resuming the trial that day. Through the glass walls of the interview room we could see a large clock. When it showed 4 p.m. I stopped the 'conversation', because I knew that in half an hour Dr Maden would have to leave and we would all be processed back into the paddy-wagons.

'Well,' I said to him, 'what do you think of it all?'

He smiled the sort of smile grown-ups use towards children or the elderly. 'Well, of course, there is no question but that the CIA does do terrible things to people. That is obvious. But on the basis of what you have told me, I have no choice but to conclude that you are insane.'

Not a surprise. Much later I checked whether a psychiatrist ought to declare a person insane solely on the basis of a single meeting – or 'a conversation' as the baroness had put it. I was told the psychiatric textbooks allow no such thing. The way it was explained to me later by a doctor who examined me and found me to be wholly sane is this:

If you were saying that God was speaking to you from the television set telling you to go out and do things, then it would be correct to diagnose a serious psychiatric condition. But that is not what you have been recorded consistently as saying. On the basis of your account of what has happened, all that a psychiatrist could conclude is that you may have a psychiatric condition. Whether you did or not depended on whether or not what you had said was true. Mentally ill patients do sometimes complain of persecution by the CIA. In your case, you had a credible explanation for why the CIA had behaved as they did towards you and a number of different people existed who could in- dependently verify your account as true. There have never been any grounds to find you mentally ill on the basis of what you have told people the CIA has done to your life.

So Dr Maden got it wrong. He did have a choice. He should have come to a quite different conclusion on the basis of our two- hour 'conversation'. If all Dr Maden knew about me had been gained from that single encounter, he should have checked the facts and then, at worst, have come to a finding equivalent to the Scottish verdict of 'not proven'.

What I told Dr Maden might have been symptomatic of insanity if and only if it had been untrue. Since my story was true – and I told Dr Maden that people independent of me could verify the truth – then my telling the story did not indicate insanity. However, Dr Maden was well briefed before he met me. That briefing must have left him in no doubt that I was insane, because it seems he had assumed, without checking, that my account of what the CIA had done to me was wholly untrue.

Dr Maden left. The paddy-wagon picked me up as usual and took me back to Brixton. However, whereas the night before I had slept in a cell in one of the general blocks with the Libyan Rajeeb as my cell-mate, without explanation I was put in solitary confinement in the hospital wing. Solitary confinement is a punishment. It was to be my usual accommodation for the remainder of my sojourn as a valued guest of Her Majesty. The prison authorities would not have isolated me without outside input. The baroness had told me the previous day that Judge Fingret had told her he had no power to tell the prison service to let me have a single cell just for one night. Somebody, though, had had – and had used – the power to fling me into solitary confinement permanently.

It was a smidgeon after 9.30 a.m. on 17 September 1997 in an interview room in the cells beneath Southwark Crown Court. Hewitt said to me, 'We have just come from Judge Fingret. We gave him Tony Maden's report on you. He has agreed to send you to a mental hospital for treatment if you change your plea to guilty to all four charges.'

Yes. I had heard aright. In the words of my pal Jimmy at Belmarsh, I had just been 'done up like a kipper'.

I said, 'You've done *what*?' After that, words failed me, and that does not happen often.

At all times since this horrible nightmare began, I had gone with the flow. I had mistrusted various people, and with good reason, as events were to show. I had always gone along with everything presented to me if, on the face of things, it was reasonable.

That Wednesday morning in September 1997, it all blew up in my face. I was finished. And I had walked straight into it with my eyes open.

I should have stayed in my cell the previous two days and refused to see anybody, starting with the baroness and going on to Gordon, Hewitt and Dr Tony Maden.

Beyond acknowledging my gullible stupidity, a number of things need to be said. There was nothing in my deal with the baroness, or in her letter to me, about a psychiatrist preparing a report after our 'conversation'. I was not told that any report of my 'conversation' with the psychiatrist would be given to Judge Fingret. Hewitt's words were the first suggestion that Maden had prepared a report. I was not even told that the report existed until after Judge Fingret had received it.

Southwark Crown Court is in central London, but Dr Maden was based at a hospital in Kent, at least an hour's drive away. He had left the court at the start of the busy London rush-hour, driven to Kent, written his report from memory, and supplied it to Hewitt early the next morning. Clearly, the report had been planned for.

Nobody had told me about the plan. Not the baroness, not Dr Maden, not Hewitt, not Gordon. I had been tricked into 'a conversation' with Maden solely so that he could write a damning report for Judge Fingret to exploit. With that report, Judge Fingret was able send me to a secure lunatic asylum for the rest of my life. That is what he would try to do.

To present a highly damaging report to a judge in the middle of a trial without the express permission of the accused client who is the subject of the report is reprehensible.

To mislead the accused client by misrepresenting a formal psychiatric evaluation as a mere 'conversation', when the true but undisclosed purpose of the evaluation is to prepare a report to be put before the trial judge during the trial is equally reprehensible.

Gordon had only been re-engaged by me at the request of the baroness because Judge Fingret had refused to ask the prison authorities to give me a pen, paper and a cell so that I could work overnight on a statement to be read to him the following morning. With that statement, I should not have needed lawyers.

Hewitt had only been re-engaged, very much against my wishes, because it was a legal rule that Gordon, the barrister, be 'instructed' by a solicitor. Both Gordon and I in open court had made it explicit that Hewitt's role was purely *pro forma*. I had not instructed him to procure a psychiatrist to evaluate my sanity, to produce a hurried report on me overnight, or to present it to the judge without even letting me know it existed.

Nominally – notionally – Hewitt and Gordon were defence lawyers. Believe it or not, they were supposed to be on my side. From where I stood, it did not look as if they were on my side.

Hewitt had not contacted any of those who could clear my name, so that I could not call them as witnesses to the truth of my account. He had not told me that Dr Maden was carrying out a psychiatric evaluation, so that I had no opportunity to decline to take part. He had not told me Dr Maden was going to prepare a report, so that I did not get the chance to read it before it was used. Above all, he had not told me Dr Maden's report was going to be put in front of the judge, so that I was prevented from instructing him that I did not wish to plead insanity.

I had already been in a psychiatric institution in Ireland until Joe Trento's telephone call had saved me. I knew that even a lengthy stretch in prison would be better than subjecting myself ever again to the lunatics who run the state's asylums.

I never heard from Baroness Williams again. Her intervention was probably well meant, in a middle-class, middle-brow, muddle-headed sort of way, but it was to lead directly to my being tortured very nearly to death – a catastrophic consequence that she cannot have intended.

Even if what I had done had been a real offence, I and everyone involved knew that the amount of jail time I should serve would be minuscule. As it was, when I was released from the psychiatric institution in May the following year, I had spent twice as much time locked up as Judge Fingret would have handed down as a criminal sentence. Secure lunatic asylums are not soft options. They are frightening, terrible places. Nobody in his right mind would choose willingly to go into one of them. I did not so choose. Yet, thanks to the seemingly well-meaning but in practice catastrophic interventions of the baroness and of my lawyers, who seemed to me to be acting more for the Crown than for me, I was not offered the choice.

There it was, then. Hewitt and Gordon, supposedly my lawyers, wanted me to plead guilty and somehow, though I had not been consulted, a deal had been done with the judge.

I said, 'What do you mean, "plead guilty"? The only reason I took you back is that on Monday you told me you could demolish the prosecution witnesses because they were so poor. Why should I plead guilty to something I haven't done and you told me you could secure my acquittal for?'

To which Gordon replied, 'That was Monday. Things have changed now.'

Yet since Monday Gordon had heard no new evidence, because the case had been adjourned. Besides, there had been no ambiguity in what Gordon had said to me in the company of the baroness on Monday afternoon. He had said the prosecution witnesses were feeble and he could win an acquittal by demolishing them. Nothing else, other than that, would have induced me to re-engage him. Instead, I had been led to speak to a psychiatrist who, without my knowledge or consent, would prepare a report which, without my knowledge or consent and against my will, would be put in front of the judge. During the meeting with Dr Maden, I had very carefully told him that I was meeting him for a 'conversation' and not a formal evaluation.

Had Dr Maden wished to conduct the conversation on any basis other than what he knew had been agreed, he should have said, openly and honestly, 'That is not the basis on which I have been paid to come here. I was told that you are suffering from delusions of persecution by the CIA and was asked to determine the extent of your psychiatric disorder. That is why I wish to take notes. If it is your wish that I do not conduct a formal psychiatric evaluation, I must accept your wishes and end this interview at once.'

Dr Maden said nothing of the kind. Hewitt, however, felt that a guilty plea would be in my best interests.

'I will not change my plea to guilty,' I said.

Astonishingly, Hewitt then said, 'If you refuse to change your plea, we will have to discharge ourselves as your solicitor and barrister.'

'I don't want you as my lawyers. You are sacked anyway.'

Disconcertingly, Gordon said, 'Mr Lehane, I don't know why, but I like you. I have enjoyed all our meetings. I don't understand it, but I like you.' There was no reply to that. I had no idea what he meant then. I don't have any today, more than a decade later. He thrust out his right hand to me. 'Goodbye, then,' he said.

I shook his hand. Hewitt grunted, huffed and whined all in one sound and movement. I shook his hand, too. They left. My Securicor friend Michael took me back to the cells.

Hewitt and Gordon, I presume, went back up to see Judge Fingret and told him that I had refused to change my plea and that – with my enthusiastic endorsement – they had discharged themselves as my lawyers.

Judge Fingret had me in a monstrous Catch 22. If Dr Maden's report was true and I was insane, then I could not be validly convicted of an offence and he could not allow my trial to proceed. If Dr Maden's report was not true, then I could not be validly locked up in an asylum for criminal lunatics. The judge, though he knew that Dr Maden had found me insane, though he knew that he was going to rely upon that report as the basis for sending me to an asylum for criminal lunatics, failed to discharge the jury and to enter a finding of insanity. Instead, he withheld the report until the jury had safely convicted me. Then, and only then, did he deploy it. For without it he would have had to release me at once, the time already served being more than enough. With it, I could be kept locked up until I died. I leave the reader to decide for himself where the 'justice' was in this elaborate judicial pantomime.

Later that afternoon, my cell was unlocked and Margaret told me that there was somebody waiting for me in one of the interview rooms. I replied that I did not want to see anybody. She said it was an usher from one of the courts upstairs so I went with her to the room. There I found a tall young man with an open-looking face standing to attention. He wore a long black scholar's gown over his suit and tie. When we were left alone, gazing off into the distance, avoiding all eye contact, he declaimed: 'Judge Fingret has ordered me to tell you that the prosecution in your trial has ended its case and if you want to present a defence to the charges you should do so now.'

I said to him: 'I want the trial stopped and I want the judge to appoint lawyers to prepare and present my defence. I have written to him repeatedly with this request. He has not replied. I want you to tell him that.'

The young man continued to stand to attention and to gaze into the distance. His eyes must have been focusing on the wall of the interview room on the other side of the narrow corridor. There were no other people in the interview rooms.

I stood straight in front of him, making sure that he had to make eye-contact with me and repeated what I had said to him. He again remained silent, his lips unmoving. Across his face came the flicker of a contemptuous smile. Upstairs was a jury of twelve good men and women true who had never seen or heard me but who would give the judge and the prosecution what they had brought them all there for. All of these twelve would be like this usher standing in front of me, a smile of superiority on his face, secure in the knowledge that British Justice is The Best In The World.

After a few more moments standing like a statue, the usher left. Margaret returned to the interview room and took me back to a cell. Not long after this, the 'bogus Arab prince', the well-educated and expensively-dressed Rajeeb, returned to the cells. During the previous few days, and the one night in which we had shared a cell at Brixton, we had got to know each other. Jail is like that. The nearest equivalent is being on a transatlantic boat for a week. In both cases one is locked up with the same people whom one cannot escape. Strong links – I won't call them friendships or relationships because they depend entirely on the circumstances which are by definition unreal and of limited duration – are forged, often very strong links.

Rajeeb had been found innocent of all the charges and was incandescent at the London daily tabloids for reporting him as 'the bogus Arab prince' caught out in a fraud. It became clear that we had the same common enemy in MI5. Rajeeb had had the best British lawyers that money could buy. The following week, as part of an emergency mail-shot to lawyers who might act for me without money, I wrote to Rajeeb's main defence lawyer. She did not reply.

But what a difference from Legal Aid! Rajeeb's lawyers had won. He had been acquitted. That is why he was back in the cells with me, delighted, in the middle of the afternoon. He was about to be discharged. I knew that he had been bitterly angry that the terms of his bail up to the trial had meant he had had to spend a year in London rather than get on with his business in Rome, where he lived. I knew that he was angry that the judge had revoked his bail on the first day of the trial and he had had to suffer the grave indignity of being housed like a common British criminal, just like the rest of us.

I had seen him in reflective, gloomy periods when he had read the Koran in Arabic, in much the same way that I had read my Bible. But all that was gone, swept away. British justice being what it is, of course, he had to continue to suffer the indignity of imprisonment, even though he had no stain on his character. But it did not matter. He was about to be free. He would be in Rome later that night. His life was now his once again.

In the hour we had before Margaret came to tell Rajeeb that the judge had signed his release papers, Rajeeb repeated his offer of a new life working for his people and wrote down a London telephone number and a code-word on a copy of that day's *Evening Standard*. When Margaret came to lead Rajeeb to freedom we shook hands. I wished him all the best. He wished me all the best and urged me to do as he had suggested. I thanked him. We had shared a few days out of our very different lives in a common nightmare. For those few days we had been friends, colleagues, comrades.

Behind the high walls and iron bars, we were all equal citizens, no matter what we had been outside. Once we went our separate ways we would lose that bond of equality in adversity, but not the memory of it. That remains evergreen. I can almost sense the presence of Rajeeb in this room as I think about him. He is presumably somewhere in Rome in his expensive suits working for Colonel Gaddafi, who seems to have become more friendly towards the USA and Great Britain since 1997.

Though I never considered taking up Rajeeb's offer, he had meant what he said. He was extending the hand of friendship and assistance beyond our shared experience, and beyond the call of duty. He told me that, as a devout Muslim, having received the unexpected acquittal, he felt bound to help others. That was why he had made his offer. We shook hands and Rajeeb left the cells and my life.

At 4.30 p.m. the paddy-wagon came and I was once again taken back to solitary confinement in the hospital wing of Brixton Prison. At least, I thought, as the vehicle threaded its way through the rush-hour south-London streets, I had done finally and for all time with Hewitt. That, at least, was a thought I had to take with me on into my future.

At 11.15 the next morning, Thursday, 18 September 1997, the Securicor boss, Margaret, came to the cell at Southwark Crown Court where I was alone reading my Bible. She told me the jury had found me guilty on all four charges. She said she was sorry. I thanked her and she left the cell and locked the door behind her.

I was 48 years and four days old, and a convicted criminal. Now I was a member of the criminal classes. Sitting alone in a locked cell beneath Southwark Crown Court, having spent the previous four months in jail, I still felt that I was better off than I had been before. I reflected on what had brought me here. I just wish it hadn't happened.

The truth is that it did get to me. I could not read the Bible. I just sat there on the bench thinking about the past, about what might have been. About the future I had no illusions: I was for 'the big needle'.

I wept. Not boo-hoo, boo-hoo, but silent tears, angrily spat out from my eyes, slowly coursing down my cheeks. Not many, but tears, real ones. Tears of enormous rage, ferocious anger at what had been done to me and what had become of my life, what had become of me, my hopes, my dreams, the desire to get married, settle down and have a family, which had led me in the winter of 1982 to resign my high-flying staff post at the *Daily Express* and go the following year to the USA on a Harkness Fellowship, to get out of the rat-race that was Fleet Street national-newspaper journalism and work somewhere where my skills as a journalist and my interest in international relations would provide me with a base on which to build a new life centred on a loving relationship with a wife and children.

All gone. All long gone. Taken away from me by Goodman, Harkness, the CIA, MI5, all those who had remorselessly, as it felt to me, plotted against me and, in Joe Trento's words, crushed me.

So I wept bitter tears, for how long I don't know. Back when I had owned a house in Oxford, I used to have a heavy punchbag hanging in the garage with a pair of boxing gloves. I used to pound away at the bag for exercise and for the sheer hell of it. God how I wished I had that bag and the gloves in the cell with me that day. How I should have pounded away at that bag!

The tears stopped and I wiped my eyes and cheeks dry. I realised that I needed a priest. In the British prison system, prisoners can ask to see a priest, imam or whatever at any time. The warders see it neither as a treat for a prisoner (which they would forbid) nor as an emotional need (which they would ignore). They see it as odd but harmless.

I knew that there would be a Catholic priest whose duties took in Southwark Crown Court, so I asked for one. I told Margaret I wanted to see 'an Irish Catholic priest'. I told her he had to be Irish. If no Irish priest were available, I did not want a British one. She said she would see what she could do.

There was a Catholic priest available. He was the Chaplain of Guy's Hospital, not far away. And he was Irish. He came to see me at about 1.30 p.m. He was sitting waiting for me in one of the visiting-rooms, a grey-haired priest in his late fifties who exuded what I needed.

The reason I had wanted a priest, inasmuch as I had a coherent idea beyond the emotional need, was that I had suddenly felt I had to have the last rites of the Catholic Church. The last rites are given to a Catholic on the threshold of passing from this life to the next. All Catholics, lapsed or devout, tend to seek those last rites on their death-beds. Lord Marchmain in Evelyn Waugh's *Brideshead Revisited*, for example, defers in the end to the power and significance of this sacrament. The dying man is shriven of all earthly sin before passing on to meet his Maker.

Extreme unction is perhaps the most solemn of the sacraments of the Catholic Church, the one we all understand in our personal lives with a totality of assuredness which goes beyond belief or lack of it. The powerful need for an Irish priest to give me the last rites made little sense to me as I sat in the cell. I was not aware that I was in imminent danger of death. I went into jail a physically and mentally healthy man. I could expect to live another 40–50 years, perhaps.

Today, of course, I can see clearly that the news of my conviction did constitute in a real way a passage from one life to the next. Not emotionally, but really. Before the jury had returned, I had been a man with no stain on his character. Now I was a convicted criminal and would carry that label and stigma for the rest of my life. To accomplish that rite of passage, I needed a priest. And I am an Irish Catholic. Not a Roman Catholic. Not an Arhh-See. I wanted a priest of the Old Religion. I got exactly what I needed.

I didn't ask for the last rites, because he would not have given me them. I asked to make my confession. I told him briefly why I came to be in jail. Then I began, as I had been taught long, long ago as a child: 'Bless me, father, for I have sinned.' The priest listened to my confession, gave me a penance, which was not insignificant, and asked that I make an Act of Contrition: 'O my God, I am truly sorry that I have sinned against Thee and, with the help of Thy Grace, I will not sin again. Amen.'

Then the priest gave me absolution. All my sins were forgiven and the weight on my shoulders and in my heart lifted. I now had the strength to go on.

The moment that Margaret told me that I had been convicted, I assumed that I should be taken from the court to a secure criminal-lunatic asylum where the forcible injections – what I called 'the big needle' – would begin at once. Therefore, I was surprised to find myself still in the cells at 4.30 p.m., when the courts upstairs closed shop and we prisoners were delivered to various jails around London as usual in the armoured paddy-wagons.

I was taken back to Brixton and put in one of the solitary-confinement cells in the hospital wing, as I had been for the previous three nights. I expected to be taken the next day to the lunatic asylum and was surprised to find myself back in the cells at Southwark Crown Court at 8.30 the next morning.

However, what happened just before 10 o'clock was an even greater surprise. The other prisoners had all gone up to the courts a few minutes earlier, having spent time with their briefs in the interview rooms, and I was settling down to the usual solitary routine, reading that day's newspapers loaned from my friends the Securicor guards. Then the door to my cell was opened and I was told that I had a visitor. I had not expected anybody and there was nobody that I could think of who might have visited me, even if such visits were allowed, which they were not.

As I was taken to the interview room, with a mixture of astonishment and revulsion I saw the solicitor Stephen Hewitt sitting at the table waiting for me. My first instinct was to refuse to see him. My second eclipsed that in a nano-second: I itched to hit him, several times – now was my chance.

I have never before 'cold-cocked' somebody, as the Americans call it. This is because every time I felt that way I made myself count to ten inside. The mechanism clicked in that morning. I counted to ten.

He was businesslike. He made no offer to shake my hand. Had he done so, I should not have accepted it. So, out of all my ammunition, all I could pluck was: 'What are you doing here?'

'The judge sent me.'

'Why?'

'I am to tell you where you stand and what is going to happen to you.'

There was no further attempt to pretend that Hewitt was somehow on my side and that only my insanity was preventing me from seeing it. He was businesslike but he was also something else. I know what he was but I don't have a word which encapsulates the blend of characteristics which he displayed. He was frightened of what he was doing. He was going somewhere he had never gone before. He wasn't comfortable. He didn't feel guilty or ashamed. There was no element of that in him. He was at once cocky and unsure of himself. He felt himself to be the master of the situation in the interview, but something told him that it was more complex than that. He had never done something like this – what he had been doing for months – and it wasn't that he never wanted to do it again, he had no problem with that, it was that he couldn't quite integrate his previous 30-odd years with his new role in life. He could not make eye-contact. He could talk, but he could not talk and look me in the eye at the same time. Strange. He was the master, I the prisoner at the mercy of my jailers. I didn't need a fist, a boot or a needle laid on me to know that. Still, something kept Hewitt from looking me in the eye and that something gave me a feeling, odd though it seems in the context, that I was the master, not Hewitt and his bosses. Just because he could not look me in the eye even once, I felt superior in some strange but essential way. Hewitt was the slave, not I. He would drive out of the car park in a few minutes after checking back with Judge Fingret and go back to his nice life. I had no life to go back to. But he was the slave, not I.

Long ago in March, after six months as my solicitor when he had, as far as I could see, done little to prepare my defence and gone on holiday for the two weeks scheduled for the committal hearing that, in his absence, I had had to abandon, I had sacked him for this.

Since then, Hewitt had seemed to me to be running with the hare and hunting with the hounds. If that had not been my conclusion up to that Friday morning, what Hewitt told me at our meeting in the cells would have left me in no doubt. What he was doing, he explained, was delivering me a message from Judge Fingret upstairs. He was just the messenger.

Judge Fingret wanted me to know what was going to happen. He was not making me an offer. I was in no position to bargain. They had me where they wanted me. Dr Maden's report had been all they needed to find me insane. Now that I was officially both a criminal and insane, there was nothing I could do.

So Hewitt told me how it was going to be. 'There is not a place for you in the secure hospital the judge wants to send you, so you will be going back to jail again tonight. When a place becomes available, you will spend three months there. Then you will be released back into the community.'

The crucial difference between a judge sending a prisoner to a jail and to a secure lunatic asylum is that a fixed term only applies to jail and never applies to a lunatic asylum. Prisoners serve sentences in jail. In lunatic asylums, there are sick and are released only when they have been made better. One of almost 200 delusions the warders reported I had in the secure lunatic asylum was that I believed I was a prisoner. Christopher Monckton, with his ruthless ability to cut away the waffle and find the main point, bluntly asked me: 'Can you walk out of the front door if you want to?' Answer:

'No.' 'Then,' Christopher replied, 'you are a prisoner, and your jailers are delusional.'

What Hewitt told me was going to happen to me could not happen under the British legal system. Never mind that this was not the first time I could say that. What matters is that Hewitt told me that I should spend an unheard-of fixed term – exactly three months – in the lunatic asylum.

What the judge almost certainly meant, but what Hewitt did not dare to say, was that the real deal was rather different: 'If after three months you have accepted that you have been mentally ill since 1983 and that your claims against the CIA have all along been symptoms of your insanity, you will be released on licence, but in law you will always be subject to the judge and, should you later decide to renew your claims against the CIA, the judge may send you straight back to the hospital for further treatment.'

Hewitt did not say that, because he had no need to. This was all taken as read. It did not occur to Hewitt or the judge that, once sent to the lunatic asylum, I should refuse to withdraw my claims against the CIA. The mere truth made no sense to the judge or the lawyers. Were I to assert the truth, I should never be released. Months before a probation officer, David Arnold, had told me all about the special unit at Broadmoor for prisoners with untreatable personality disorders. He had advised me to give in, so as to avoid being sent to Broadmoor for life. He had argued that, whether I was mad or not, it made sense for me to give in because I was faced with the overwhelming, irresistible power of three police states that pretended to value freedom – the United States, Ireland and the United Kingdom.

Strangely, as I listened to Hewitt, I gradually but perceptibly began to feel sorry not for myself but for him. I began to pity him, and it would not go away. He did not want my sympathy, and I did not want to give it. Yet, as he outlined my future, I got a growing feeling of complete unreality. It was Hewitt, not I, who was the lunatic: he, not I, needed a better psychiatrist.

With hindsight, I can see that what caused these unexpected feelings in me was that the fundamental premise on which Judge Fingret had given Hewitt his instructions was false. It was exactly the same false premise that Goodman of the CIA had used as the basis of dealing with me all those years ago: Lehane is under my control, because I can hurt him badly and he cannot stop me, therefore Lehane will do whatever I tell him. No. It had not been true in the spring of 1984 in Washington. It was not true in the autumn of 1997 in London.

None of the things that Stephen Hewitt said to me inclined me to accept the future as Judge Fingret had told him to tell me it would be. I could not have what I wanted: that was clear. But I was not going to accept something I did not want.

I do not recall how Hewitt and I parted that morning. I think I just got up and left and walked back to the cells when Hewitt had finished what he had come to say. What I do remember vividly are two things. First, Hewitt was convinced that I was going to accept the judge's offer of three months in the lunatic asylum, agree to withdraw all my claims against the CIA and then be released into a council flat in Lambeth and work in the council library. Secondly, that if I refused to give up the truth I should be sent to the special unit for intractable personality disorders at Broadmoor, where, along with the Yorkshire Ripper, I should spend the rest of my life.

I had been defeated. I had lost. I had lost over and over again since the spring of 1984. These people were too powerful for me. I had failed in my attempt to overcome what they had done to me in 1984. Now they were going to lock me up for good and destroy my mind with powerful drugs. Fair enough. I couldn't stop them. There was nothing I could do. They had won.

18

Fellowship of the Damned

'You are afraid,' said O'Brien, watching his face, 'that in another moment something is going to break. Your especial fear is that it will be your backbone. You have a vivid mental picture of the vertebrae snapping apart and the spinal fluid dripping out of them. That is what you are thinking, is it not, Winston?'

from *Nineteen Eighty-Four*, GEORGE ORWELL

In February 2001 I attended by appointment St James's Hospital, Dublin to have a gastroscopy. A camera on the end of a cable was inserted down my throat into my stomach so that real-time pictures could be taken. It is an uncomfortable but painless experience. Most people manage to handle it. I disliked it but I, too, could handle it.

Yet after no more than a few seconds I had to call a halt. This was because, for safety, a strong male nurse pinions the patient, who is lying on his side, to the examining table in such a way that the patient is unable to move. This I could not take at all.

I had been beaten by warders in both jail and the criminal-lunatic asylum. Before each of these beatings, I had always been completely physically immobilised.

St James's Hospital is one of Dublin's major general hospitals. It has no prisoners and no warders. Its doctors are real doctors acting solely to give aid and comfort to patients. I knew this. Yet, I could not cope with the gastroscopy. The moment the nurse gripped me that day, I had an immediate and terrifying flashback to my incarceration. It was something with which I could only cope by breaking off the procedure.

Nor did it end there. I was in a state of shock all day. I went from

St James's to see a very holy Dominican priest who had befriended me and who knew what I had gone through in Britain. That is the reality of torture. The memory never leaves one. It remains just beneath the surface and can be reawakened without warning at any moment. One learns to live with it, but sometimes all the pre-cautions one takes count for nothing when the unexpected happens.

The decision to categorise my treatment as torture was made by Christopher Monckton in a 24-page report on my case that he submitted to Judge Fingret at Southwark Crown Court on 21 March 1998. He based his *ratio decidendi* on the United Nations Convention on Torture, which defines as torture – 'Any act by which severe pain or suffering, whether physical or mental, is intentionally inflicted on a person for such purposes as attaining from him or a third person information or a confession.'

The United Kingdom is one of 127 nations that have signed and ratified the UN Convention on Torture. The international judges at the Hague Tribunal in the Netherlands have ruled that the Convention 'signals to all members of the international community that the prohibition on torture is an absolute value from which nobody must deviate.'

Aleksander Ginsburg, a dissident in Soviet Russia, once said of his KGB torturers, 'I knew they would not try to kill me before the trial. This is because I was a "defended person", someone whom the West knew about and was likely to make a fuss about. Without this form of defence, political prisoners just die.'

However, when I had been arrested on 3 May 1996 I had not been a 'defended person' in the sense that Aleksander Ginsburg meant. As William Corson had told me once, nobody cared about me. I was heading for oblivion. I avoided oblivion solely because of the actions of Christopher Monckton in March 1998. From the moment of his impeccably-targeted and decisive intervention, I became a 'defended person', somebody about whom Christopher would and did make what he calls a 'stramash'. But, before his spectacular *coup de main*, in the face of gross criminality by the British judicial system, manipulated by MI5 on behalf of the CIA, I was quite defenceless and, to put it bluntly, months or even weeks from death.

Prisoners in jail are informed the previous night if they are to leave the jail the next morning. On the night of Sunday, 4 January

1998, in solitary confinement in Belmarsh, I was told I should be leaving next morning for the Crofton Clinic in the Bracton Centre attached to Bexley Hospital, under the jurisdiction of what is now 'Oxleas' Council, whose motto, an interesting instance of the pietistic present participle, is 'Improving Lives'. Next morning, in handcuffs, I left Belmarsh. No paddy-wagon this time, just a small prison van. The passengers were two warders – to one of whom I was handcuffed – the driver and myself.

When we arrived at the criminal asylum, the two warders took me through the numerous security gates and doors into the unit where I was to be held. We were met by two warders, one male and one female. They signed the Belmarsh paperwork, my handcuffs were unlocked and the Belmarsh warders left. The two lunatic-asylum warders told me their Christian names, offered me their hands, which I declined, and asked me what I wanted them to call me. I made no reply. They told me they would call me 'Denis'.

I note in passing that when Batman and Robin had arrested me in May 1996 they had used my Christian name in a crude attempt to demean me psychologically.

I was taken to my cell. A few minutes later a female in her forties arrived. She identified herself by her Christian name and told me that she would be my 'designated warder'. She said that prisoners made their own lunch but that the right to use the kitchen had to be earned and that, as I did not have this right yet, a meal would be provided. She gave me a brochure and left.

I read the brochure. It outlined the process whereby I should travel from my then state of 'serious mental illness' to 'cure' by the treatment appropriate to my 'condition'.

Major Hollywood film studios these days make blockbuster films in Ireland because of huge tax breaks. Had the makers been offered the use of Dublin's Grangegorman Lunatic Asylum for the making of *One Flew Over the Cuckoo's Nest*, they would have rejected it out of hand. A site of several hundred acres with enormous, run-down, nineteenth-century buildings, the furniture and fittings made of iron, the food rotten and insufficient – Hollywood would have rejected Grangegorman as a cliché, a caricature of the grim and forbidding Victorian mental institution that it had once been.

Yet, in my five months there more than a decade earlier, I had known more love and kindness from the staff than one could imagine. Their attitude towards us all was, 'There but for the grace of God go I.' Anybody could become insane, themselves too, and we were just the unlucky ones. Sleeping in an iron bed, which could be half a century old, in a large dormitory with other unfortunates is not disagreeable, and the food is bearable, when the people looking after you are like Dinny Neville, Eamon and all my other friends at Grangegorman. Nobody ever gave me 'a good kicking' there. True, they had injected me with large doses of powerful psychotropic drugs against my wishes, but they had done so with kindness. I offered no force to them. They inflicted none on me. They are good people.

The Crofton Clinic at the Bracton Criminal-Lunatic Asylum was something else. Unlike Grangegorman, the place was modern and well equipped. There were carpets on the floor. There were no dormitories: everybody had a cell to himself. The cell doors were never locked.

In all of the jails in which I stayed, there was often humour and fun. It is part of the human condition. I will remember till the end of my days the night in Belmarsh when the black ex-heavyweight boxer from Brixton, Dave, the white man, Pete, and I were up till the early hours watching an amazing electrical storm above Wool-wich Marshes. We oohed and aahed like children. Most prison warders were good skins. It was possible to have a joke with them.

The Crofton Clinic was in no way comparable. There were no jokes. There was fellowship and friendship between prisoners, but even among us there was no humour. It was the fellowship of the damned. There was no place for humour there. Even in death there is gallows humour. Crofton, for me, was about torture first. There can be no humour in that.

For more than six weeks I lived in the Crofton Clinic. With one important exception, I refused to talk to any of the 'doctors'. Shortly after my arrival, I had agreed to meet one of them, Dr Simon Pryor-Proctor. I had agreed to meet him for the sole purpose of telling him that I should not cooperate in any way in any psychiatric evaluation, that I was not guilty of the trumped-up charges, that I had been convicted in a defective show-trial and that my claims against the CIA and MI5 were true and, therefore, not symptomatic of any psychiatric disorder.

Dr Pryor-Proctor cut the meeting short by telling me that he needed to go because he had a puppy at home that needed feeding. He was a man of around 30, about 5 ft 6, obviously from a good upper-middle-class public-school background. He was vapid and shallow. He struck me as the sort of man who, having fed his puppy, would put on Radio 3 and settle down to read a good John Le Carré or Len Deighton spy novel without noticing that the imagined 'criminal lunatic' he had left behind in the torture centre had been talking to him of just such events happening in the real world.

Dr Pryor-Proctor's boss, Dr Roy Simpson, a decade or so older, was altogether more frightening. Simpson came on with charm and smiles and regarded himself as something of a communicator. However, once he realised that he was making no headway, the toothy smiles and the false bonhomie would stop.

The way my non-cooperation affected how I was treated in those first six to seven weeks concerned wages, exercise and personal toiletries. In jail at that time, everybody had to work for a wage of less than five pounds a week: the minimum wage does not apply to prisoners' earnings. In addition, all basic needs are catered for. They feed you, they clothe you, they provide you with toilet rolls, razor blades, soap, shampoo, deodorant, all for free. The free stuff is basic, though. If a prisoner prefers a better type of soap or shampoo, he can buy it out of his wages from the shop.

By law, all prisoners must be clothed and fed and they must have an hour's exercise each day. The first problem at the Crofton Clinic arose when I refused to undergo a training programme to learn how to cook and clean. I did not want to do this, I told them. They had to feed me and, if they didn't want to, fair enough, I wasn't that bothered. Lessons such as those in cooking and kitchen-cleaning would have filled all my days there had I cooperated with them.

My refusal to play was a difficult one for the authorities at the torture centre. They solved it by permitting me to use the kitchen to cook for myself without taking any lessons. It saved them cooking for me. When I asked for my hour's exercise each day, they just said no and that was the end of that. Had I cooperated with the programme, they told me, I could have gone to the gymnasium once or even twice a day. No, I told them, I was not going to cooperate. This made them cross, because they had hoped that if I wanted exercise I was going to respond like one of Pavlov's dogs and do exactly what they wanted.

In theory, of course, the Crofton 'Clinic' was not supposed to be a place of torture. It was a 'hospital unit' for 'psychiatric patients' who needed to be 'protected' so that their 'treatment' would make them 'better'. It purported not to be a jail. *Ergo,* there were no warders and no prisoners.

There was no prison work to be done and no prison wages. However, the Department of Social Security paid the prisoners. A few days after my arrival, I was given a government form to be filled in by patients wanting to receive social welfare during a stay in hospital. I wrote my name and my prison number. In the section where the applicant had to outline the diagnosis of his illness, I wrote, 'I am not mentally ill. I am a prisoner being held in this place against my will.'

The form was duly signed and sent off. My application for benefit was rejected on the ground that I claimed to be a prisoner and to be suffering from no illness. The warders greeted this rejection with triumphant joy, their reasoning being that, having denied myself money by insisting I was not mentally ill, and having suffered as a result, I was now going to knuckle down and cooperate. They were convinced they were 'winning'. They were certain that, for the sake of getting welfare money, I should inevitably fill in a new form, this time admitting that I was a voluntary patient who accepted that he was mentally ill and in need of psychiatric treatment. They got that one wrong, but for a day or so they were cock-a-hoop.

18 February 1998 would have been the fiftieth birthday of my elder sister, Mary Ann. Though she lived less than a week, I have always had a sense that she is with me all the time, especially in times of deep despair.

Mary Ann was in my thoughts. I had no hope of ever being released. Early that evening, six thugs of warders came to my cell. All but one of them did not work in my wing. I recognised them at once as being like the 'block screws' – warders specially selected for their sadism and love of savage violence, the 'special forces' of Her Majesty's Prison Service, who run the punishment blocks in jails and carry out the premeditated beatings.

These six were the same category of thugs. They were the hard men among the warders in the asylum for criminal lunatics. They had come to fight. They told me that they had been ordered to give me an injection and that I was on record as saying that I should resist any such injection violently. A nice touch, that. They had written in their records that I had told them that I intended to resist by force should they seek to inject powerful drugs into me against my will. In fact, I had spent almost six weeks refusing to talk to them at all.

I had not seen five of these Neanderthal block screws before. They had come from different parts of the lunatic asylum to give me a lesson. When I was told that their records showed that I had told them that I should resist violently any injection, I said, 'That is not true. I have no intention of attacking anybody and never have had.'

The chief grunt, who was no more than 30, was cocky and arrogant. His taunts and abuse would hurt me more than the beating. He told me to take my trousers down and lie face down on my cot. I said, 'No. I won't.'

There was a pause. Then he said in a very loud voice, 'The prisoner is about to attack. He must be restrained.'

Then the beating began. It was not my first beating but it was by far the worst. I am not really able to describe what happened. What I can say is that anybody who watches the action films where the hero takes on and defeats any number of attackers are total nonsense. Two would have been enough. Six were sent. I was trussed up like a chicken. My arms were twisted behind my back and my fingers were turned the wrong way around. My legs were forced into my back. I was helpless. I made no attempt to strike any of the attackers.

In the split second between Australopithecus's announcement and the start of the boneheads' attack, it flashed into my mind that, if I acted at once, I could hurt one of the attackers. But, I knew that that would be the end of my resistance. I chose not to attack any of them. I did nothing. And so I took my 'good kicking'. The whole thing is a sort of muddle in my mind today, just as it was then. During the beating, there was a running commentary of abuse: 'You think you are not mentally ill. That is the first sign of mental illness. We're going to make you realise that you are mentally ill!'

I remember those words from Australopithecus, because they

recalled the Lobotomy Man's *obiter dictum*: 'Believing you are not paranoid is a symptom of paranoia!'

I remember clearly one of the thugs, while I was trussed by his other colleagues, grabbing the hair on my head and violently twisting it, using it to bang my head on the ground. Grabbing the hair of an immobilised man and using it to raise his head and then to bang it as hard as possible on the ground is a gratuitous act of violence. All of the beating was of course gratuitous, but that particular event stood alone as one where the perpetrator had made a premeditated decision to hurt me as badly as possible when I was not a threat to any of them and had offered no defence to their attack.

The pain from what that warder did to me was instantaneous and awful, quite apart from the pains I was suffering at the hands of all the others. Being secured by my hands and feet in a contorted position was certainly painful. The various parts of my body upon which they had rained down blows of every kind were numb at first. The pain would come to all the body when the various endorphins, serotonins and adrenaline had ceased to course through my veins and into the brain. That pain was going to be bad. But that single act of twisting my neck and slamming the back of my head on the ground was a quite different pain from all the others.

After several minutes, they stopped. They had me trussed up on the ground, unable to move and in great pain.

'Go on then, give me the injection!' I screamed at them. By now I was desperate to be set free.

'Oh no,' said Australopithecus. 'You've been a bad boy.' Then he said to his fellow Neanderthals, 'Get him on his feet!'

I was brought to my feet and doubled over in great pain, with my arms pulled way up behind my head and my head almost knocking on my knees. Then I was beaten as I was dragged out of the cell and through the area where the prisoners could associate freely.

My fellow-prisoners were there and saw what was being done to me. They knew what was happening. There was nothing they could do.

I was dragged into an isolation cell which contained nothing other than a filthy old mattress on the floor. There I was forced face-down, still held trussed-up, while one of them pulled my trousers and underpants down. Finally, another stuck a needle into my upper thigh.

Then they did something that I did not think much about at the time but which later gave me something to hang on to. They took my blood pressure. While I was trussed up like a chicken, unable to move, they put the cuff around one of my arms, pumped it up and took my blood pressure. It was off the wall and beyond. What had they expected?

I realised later exactly what they expected. They expected me to let them take my blood pressure when I was not trussed up like a chicken. No check for blood pressure on a man who has just been beaten savagely is going to have any value unless it is followed by regular checks when the victim is not under stress. They needed me to cooperate with them for this to work.

They could kick me and beat me and grab me by the hair and smash my head against the floor, but they couldn't do that and take my blood pressure at the same time. They needed me to cooperate. Yet they had no power to make me cooperate in this regard because, for all their overwhelming numbers and their brutal savagery, their violent methods meant that they could not get a reliable blood-pressure reading from me.

Likewise, I learned that they needed feedback from me about the effect of the psychotropic drugs they were forcibly injecting into me, so that they could work out how far they could get away with increasing the dosage. They needed me to cooperate of my own free will. But I wouldn't.

The drug they were giving me was Depixol, a strong psychotropic medication. 'Psychotropic' is Greek for 'mind-altering'. They were trying to alter my mind so that I should no longer recognise the truth.

I couldn't defend myself against them because I lacked the force required to deal with them. But I could refuse to talk to them, as I had done, and they could kick and beat and harm me, as they did, but that was all they could do. Their power was great, yet it was limited. My power was small, but I could and did withhold my co-operation.

'Now, you've been a bad boy but we want to be friends with you,' said Australopithecus. 'You're an educated man and you know you shouldn't behave like this. You are mentally ill and we are your friends and we want to help you. There is no need for this to ever happen again. All you've got to do is talk to us and let us help you.'

I was still in the iron grip of three of his fellow thugs, my face in the mattress, my arms twisted unnaturally up and behind my head so that it was forced faced down into the mattress. My naked legs, with my trousers and underpants at my ankles, were forced into my back at an unnatural and painful angle.

The grip on my arms was released so that I could talk. Australopithecus put his face close to mine and looked me in the eye. I said nothing. No, that is wrong. I did not speak. But I looked. I was in agonising pain. I just looked deep into the blackguard's eyes. He did not like what he saw there. He jumped away from me as though I had struck him. 'Aha! I see we've got a hard man here. He doesn't want to be helped. He thinks he's not mentally ill, an educated man like that! Leave him here to stew for a bit.'

So they all left me. There was a large picture window in one wall. They placed a warder on the other side of it looking at me permanently. He was not one of the 'special forces' warders who had just assaulted me with intent to cause grievous bodily harm, but one of the others.

For reasons I did not ponder at the time and cannot explain today, I sat on the floor in the cell in a Buddha posture; that is to say, my legs were crossed, my hand were cupped in front of me, my back was straight and I looked at the opposite wall. I sat at right-angles to the warder observing me through the picture window. I didn't think a great deal. Or rather, my thoughts were confined simply to coping with the situation. I did not ponder that what had just been done to me was likely to occur on a regular basis thereafter.

My watch had been taken, so I had no idea of time. At some point, the cell door opened and Australopithecus and his pals were back. I saw them out of the corner of my eye. My gaze did not move from the opposite wall. I have distinct memories of only two warders. The other four are what they were then, just a blur, people I had never seen before. As well as Australopithecus, there was *homo erectus*. He squatted in front of me seeking eye contact.

I did not want eye contact with him, so I focused on the wall directly behind him and above his head. It was not a great angle of elevation for my eyes. This phrase that I had heard used a number of times during the beating – 'you're an educated man' –

was something that the warders believed was the key to unlocking my hostility towards them. I have no idea what had been their instructions and what preparation they had made before the attack. All I knew was that they had come to beat me.

Next, *homo erectus* squatted in front of me, still trying but failing to make eye contact, while Australopithecus sat on my right, his body touching mine. I had no doubt that this tactile experience was not an accident. Australopithecus, who had been aggressive and threatening in his tone to me in the first round, chose a kinder, gentler tone this time.

'Denis, we want to take your blood pressure. Will you let us do that? Please?'

I said nothing. I just stared at the wall above *homo erectus*'s head. He started again on the mantra, 'Denis, you are an educated man. We only want to help you. We don't want this.'

Again silence. As *homo erectus* was failing to engage my unseeing eyes, Australopithecus was touching me. The left-hand side of his body was in permanent contact with my own. His right hand started caressing my right forearm just below the elbow. He cooed at me, like a lover, 'Ah, come on, Denis, we only want to help you. This isn't the way an educated man like you should behave.'

The other four warders encircled me and the two warders who were doing the talking. I had no personal space. There was a warder blocking all access out for me. The two warders who took it in turns to tell me how educated I was kept up a non-stop barrage. Their four accomplices were squatting on their heels around me, exuding menace. But I didn't pay much attention to five of them. Australopithecus had all my attention. His hand progressively moved down my right forearm. I was sitting in my Buddha position.

He reached my wrist and went beyond it into my cupped hands. He started rubbing his fingers in my cupped hands. It was a slow, deliberate process. Strangely, I was equally deliberate. It wasn't much of a decision to sit immobile in my Buddha position while the six warders crowded around me, and not to respond to any-thing they said or did. I was not going to be able to stop them beating me again. The previous beating had left me full of all the body's flight-or-fight chemicals. If they were going to beat me again, the body was as ready for it as it could be.

But my decision to do nothing was not enough. As Australopithecus's hand travelled down my forearm towards my hands, rubbing and soothing my bare flesh with his fingers, his body leaning into mine, I waited. Australopithecus stopped at my hands. After whatever period it took them to conclude that I did not want to be friends and that I was not going to let them take my blood pressure, Australopithecus withdrew his hand and huffily said, 'This man is mentally ill and does not understand that we are here to help him. We are wasting our time.'

With that, they left the cell. I remained there for several hours. To start with, one of the non-special-forces warders, who took it in turns to watch me through the picture window, every half an hour or so would ask me if they could take my blood pressure. I never said a word to them. It wasn't difficult. Hatred and anger are good for that. I have never been a great one for loving my enemies, no more than I think that turning the other cheek is always the best thing to do. Had Australopithecus and I been alone in a cell, that is something he would have learned.

By the evening, they had given up, at least for that day. I was told that I was to be taken back to my cell. I didn't want to go. I was happy enough where I was, I told them. They had the answer to that. If I didn't go back to my cell, they would summon the block screws and beat me once more and dump me there. I went back to my cell.

In the final report submitted to Judge Fingret on 21 May 1998, the chief torturer who had designed the entire procedure applied to me by his team of psychopaths said that my attitude towards all of them 'has at all times been one of disdain'. He got that right.

I had rejected their advances. I could not stop them beating me and sticking needles wherever they chose. But I could refuse to make friends with them, which was their objective. I hated them ferociously. One may say that beating a stranger without mercy is not the best way to become his friend, but that is not what history says. As a journalist I was familiar with what is called 'Stockholm Syndrome', named after a 1973 bank robbery in Stockholm which went wrong. The bank robbers took four hostages – three men and a woman – and held out against the police for six days. When the four hostages were rescued by the police, they sided with the robbers who had held them hostage and tried to help their former captors escape punishment.

When the incident was analysed by psychologists it soon became clear that what had happened in Stockholm was not an isolated incident. In the years which followed, when terrorist hijackings of commercial airliners became relatively frequent, the same phenomenon was frequently observed. Stockholm Syndrome comes into play when a captive cannot escape, is isolated and threatened with death, but is shown token acts of kindness by the captor.

The doctors and warders in the lunatic asylum did not go so far as to threaten me with death. Perhaps that is why Stockholm Syndrome never kicked in. By the winter of 1998 it was well established that switching from beatings to kindness and back again could break down a prisoner's will so that he could reasonably be expected to love his captors. I was never tempted. I hated them all then. I hate them all today. Perhaps hatred is the antidote to Stockholm Syndrome.

When I was returned to my cell that night I made two requests to the warders. I was entitled, according to the rules, to make both requests. The first was that they find an Irish Catholic priest somewhere to come and see me that night and bring with him a set of rosary beads. The warders regarded the request to see a priest with the same bemused indifference as their predecessors in the various prisons had. Margaret, the Securicor boss at Southwark Crown Court, had treated me differently and had telephoned around until she had found a priest for me. But she and her Securicor colleagues were not British prison warders.

The warders, products of a Godless, secular society, thought the request to see a priest the crowning proof that a prisoner was insane and certainly not as intelligent as they thought they were. To them all religion was merely superstition; the tag 'hocus-pocus', which derives from the Latin words said in the Mass, *Hoc est enim corpus meum* ('This is my body'), was invented after the Protestant Reformation as a way of insulting and abusing Catholics. I believe in the Catholic faith because my grandparents believed and all belonging to them before and since have believed. The faith is a comfort in times of trial when we feel weak, vulnerable and defenceless.

At 7.30 that evening the warders delivered me to the interview room. There I found Father Jack Madden, an Irish priest in his fifties who, he told me, knew Father Malachy O'Toole, whom I had seen the previous September in the cells of Southwark Crown Court. Father Madden, like Father O'Toole, did not care that I was a convicted criminal. He did not care that I was officially criminally insane. All he cared about was that I was an Irish Catholic who had called for a priest in a time of great anguish.

The first thing Father Madden did was give me a set of rosary beads in a small leather case. When I opened the case and took out the rosary beads I saw that on the reverse of the crucifix was printed MADE IN IRELAND. That comforted me. I still have those beads. I try to say the rosary every night. It is the only thing from my year of incarceration that I can bear to keep with me. The horror of what was done to me fills me with revulsion and I cannot cope with anything that reminds me of it. But those rosary beads are different.

As I had done with Father O'Toole in September, I asked Father Madden to hear my confession. I had not had absolution for several months. This was because when I had asked the warders when I was kept in solitary confinement at Belmarsh for the Catholic chaplain, Father Kevin, to come and hear my confession, he had sent a woman and I had refused to confess to her. Father Kevin is a good man and a conscientious priest but his Catholicism and mine are not the same. He was very popular in Belmarsh with the Afro-Caribbean prisoners, not because they were Catholics but because Father Kevin had a seemingly inexhaustible supply of short versions of the rosary beads. The black prisoners liked wearing them as necklaces.

The rules forbade necklaces *qua* necklaces, but if the coloured beads ending in a crucifix hanging around a prisoner's neck had been given to him by a recognised padre there was nothing the warders could do. My gut reaction was that this was blasphemy. After Belmarsh, I spent time in Wormwood Scrubs. The Catholic priest there was British and we did not get on. I did, however, meet the late Cardinal Basil Hume, Christopher Monckton's old friend, who celebrated Mass on Christmas Day there. It was only a matter of weeks before he learned that he had terminal cancer. I found him a kind and holy priest. At the end of the Mass, he shook hands with every one of us. In the homily, he told us that he was there because the Scrubs was his local prison and he could not think of a better place to celebrate Mass on Christmas Day than with us.

So I had not been given absolution for various reasons and I wanted it. I made my confession and Father Madden gave me my penance. Then we talked. I told Father Madden my story. As elsewhere in the prison system, the walls of the interview room were made of glass so that warders could observe what went on. Strangely, whereas before I had found these windows offensive I found them to my liking at the 'clinic'.

The warders could see us but they could not hear us. They would not have understood if they had heard. But they could not hear, so the windows came to be a real barrier between me and the warders, all they did to me and what they stood for. The interview room, transparent though its walls were, became a place of refuge. Father Madden visited me regularly. We would sit in the interview room for an hour, maybe more. The warders would look on at us with that blank, puzzled expression of the barely-intelligent British working class. And I was away from them. I had a personal space with Father Madden which I did not have at any other time.

Father Madden's visit that evening helped me cope with the pain and distress that the vicious beating by the warders had caused me, just as in September his friend and colleague Father O'Toole had assuaged my despair. Before he left, Father Madden told me that one of the other prisoners, Danny Barr, a native of Belfast in his late thirties, was a very devout Catholic and said a decade of the rosary each night. He said he would speak to Danny after our meeting and see if he could help me in any way.

Danny and I spoke later that night. Like all the other prisoners on that wing, he knew what the warders had done to me earlier in the day. Like all the others, he felt revulsion at it. He told me that he had been forcibly injected with the same psychotropic drugs and that it had been a truly horrible experience for him. Danny had a pure and powerful Irish Catholic faith which shamed me. He knew the truth. He was never beset by the doubts, puzzles and questions that bothered and sometimes tormented me. He left a lasting impression in me. I remember him every morning in my prayers, as I remember others who have helped me.

The second application I made to the warders that evening was to be allowed to telephone my nominal solicitor, James Nichol, who had finally become my solicitor at the end of 1997, when Judge Fingret had agreed to his being paid Legal Aid. There is a public payphone on the wing and one of the warders stood by me as I made the call. Prisoners in Britain, whether in jails or lunatic asylums, have no privacy. All letters and outgoing telephone calls can be, and often are, monitored. Calls to lawyers, though, are supposed to be private.

Nichol would not be there because it was after office hours, but I knew that there would be an answering machine and that Nichol would call in to collect messages. So I left a message on the machine to say I had been savagely beaten and was in pain and that I wanted him to come and see me that night and bring with him an independent doctor to examine me. Nichol did not respond. I contrast Nichol's decision to ignore my call for help with that of the Irish Catholic priest who had come at once when the warders told him a prisoner he did not know needed him.

Had an independent doctor examined me that night, he would have found that my blood pressure was elevated to dangerous levels. Given the savage attack, this would not have surprised the doctor. However, he would have wanted to check the blood pressure the next day and at regular intervals over the following days to see if it had returned to normal. Such checks would have shown that my blood pressure was permanently high and that I was developing heart disease which made it likely that my heart, if untreated, would fail – as it did after my release. I ran the risk of a heart attack or a stroke if the condition were not treated. As I was a lifelong non-smoker, had been a regular blood donor until comparatively recently, had for decades gone jogging for exercise, and had no history of heart disease in my family, it is reasonable to conclude that the elevated levels of blood pressure were probably caused by stress. In addition, had an independent doctor examined me on the night of 23 February 1998 he would have found something wrong with my spine. This problem was indicated by a severe pain in the back of the head, to the left, behind the ear and close to the cerebral cortex, and was caused by damage to the left occipital nerve, which runs from the spine into the brain. This would have been clear to an independent doctor, had one arrived.

This injury persisted even when the bruises went away and the pain in other parts of my body diminished. An independent doctor that night would have found that during the savage beating one of the vertebrae in the thoracic spine had been forcibly compressed into the spinal column. The force had been sufficient to cause serious damage to the spinal cord. Had the force of the attack been greater, it could have killed me or left me a paraplegic. I needed immediate treatment for this injury. Today, more than a decade later, I suffer constant pain throughout my body which the doctors tell me I will have to live with for the rest of my life.

Because of the location of the pain I associated it with the forcible injections which had coincided with the beatings. I was suffering visibly from the effects of this powerful drug when Christopher Monckton's doctor, David O'Connell, examined me after Christopher had had me released. I did not mention the pain in the back of the head to Dr O'Connell, because I assumed it had been caused by the injections and that it would go away in due course as all the other symptoms did within six to eight weeks. It did not go away. The pain was not caused by the drugs they had injected into me. It was caused by the damage they had done to my spinal cord.

I am still officially insane in Britain. I could be arrested and thrown into a criminal-lunatic asylum at the whim of any judge, without any trial or any further alleged offence, as long as two doctors signed a form to say that I had become a danger to myself or to others. The state has plenty of doctors ready routinely to sign such forms when asked to do so. This is why I have no intention of ever returning within Her Majesty's realms – I do not ever want to endure her hospitality again.

Dr O'Connell, would notice my high blood pressure when he examined me later in the year. Astonishingly, a doctor in Cork City who took my blood pressure on three successive weeks, following Dr O'Connell's finding, concluded that the blood pressure was fine. It was not fine. I came close to death twice the following year because the hypertension caused by the stress of my life as a member of the underclass and an insane criminal had not been treated.

On 10 April 1998, the governments of the United Kingdom, led by Tony Blair as Prime Minister, and the Irish Republic, led by Bertie Ahern as Taoiseach, plus the leaders of all the main Northern Ireland political parties, signed the Good Friday Agreement which brought devolved all-party government to the Province. It would prove to be a major step towards ending the Provisional IRA's terrorist war against Britain, and would set Northern Ireland on course for peace and economic renewal.

I heard the news as a prisoner of Tony Blair, confined by his government at the behest of the US government in a criminal-lunatic asylum, enduring judicially prescribed torture which was destroying my mind and hastening my death. That peace agreement could not have been signed without the resolute and determined activities of President Clinton in the US. On numerous occasions he cited the debates he had attended on Northern Ireland at the Oxford Union as giving him his enduring interest in the Province. He was at Oxford between October 1968 and June 1970. In the academic year 1968–69, the Oxford Union did not debate Northern Ireland once. In the next year, it did so twice, on both occasions, it will be remembered, at my insistence. Before those debates, I had repeatedly tried to obtain adjournment debates on Northern Ireland.

It was a strange feeling. Clinton's interest in Northern Ireland's affairs had begun with debates at the Oxford Union instigated by a man who was now a political prisoner undergoing torture in Bexley. The small seed that I had apparently sown in a young American student's mind had blossomed into the fruit of peace in Northern Ireland. I did not dream of suggesting to the warders that it was all my doing. They would have thought I was insane, and a note would have appeared in their records to the effect that 'he is now claiming that he is responsible for peace in Northern Ireland'.

19

Freedom

Freedom is the freedom to say that two plus two make four. If that is granted, all else follows.

from *Nineteen Eighty-Four*, GEORGE ORWELL

After a year in jail and in the 'clinic' for the criminally insane, I did not know where to turn. Then I heard Christopher Monckton on the radio. I cannot remember what he was talking about, but I was reminded that he had said he would help if my lawyers contacted him. I had no lawyers any more, so, in February 1998, I queued for the single telephone which the inmates of the Crofton Clinic in Bexley were allowed to use. In the hearing of my torturers, I telephoned Christopher.

He took the call in the vast library of his Scottish mansion. I told him the latest chapters in my story. Even in my confused state, chemically lobotomised by the forcible injection of a drug known to prove fatal over a period of time, I could hear how horrified he was. Then he asked one simple question, and I knew I was going to be free.

This is what he said. 'Denis, you're a journalist. If someone had telephoned you and said the CIA was out to get him, you'd suspect he was a paranoid schizophrenic. So put yourself in my shoes, and tell me how I can check out your story about the CIA.'

There in the telephone queue, in front of my brother criminal lunatics, hard men all, with the phone in my hand, I burst into tears. I couldn't stop myself.

'Why are you crying?' asked Christopher. I suspected he already knew the answer.

'Because,' I said, 'you're the first person since I was locked up who has ever asked me how he can verify from independent sources that my account of events is true. And I can answer it.' I gave him the telephone number of Joe Trento in the US, and told him that through Joe he would be able to reach everyone else he needed to speak to.

In the last week of February 1998, shortly after my telephone call from the 'clinic' to Christopher's Scottish pile, the documentary film-maker Sean McPhilemy also contacted Christopher. When Sean told him what was happening to me, he flew down from his home in Scotland to see for himself. He met me in the canteen at Southwark Crown Court and was profoundly shocked at what he saw. Only a year previously I had been black-haired, clean-shaven and trim. Now I was a mess: heavily overweight because weight gain was one of the many side-effects of the psychotropic drugs; white-haired because of the stress caused by the beatings; confused because the drugs interfered with rational thought; and in constant pain from my injuries at the hands of my torturers.

Christopher set about getting me out of the secure lunatic asylum. It is obvious that he succeeded, because today I am alive and free in Ireland and not dead in custody in England.

He came down to London when I was next due to appear in court for the monthly review of my incarceration under the Mental Health Act. When we met he was visibly moved by my condition. He took my hands in his and said, 'Denis, I won't let you down.'

He was true to his word. He didn't let me down. After so much betrayal, constancy was something to which I was not used. He later told me that I had aged 20 years in the fifteen months since he had last seen me. He had no need to be told the details of what was being done to me. One look at me was more than enough.

Christopher undertook a painstaking investigation of every aspect of my case. He ran what he called a 'Robin Hood' consultancy: the fees of his rich clients subsidised his numerous *pro bono* cases. I did not get away without paying, though. Christopher told me sternly that there was nowt for nowt and not a lot for sixpence, so his fee for springing me out would be a pint of Guinness in a Dublin pub once I was free. It turned out to be good value for me, that fee: Christopher and his staff put in hundreds of hours on my case.

First, he obtained all the paperwork. He told me to send him all the psychiatric assessments that the Crofton Clinic had prepared.

On the telephone, I asked him what he made of them. He said, 'The technical term for all of these reports is "gibberish".' He did not tell me until long afterwards that it looked very much to him as though the reports had been very carefully contrived so that when, in a few months' time, I keeled over and died, the 'clinic' would be able to produce a complete paper-trail to show how blameless, diligent and caring Her Majesty's government and all its function-aries had been. Christopher is seldom vulgar, so that it is quite startling when he departs from the canonical vocabulary of the Queen's English. 'There are four psychiatric assessments of you, Denis,' he said, 'and each of them is a craftily machined piece of arse-plating for Big Brother's wobbly bot.'

For instance, Christopher was tickled to discover that one of the four 'psychiatrists' had written the following priceless gem: 'This man is very intelligent. It is a marked symptom of his condition that he has been able to convince many people that his claims against the CIA are true.'

This was another way of saying what the Lobotomy Man had said to me back in July of 1984: believing that one is sane is a symptom of insanity. Thus an articulate lunatic, so the 'psychiat-rists'' argument ran, can fool normally well-balanced people into believing that he is telling the truth and must accordingly be sane. Christopher later told me that one of the strongest arguments he had been able to put in front of the judge was that not one of the four shrinks had bothered to lift a telephone and check the truth of my account with Joe Trento or William Corson or anyone else. 'Judges work on facts,' he said, 'and the moment they realise the people who ought to have checked the facts haven't done their homework you're past first base.'

Over the following weeks, Christopher spent hours on the tele-phone with me going through what he found in the paperwork and asking detailed, careful questions. I could only manage to talk to him for a few minutes at a time, but he said I was not to worry: I should ring him whenever I felt strong enough, day or night, and he would be listening.

I told him everything that had happened since we had last been in touch. I said I had been told that, if I did not withdraw what I had said about the CIA and MI5, and if I refused to go along with the falsehood that I had been insane since 1983, I was never going to be released. Instead, I had been told I should be sent to a special unit at Broadmoor.

I told Christopher that I understood the Crofton Clinic in which I was living to be a halfway house to Broadmoor. Were I to give in and publicly admit the lies were the truth, I should be released on licence and given a council flat on an inner-city estate in Lambeth and employment as a librarian or something similar would be provided for me. But if I refused to capitulate, my cell in Broadmoor awaited me.

Because of the effects of the psychotropic drugs I could not spend more than 20 minutes on the prisoners' phone at a time. Each time I had to go and rest before the next period of relentless questioning. Christopher asked me detailed questions about my symptoms, which included headaches, rapid weight gain, disorientation and inability to concentrate. Christopher also took the name of the drug that was being forcibly injected into me.

His first step in verifying my account was to ask his doctor, David O'Connell, about Depixol. His doctor confirmed that each and every one of the symptoms I described to him was listed in the pharmacopoeia – a medical encyclopaedia of drugs. The symptoms included loss of concentration, headaches, confusion, sluggishness and morbid weight gain.

Christopher was appalled at what I told him about the forcible injections and the beatings. The warders looked on with mounting terror as I spoke to him. They heard everything he and I said, but there was nothing they could do. They could hardly attack Christopher. He was invulnerable to them. When I saw the naked fear in their miserable, shrimp-like faces, I began to realise for the first time what the power of true authority is. Christopher had it. They did not. And they knew it. And so did he, though he was far too polite to say so.

That meeting at Southwark Crown Court gave me hope. Privately, Christopher's main concern, as he told me later, was that I was going to die at the hands of my torturers before he could rescue me. David O'Connell had told him that more than one or two months' exposure to the forcibly injected psychotropic drug would be very likely to kill me. But Christopher said nothing of that to me at the time. He smiled, told me not to worry, and said – in the hearing of the now gelatinous warders – that if there were any more violence he was to be notified at once. As the warders led me away, Christopher watched until we were through the door, giving me a wave and a wink as I went.

I hoped – at last I hoped – but I did not dare to allow myself too much hope at that stage. For a start, the effect of the drug was mind-numbing and it was difficult to react to anything in a normal way. And there had been plenty of false dawns before. I did not want to get my hopes up too high only to have them dashed again.

After our meeting, Christopher telephoned Joe Trento in the US, who answered all his questions without hesitation and confirmed my account of events on all points.

Christopher also spoke to my father, who told him that there was no truth in the claims made about me in the official record and that he himself had been told by Joe Trento in 1987 that the CIA had, indeed, done the things I said it had done and that consequently my account was not prompted by psychotic delusions. Christopher told my father how sorry he was for the misery that as a parent he had suffered because of what had been done to his son.

Christopher concluded that I was the victim of inhumane treatment amounting to torture. Mine was an appalling story, but nothing that four years dealing with the festering tentacles of the British state on behalf of Margaret Thatcher had left him unprepared for. The most important thing, he said, was to get the torture stopped at once and then to secure my release. At that time, Christopher was still just able to work as an independent consultant dealing with governmental abuses of power, usually for businesses, sometimes for governments. Despite his increasingly precarious health, he set out at once to produce a report on what had been and what was being done to me.

Christopher's 24-page report was completed on 26 March 1998, remarkably soon after I had first contacted him. It was thorough, complete and devastating. His conclusion was that there had never been any justification for what had been done to me; that I had told the truth throughout; and that there had manifestly been no basis in fact or in law either for prosecution or for incarceration in the 'clinic'.

His report found unequivocally that I had been and continued to be systematically, deliberately and premeditatedly tortured and subjected to inhumane treatment (his own words) over a period of months in 1998 with the intention of compelling me to withdraw my truthful statements against the CIA, which had destroyed my life because I had refused to work for it as a spy under the cover of my career as a journalist.

Christopher saw to it that his report was delivered to Judge Fingret, and he followed up the report with a telephone call to the judge to make sure he had got it. He also sent a copy to me, but I was so ill under the influence of the drugs that I was unable to read any of it. I managed to read his covering letter, though. This is what he wrote:

> Have courage! Don't let your torturers undermine your spirit. We have completed and revised our report and, after speaking to Judge Fingret this morning, have sent him a copy, together with a covering letter. I have also written to Shirley Williams as the first stage of preparation for the parliamentary assault which will ensue if the judge does not act decisively enough or quickly enough on the basis of the report. The four so-called 'psychiatrists' will be lucky to get jobs grading turnips after their disgraceful per-formance, and the Crofton Clinic will probably be closed as well. In due course Her Majesty's Chief Inspector of Prisons is going to be very interested in what has been done to you there. The media can also be expected to give things a certain amount of coverage when the time is right. Torture at the hands of psychiatrists is something which might have been expected in Soviet Russia or Nazi Germany but in Blair's Britain at the end of the twentieth century it is A Story. Keep in touch whenever you feel like it. I will always respond as quickly as my unreliable health permits.

Also included was his letter to the Baroness Williams of Crosby, of the same date, the substance of which ran as follows:

> I spoke to Carol Savage, who was very much on the ball, in your office today. She thought you might be interested to see a report we have prepared, which is highly critical of the four psychiatric 'assessments' carried out on Denis Lehane, to whom you have been very kind. The report has been sent to the judge in the case, His Honour Judge Peter Fingret, at Southwark Crown Court. I have given the judge a week to order an end to the torture which the gruesome psychiatric experimenters at Bexley Hospital are

inflicting upon him on the mistaken assumption that his story about his mistreatment at the hands of a rogue CIA agent in the early 1980s is false. The story has in fact been researched for CNN by Joe Trento, a television reporter, who has confirmed to me that it is all true.

I am deeply concerned about this case. Denis is being tortured, in Britain, in the late twentieth century, and with the apparent approval of the judicial system, on the basis of sloppy and grievously inadequate psychiatric assessments, in retribution for an alleged 'offence' so laughable that the CPS had to dredge up an obscure provision in a near-defunct Act of 1861 in order to get away with a conviction in the obvious total absence of *mens rea*. In our report you will find a brief account of the painful and distressing symptoms induced by the psychotropic drugs which are designed to change Denis's mind so that he is falsely induced to believe that his story, which is true, is false. Denis is deteriorating fast under this gross medical abuse and I fear that he may come to permanent harm unless decisive action is taken.

Carol Savage tells me you are back from Siberia on 6 April. If by then I have not had a satisfactory response from the judge, and if Denis is still being tortured, I shall approach you and ask you to put down some penetrating Parliamentary Questions on his behalf. He ought not to have written the silly letters which led to his conviction but no one takes them seriously and his current plight is far more severe than his alleged offence merits. He has suffered more than enough already.

For the time being, this letter requires no action on your part: it is for your information only and there is no need even to reply. I shall send another signal if I think that action would be helpful. Once again, many thanks for the enormous efforts you have already made on Denis's behalf.

Christopher's covering letter to Judge Fingret, also of the same date, was devastating to the reputation of British justice:

YOUR HONOUR – We spoke this morning. Please forgive this direct letter, but I am deeply concerned at the inhumane treatment to which Denis Lehane, a former journalistic colleague, is being compelled to endure in the Crofton Clinic, which is a division of the Bracton Psychiatric Centre in Bexley Hospital.

Mr Lehane, on the order of the court, is undergoing what is supposed to be a psychiatric evaluation but in the circumstances amounts to torture. That torture must cease. This letter proposes a course of action which should provide sufficient reassurance to enable Your Lordship to make the necessary order *without waiting for the case to call again in court.*

The enclosed report, which we have prepared after studying the four so-called 'assessments' of Mr Lehane done by psychiatrists for the courts, shows that the 'assessments' are founded upon more than 180 instances of material error of fact or opinion and that there are strong grounds for believing that Mr Lehane's story of mishandling in the early 1980s at the hands of a rogue agent of the CIA is in substance true.

In particular, I spoke last year and again some days ago with Mr Joseph Trento, a television journalist who worked for CNN in the mid-1980s and spent several months researching and filming a documentary about what happened to Mr Lehane. On both occasions Joe Trento confirmed that Mr Lehane's story is true and that he had personally verified it in conversation with Dr William Corson, a former CIA liaison officer to three Presidents of the United States, who had studied Mr Lehane's Intelligence file.

Yet all four of the psychiatrists, in flagrant defiance of the rules of their profession, have made not the slightest attempt to lift a telephone and check the veracity of Mr Lehane's story. Instead, they have lazily assumed his account of events to be false and, on that assumption, are subjecting him to a painful and distressing regime of enforced injections with powerful psychotropic drugs intended to change his mind. The drugs are, as you may know, administered by force, and you will find some of their pernicious side-effects described in our report, which will in due course be placed before the Home Secretary with strong recommendations that the procedures for psychiatric evaluation be radically reformed to prevent further abuses of this kind and that the four psychiatrists be in future debarred from carrying out such 'assessments' on behalf of the courts.

There are so many factual inaccuracies in the four psychiatric 'assessments' that they provide no reasonable foundation whatsoever for the conclusion that Mr Lehane is mentally ill, for his

continued detention or for the enforced administration of psychotropic drugs in a futile attempt to try to convince him that what is
in fact the truth is not the truth.

However, as a judge you will no doubt be anxious to protect the
public interest, just as you will wish, in your capacity as the chairman of a mental health tribunal, to protect Mr Lehane from
further torture. I have thought a great deal about how to give
Your Lordship the necessary reassurance, while at the same time
giving effect to your finding, at last Friday's hearing, that Mr
Lehane should be given a proper psychiatric evaluation before
the case calls again in court.

I have, therefore, discussed the position with Mr Lehane, who
has so far declined – in my view understandably – to give any
assistance whatever to his torturers, who appear to me (for
reasons set out in our report) to have acted not merely with gross
negligence but with demonstrable bias and unpardonable cruelty.

Mr Lehane is now prepared to undergo a thorough psychiatric
evaluation, and to cooperate fully in that evaluation, subject to
the following conditions, all of which seem to me to be both
reasonable and, in the circumstances, necessary. First, Mr Lehane
cannot be expected to cooperate while he is ill and in constant
pain and distress as a direct result of the grossly inappropriate
regime of enforced psychotropic medication to which he is being
subjected. Therefore, I hope that Your Lordship will *immediately*
order that this misconceived, scandalous, objectionable and inappropriate mistreatment cease forthwith.

Then, after a suitable period of recuperation, we recommend
that Mr Lehane should be interviewed by an independent psychiatrist unknown either to Mr Lehane or to any of the four
who have 'assessed' him hitherto; and the psychiatrist should be
appointed by the governing body of his profession to guarantee
his objectivity, independence and standing. Before the interview,
the psychiatrist should be given a copy, not only of the four
'assessments', but also of our report, so that he can understand
why this unusual challenge to the competence of his fellow psychiatrists is thought necessary and so that he can grasp quickly
the facts underlying the case. At the interview, I propose to be
present to reassure Mr Lehane that the procedure is fair; as you
will see from our report, he has very good reason to be deeply

suspicious as matters now stand. Since I knew Mr Lehane before the events complained of, it may be that I can be of some assistance to the appointed psychiatrist – one of the four psychiatrists has commented that a perspective from someone who knew Mr Lehane long ago would be helpful.

Mr Lehane has agreed to cooperate provided that the above conditions are sensibly and fairly met. They are not unduly onerous and, in the circumstances, they do make sense. In this manner, I believe that the best effect can be given to Your Lordship's direction at last Friday's hearing that before the case calls again in court a proper evaluation of Mr Lehane should be carried out.

I trust that Your Lordship, on reading our report, will be sufficiently sympathetic to the interests of justice to ensure that its recommendations be carried out *without further delay*. From my telephone conversations with Mr Lehane, I believe that the torture (my word, not his) which is being inflicted upon him is doing him real harm and I cannot stress strongly enough the importance of bringing the torture to an end *at once*.

I must, of course, make it plain that I am not accusing the court of ordering or condoning torture. Until our report came into Your Lordship's hands, you had no means of knowing that the scientific basis upon which the psychotropic mistreatment is being administered is woefully unsound, and it may be that the drastic side-effects of the drugs had not hitherto been brought to your attention.

It is fair to point out that I am writing to you on my own initiative and at my own suggestion. I have discussed this proposed intervention with Mr Lehane and have copied this letter and the report, both to him and to James Nichol, his solicitor. I am acting in this way solely because I believe that Mr Lehane will come to permanent harm unless the psychotropic treatment is immediately stopped and you are the only person with the power to act immediately.

I imagine that you will be reluctant to reply to this letter. However, I shall be keeping in touch with Mr Lehane and I shall hope to hear from him within the week that you have intervened, failing which I shall have to take the matter up in Parliament.

The court acknowledged Christopher's letter, but Judge Fingret did not act immediately upon receipt of his report, despite the clear and compelling evidence with which he had been provided that I was currently the victim of cruel and inhumane treatment, and that my condition was deteriorating so rapidly that he was in real fear for my life. Consequently, there was no independent psychiatric assessment. Instead the torture continued. A couple of weeks later, at the next monthly review of my case, Judge Fingret mentioned that he had received Christopher's report but nevertheless committed me straight back into the hands of my torturers in Bexley.

Christopher was furious. He wrote to Judge Fingret again, this time very bluntly, saying that now that the judge knew from the report that I was indeed being tortured he was himself guilty of torture because he had sent me back to my torturers without even going so far as to order the independent psychiatric assessment which Christopher had asked for. Christopher wrote that unless the judge released me into his custody within fourteen days he would personally write to the Attorney-General requesting that the judge be removed from the Bench, disbarred, and prosecuted for torture under the Criminal Justice Acts.

Christopher, unlike the various lawyers who had been paid to help me and had simply not bothered, never spent an instant worrying about whether coming to the aid of a convicted criminal lunatic might prove to be a bad career move for him, or might look bad on his MI5 file. And he had calculated Judge Fingret to a nicety. He had surrounded him in what he calls 'a cage of paper'. Once the Judge had acknowledged receipt of Christopher's report but had failed to act immediately upon it, despite the extreme urgency of the threat to my life and well-being, Christopher was able to slam the ball into the back of the net by giving the judge two choices: release me into Christopher's custody, or lose his job and his fat judicial pension, with the possibility of himself being put on trial on a charge of torture. Seen in those terms – the terms that Christopher had defined with his 'cage of paper' – Judge Fingret's decision that he had better set me free was, as Christopher had intended, a no-brainer.

Afterwards, Christopher explained to me how his strategy had worked. 'First,' he said, 'the judge needed compelling reassurance from an independent source that you had been telling the truth throughout and had suffered monstrously for it. Next, he needed clear medical evidence that the drug being administered to you in that "clinic" was having adverse effects on you. Finally, he needed to understand that this was a matter of life and death that required an immediate reversal of his previous decision.'

Christopher continued: 'The third of these points – the need for speed – is always the hardest to get across to the British judiciary: if they have a word for *mañana*, it doesn't convey quite the same sense of urgency. So I administered a very direct, and rather dangerous, kick in the pants. There was a risk – which I calculated to be small – that the judge would have me arrested and banged up for contempt of court when I threatened to report him to the Attorney-General for torture. Any lawyer would have been struck off for doing that. However, that was where my 24-page report came in. Most judges, if push comes to shove, can be trusted to remember that, in the late Lord Denning's words, they took the oath not to do law but to do justice. Before I wrote to the judge, I spoke to one or two people who knew him, and my impression was that – albeit with a fire-cracker up his fundament – he would read my report, realise it was true and then do justice, and do it in time to save your life. Give the old bird some credit: he done the right thing and sprung you out.'

On the thirteenth day, 21 May 1998, just 24 hours before Christopher's ultimatum to the judge was due to expire, the judge ordered my release. Christopher and Juliet Monckton came to Southwark Crown Court and waited patiently while the creaking bureaucratic paper-shuffling necessary to let me out was completed by various officials of the court, the police and the torture-chamber at Bexley. All of them were goggle-eyed. They had been caught by surprise. None of them had expected that I should ever be re-leased, still less that the agent of my release would be a sober-suited aristocrat in a bowler hat. The psychiatrists had hoped to get away with pretending that I was permanently, incurably mad and should not be let out. So there were a number of sour, nervous and, above all, startled faces in the shabby corridors of the court that morning.

Upon my release Christopher and Juliet flew me up to their country house in Aberdeenshire, where I stayed for several months while recovering from the torture. At the end of May, Christopher's doctor, perhaps the most distinguished and well-qualified GP in Britain, Dr David H. A. O'Connell, MB BCh BAO DRCOG MICGP FRSH FRIPHH, flew up to join us. Dr O'Connell has had experience in psychiatry. Over a period of four days, in the relaxed atmosphere of Crimonmogate, the independent psychiatric evaluation that I had agreed to in March and which Christopher Monckton had offered to Judge Fingret took place under the auspices of Dr O'Connell, who had the opportunity to observe me at close hand in a variety of activities. His final report on me is interesting:

I had the opportunity of observing and talking to Mr Lehane informally on 29, 30 and 31 May 1998, and carried out a formal examination on the morning of Monday, 1 June 1998.

During the first three days, I had the opportunity of discussing many and varied topics with Mr Lehane. In particular, he was able to give a logical and coherent account of his past personal history, including the events that had led up to the present situation. I was able to satisfy myself that his account of matters in no way differed from the account given me by Mr Monckton, which, in turn, relied upon third-party corroboration.

Throughout the days of my observation, Mr Lehane was dressed appropriately, and was clean and tidy in his personal appearance. I understand that when he emerged from the secure unit he had only the clothes he stood up in and that the Honourable Mrs Monckton had taken him shopping and supplied him with the appropriate apparel. His facial expression was appropriate throughout, with the exception of some slightly dystonic movements of his face, which lessened over the days. He exhibited a certain amount of restlessness of the legs when initially seen. This equally regressed over time.

[As to his mood] Mr Lehane struck me as having a normal affect. He found jokes and funny situations amusing but equally well, he was saddened by the manner in which he had been treated over the previous years. He did not appear anxious, tense or agitated.

He spoke in a uniform and regular manner and his speech was neither slowed down nor speeded up. There was no obvious pressure of thoughts or ideas.

His speech was spontaneous, reasoned and logical. There was

no evidence of thought disorder. He did not perseverate with particular ideas or phrases. His speech content was normal. In particular, there were no obsessional ruminations, no ideas of reference, nor ideas of influence. There was no evidence of thought insertion or thought withdrawal, nor were there any abnormal perceptions or hallucinations.

His cognition was normal; he appeared fully orientated in time, date and place. He was able to join in a number of social activities, including a large dance, and his interaction with strangers was throughout the time of my observation entirely normal.

Dr O'Connell's conclusion as to my mental health was clear and emphatic: 'I could find no psychiatric abnormality in Mr Lehane whatsoever.'

I have not the slightest doubt that had Judge Fingret agreed to the reasonable request for an independent psychiatric examination of me by a psychiatrist appointed by the appropriate professional body that doctor would have come to the same conclusion as Dr O'Connell in his report of June 1998. Had Judge Fingret so acted, I should have been spared the two additional months of cruel torture and inhumane treatment at the hands of what Christopher terms the gruesome 'psychiatrists' and the warders at Bexley secure unit and I should not have suffered so much.

In addition, informally, Dr O'Connell told Christopher and me that, in his view, the Mental Health Act did not allow forcible injections of any drugs let alone psychotropic ones. He also said there were no grounds whatsoever for any competent doctor to have found me to be suffering any psychiatric condition and told us that there were grounds for major legal actions against numerous of those involved in labelling me insane when I was not only not insane but demonstrating no symptoms that any properly qualified psychiatrist could have legitimately misunderstood as indicating a psychiatric condition. In short, Dr O'Connell's opinion on my mental heath is in layman's terms what Christopher told *The Examiner*, an Irish daily newspaper, in August 1998: 'Denis's mental health is perfect.'

I was in a physical mess when I was released. I spent the next two months in Scotland as a guest of Juliet and Christopher at their country house. I once lost one of their dogs when out for a walk in the grounds. I was mortified. Thank God, he turned up a few miles away on a farm. I should be remiss were I not to note here one side-effect of the horrible psychotropic drugs I had endured. One loses one's sense of taste. The first couple of weeks I spent at the Moncktons I sat on a sofa in front of a roaring fire in the library. At all times I was aware that a few yards behind me on the dining-room table was a vast array of the finest single malt Scotch whiskies that one could possibly want. Nothing would have complemented my days there before the fire better than the odd wee dram but I did not partake. I should not have been able to appreciate what I was drinking.

The Moncktons even took me with them on holiday to the Highlands of Scotland. I don't have the words to express my debt to them for their great kindness. For somebody whose trade is words it is an admission of incredible ineptitude. Christopher is fearless, kind, generous, honest and honourable. Without him, today I should undoubtedly be dead.

I had thought I had coped with my year's incarceration. I was wrong. I had gone into jail a fit and healthy middle-aged man. I left Bexley a sick man. In the summer of 2003, I welcomed Christopher and Juliet Monckton to Dublin. We did the Bloomsday Weekend together. During that weekend I had the pleasure of paying Christopher in full the only fee he has ever admitted incurring – a pint of Guinness in Dublin's famous Davy Byrne's Moral Bar, a haunt of Leopold Bloom in Joyce's *Ulysses*.

Great is Truth, and mighty above all things!

> The relationship between a journalist and a politician should be that of a dog urinating against a tree.
>
> H. L. MENCKEN,
> American editor and writer (1880–1956)

So, what can I say to wrap this all up? Well, I have always been a deeply private person. My privacy has been a casualty of the past two decades. This book itself is a profound intrusion on my privacy. I have accepted this as the price I pay for writing it, because what happened to me must not be allowed to happen to anyone else. If this book leads to reforms of the criminal 'justice' and psychiatric 'care' systems in Britain, Ireland and the US, the agony of writing it will not have been in vain.

I have omitted much concerning my family and former friends. Many abandoned me because they could not cope except by doing so. I had to cope. The abandonment hurt, and still hurts. Family and friends are for life, not just for Christmas, and not just for the good times.

I should also state that I have been let down, too, by the good and great, by official government and political persons and institutions who or which, in theory, should have helped me but, in practice, passed by on the other side.

Ditto the numerous costly quangos which exist, because it is notorious that government departments and politicians treat people in need the way I was treated when I made appropriate applications to them. Their worth is founded on their service as a safety-net to save people like me. No safety-net, no point.

I wrote to the Irish Ambassador at the Court of St James to say I had been convicted on trumped-up charges at a political show-trial that I had not attended because I had been denied lawyers to present my defence and was going to be sent to an asylum for the criminally insane where I should be tortured.

I received a reply from a junior official at the Irish Embassy enclosing a list of Legal Aid solicitors and offering no other help whatsoever. Perhaps only a lifelong nationalist like me can be permitted to say that if Ireland wants to make herself out to be an independent state then she must learn to stand up for her citizens' rights, otherwise she is nothing.

When I wrote from Wandsworth Prison in September 1997 to Pierre Sané, the Director of Amnesty International, at Amnesty's world headquarters in London, I received no response. Amnesty International had only recently won the Nobel Peace Prize for its work. My case fitted squarely into its remit. In the year 2000 my wonderful GP in Dublin, Dr Eithne Flood, was sent a circular from an organisation called Spirazi which looked after foreign asylum seekers in Ireland. Dublin GPs were invited to refer patients who had experienced torture to a newly created Survivors of Torture programme. I had previously written to the Irish Council for Civil Liberties (ICCL), which, like Amnesty, had ignored me. Dr Flood referred me to Spirazi and I met the programme director, Richard Tompkins, a young Englishman. He listened to all I had to tell him and replied, 'There is nothing you have told me that I have not heard before.' Of all the survivors of torture that Spirazi had dealt with, I was the only one with any evidence of what had been done to me.

My only reason for hope since my release has been the assistance of a handful of people who believe in truth and right. Conspicuous among these are Phillip Knightley and Brian Glanville, men with enormous reputations in the field of journalism on this side of the Atlantic who were colleagues at the old *Sunday Times*. These two gentlemen have between them won numerous British Press Awards. In addition, Phillip Knightley is a noted authority and writer on spy agencies who has twice been named Journalist of the Year in Britain, one of only two journalists to score the double whammy.

I recognise that, for the vast majority of the 300 million people of the United States, the CIA is sacrosanct and can do no wrong.

Its agents are American heroes. Everything they do is right. One needs only to watch the immensely popular TV series *24* to know this. Lies, control of the press and torture of prisoners are routine in the security services of the US. The American people approve. Their government has repudiated the Geneva Convention on the treatment of prisoners of war, international treaties on human rights and habeas corpus, regularly flies captured combatants to other countries for interrogation and has set up a concentration camp in Cuba for the detention without trial of alleged terrorists. In defiance of the US Constitution and its Bill of Rights, the US government has planned to court-martial the suspects according to 'judicial' procedures repudiated by the rest of the civilised world and then to execute them with no right of appeal to any properly-constituted court, least of all the Supreme Court.

US military lawyers assigned to defend these men abhor and reject this process and everything that has led up to it. In so doing these lawyers deliberately choose to destroy their military careers by holding to an American ideal of justice which their government and the vast majority of its people have long ago abandoned. The mass of the American people approve of all of this. The reputation of their country abroad has never been lower. Americans don't care. Historically they tend to despise and ignore the opinion of the rest of the world, believing themselves to be possessed of a God-given right to pursue a distinct and ruthless policy of pro-pagating what they genuinely believe is Democracy and Freedom.

In this context, the idea of an American publisher choosing to publish this book would appear preposterous. Nevertheless, I hope it will be published in the US as well as in the rest of the world. The American people, above all, must be given access to the truth of what the CIA does in their name.

I have been greatly encouraged by the recent publication in the USA of *Legacy of Ashes: The History of the CIA* by Tim Weiner. Just one quote from a review in London's *Daily Telegraph*:

The record of the CIA as Tim Weiner explains in this racy history is truly dreadful. Its annals, Weiner writes, are full of failure, folly and misfortune, the Agency having squandered billions of dollars and thousands of lives and bequeathed a 'legacy of ashes' – literally so in Manhattan after its wretched failure to track down

Osama bin Laden. This breezy, anecdotal book tells the story of an agency run by bickering bureaucrats, wallowing in cash, banging and crashing its way around the world at immense human cost. It is both an entertaining read and a deeply distressing one. . . . The only sensible solution now is to put the Agency out of its misery and start over.

Phillip Knightley, Brian Glanville and Christopher Monckton each read the draft of *Unperson* and kindly recommended that it should be published. Brian Glanville has written to me recently, 'This shocking, moving and important memoir should be published, and as soon as possible.'

Phillip Knightley has promised to write a Foreword for the book and will waive any payment for this. Lord Monckton, at the request of Naim Attallah, my brave publisher, edited the manuscript in record time and without even levying so much as another pint of Guinness by way of a fee.

Others who have helped this book towards publication include Neil Middleton, who published as Penguin Specials *Thalidomide and the Power of the Drug Companies*, which led to major award-winning investigations at the pre-Murdoch *Sunday Times*, the *Insight* team's acclaimed *Ulster* book, and my own book, *Political Murder in Northern Ireland*; Lord William Rees-Mogg, the former editor of the pre-Murdoch *Times* and, like Christopher Monckton, a pillar of the British Establishment; and John Pilger, another distinguished British-based journalist who has won numerous British Press Awards and is the second reporter to have won the prestigious Journalist of the Year Award. Lord Monckton drew up the synopsis of the book to tempt publishers.

Phillip Knightley has written an article, *The CIA's Destruction of a Journalist*, which has yet to be published. While I cooperated in its production, I have not read it because it would have been too painful. However, I have total confidence in him. The late Hugo Young, a colleague at the old *Sunday Times*, who was the head man at London's left-liberal *Guardian* and *Observer* newspapers, turned the article down when Phillip Knightley approached him personally on the ground that to publish the article would put the lives of all Harkness Fellows in danger because it would lead people to suspect that they might be CIA assets recruited while studying in the USA on their Fellowships. Hugo Young was himself a Harkness Fellow.

The logic of his reasoning is that the CIA should be allowed to get away with all the wrongdoing because to expose that wrongdoing would be to endanger those who might have been targeted as assets. It clearly made sense to him, but can it be defended as good journalism? Where, in Hugo Young's moral universe, was there a place for the freedom of the press and a journalist's duty to report the truth without fear or favour at all times in all circumstances? As Housman's Greek chorus used to maunder, 'I only ask because I want to know.'

I am now aged 59 and my life is in something of a mess. I am disabled by heart disease and due to my spinal injury I am virtually paralysed, housebound and in great and constant pain throughout my body.

At first I was told that I needed major and complicated surgery if the injury was to be corrected. The surgery would involve cutting through the chest and splitting the sternum as though for open-heart surgery, so as to get at the thoracic vertebra – T8 – which was compressing the spinal nerve. It was a risky procedure, but there was no alternative if I was to regain my mobility.

My health progressively collapsed during 2008. I had an 'urgent' appointment at the start of July with a young neurosurgeon at the Department of Neurosurgery at the Beaumont Hospital, Dublin. He told me that he had reviewed the MRI scans and that the spinal surgery would not cure my condition, which is far more extensive than the damage to the thoracic spine. He said the hospital could do nothing more for me and referred me to the Pain-Management Centre at Tallaght Hospital, at the last stop on the tramline some 15–20 miles away. At the time of writing, I have an initial assessment there in just over a week's time. The centre is one of only two in the country for the treatment of chronic pain. For me it is the Last Chance Saloon.

My injuries now restrict me to my apartment except for one brief, painful trip to the corner shop each morning, which requires three rests to travel about 100 yards. I am in searing pain as I put on my socks, trousers and shoes and when I tie my shoelaces. I have nobody to go on walks with and, even if I did, I would not ask them. I have nothing to offer other people.

Now it is difficult for me to read. I spend most of my daylight hours lying in bed listening to the wireless. The young consultant neurosurgeon at Beaumont has told me that the initial injury to the spine which occurred during one of the Bexley beatings in February 1998 and went untreated has progressively triggered reactions from pain receptors throughout the body, so that now these receptors are firing off as though there are injuries all over the place.

I have started saying five decades of the rosary in the morning when I wake up. Not every morning, though that is the plan. I got the idea after meeting the young consultant at Beaumont in July. He told me that some of the patients treated at pain-management centres by the use of psychology had experienced significant reduction in pain, which was reflected in changes in the structure of the brain shown on MRI scans, even though the doctors cannot explain it or guarantee that every patient will benefit.

The young doctor was trying to give me some hope when he went on to talk about the different perceptions of pain of different cultures. I remembered reading of a rather gruesome experiment which took place in Italy towards the end of the last century. A university department of neurology did a deal with an enclosed order of very traditional nuns. It involved regular brain scans of all the sisters and, when they died, they did autopsies on their brains. Quite how they persuaded the nuns to agree I cannot imagine. The results over many decades were astonishing. The nuns tended to live to great and active old age and to die of natural causes. However, their brains defied traditional medical knowledge. The neurologists found that, according to the rules, the nuns' brains could not have functioned as well as they had clearly done. Either the nuns would have been dead long before they died or they would have been severely physically disabled. The conclusions were that the brain is a more complex organ than we know and that the daily discipline of prayer and religious observance had probably played a key role in keeping them mentally fit long into old age.

So, when the doctor started talking to me about different strategies of dealing with pain and the role of lifestyle, the idea of saying the rosary occurred to me. I like doing it. I am afraid I don't contemplate the various mysteries which one is supposed to when reciting the rosary, such as the resurrection, crucifixion and all the traditional Marist devotions. Rather I just think about how to organise my day and the things which are on my mind. It is really a form of meditation, just like Buddhist chanting, I guess. It helps me get by and is part of the mechanism I have constructed to making living possible.

Publication of *Unperson* will not bring back my lost years. They are gone. Never mind. What I hope is that the book will be seen as my attempt to fulfil my duty as a journalist to report the truth of what has happened. I believe that it is a journalist's duty to report the truth without fear or favour at all times in all circumstances. A journalist must never, ever work for a spy agency under the cover of his writing.

William Corson told me in 1987 that I was the only journalist who had ever refused recruitment. My refusals had apparently caused astonishment. Yet I am proud to be a journalist. Harry Evans was proud that I had been one of his journalists at the *Sunday Times* when he wrote of me, 'Denis Lehane is a reporter. He exemplifies all that this title should mean.' There could be worse epitaphs than that.

For bleak periods during the past decades I was convinced that we live in a Godless universe and that human life has no meaning at all. At other times, it seemed to me that the question was not, 'Is there a God?' but rather, 'Does God give a tinker's blinkers about me? Is He even aware that I exist?'

My friend, Father Moran OP, died suddenly in his sleep in his mid-eighties in August 2004. When he was alive, I used to visit him at the Dominican Priory in Dominick Street and he would give me tea and biscuits and we would talk. He told me that he enjoyed my visits. I certainly enjoyed them. When I was with him I felt very close to God indeed, and all my questions seemed irrelevant in the face of the truth and reality I found for an hour or so in the company of that holy priest. But when I am outside 'in the world', I do not feel close to God at all. I miss my holy friend very much.

Earlier this year I was talking to another elderly priest I know, whom I met in 2001 via the Spirazi Survivors of Torture programme that my GP, Dr Flood, had referred me to and which had helped me a good deal. The priest gave me a book to read: *Man's Search for Meaning* by Professor Viktor E. Frankl, a Viennese psychiatrist who was Professor of Neurology and Psychiatry at the University of Vienna Medical School. He had founded what is called 'the Third Viennese School of Psychiatry' after Freud and Adler.

Professor Frankl, who died in 1997, had survived various concentration camps, although his wife had died at the hands of the Nazis, and his book is both an autobiographical account of that concentration-camp experience and an explanation of how he was able to survive when so many others did not. I read *Man's Search for Meaning* in two sittings, the first immediately upon returning home from my visit to my friend and the rest the next morning. Professor Frankl writes:

Man's search for meaning is the primary motivation in his life and not 'a secondary rationalisation' of instinctual drives. This meaning is unique and specific in that it must and can be fulfilled by him alone; only then does it achieve a significance which will satisfy his own *will* to meaning. There are some authors who contend that meanings and values are 'nothing but defence mechanisms, reaction-formations and sublimations'. But as for myself, I should not be willing to live merely for the sake of my 'defence mechanisms', nor should I be ready to die merely for the sake of my 'reaction formations'. Man, however, is able to live and to die for the sake of his ideals and values! . . . Not every conflict is necessarily neurotic; some amount of conflict is normal and healthy. In a similar sense, suffering is not always a pathological phenomenon; rather than being a symptom of neurosis, suffering may well be a human achievement, especially if the suffering grows out of existential frustration. I should strictly deny that man's search for a meaning to his existence, or even his doubt of it, in every case is derived from, or results in, any disease. Existential frustration is in itself neither pathological nor pathogenic. A man's concern, even his despair, over the worthwhileness of life is an *existential distress* but by no means a *mental disease*.

On the meaning of suffering, Professor Frankl says:

We must never forget that we may also find meaning in life even when confronted with a hopeless situation, when facing a fate that cannot be changed. For what then matters is to bear witness to the uniquely human potential at its best, which is to transform a personal tragedy into a triumph, to turn one's predicament into a human achievement. When we are no longer able to change a situation – just think of an incurable disease such as inoperable cancer – we are challenged to change ourselves . . . There are situations in which one is cut off from the opportunity to do one's work or to enjoy one's life; but what can never be ruled out is the unavoidability of suffering. In accepting this challenge to suffer bravely, life has a meaning up to the last moment, and it retains this meaning literally to the end. In other words, life's meaning is an unconditional one, for it even includes the potential meaning of unavoidable suffering.

I wonder what those quotations mean to the reader of this book. Probably very little. To me they constitute an overwhelming light on my life and what I need to do to change it. It was as though the late Professor Frankl was addressing me personally when I read his book. These examples of what he said to me provide a plan of action which I have decided to follow. He makes sense of my predicament and offers me a way out of it. He prompted me to return to *Unperson* and make a further determined effort to find a publisher for it. It gives my life meaning. Professor Frankl has convinced me that my life can still have meaning if I can strive to publish my story.

When I began this book I had wanted to write a blow-by-blow account, leaving no question unanswered, no stone unturned, no-where where the bad men could say I had not addressed each and every issue. After six months, I had written more than a million words and the extent was well on schedule to be four or five million words, say Tolstoy's *War and Peace* and Tolkien's *Lord of the Rings* combined. I was happy with that. But no publisher realistically would have even considered such a series of volumes.

So I started afresh. It pained me to pass over years of my life in a few words. But I have done it because the book is important. Without it, the bad men would have won. I don't want the bad men to win – not if I can help it. This is because I believe in a free press in a free society. That is why I became a journalist rather than a lawyer or a politician.

My objective in writing this account of how I came to sleep rough and live in hostels for the homeless and eventually in a prison for the criminally insane has not been to change the views of society towards those human beings, such as myself and my fellow residents, who live in the underclass. That would be the subject of another book. My objective is focused on something else of equal importance: the consequences for society of its failure to care for those who fall through the cracks.

My account here of what has been done to me is a harrowing tale of personal tragedy and human suffering which will not end with publication. What has been done to me is a testimony to man's inhumanity to man. *Unperson* is an important account because it highlights vital ethical issues: not only journalism's unhealthy relationship with the world of secret Intelligence, but also the way justice can be denied to anyone who is brave enough to protest about wrongdoing in our society.

The furtive destruction of a journalist's life and career by the state for the 'crime' of declining to prostitute his profession by using it as a cover for espionage is everybody's business in a free society. The West is supposed to be a free society. All Western states are supposed to be democracies. The people are supposed to be sovereign. Governments are supposed to work for the people. The people are supposed to decide who shall and shall not govern them. The people are supposed to be able to remove bad governments. Western states are supposed to be governed by the rule of law. Judges are supposed to see to it that the rule of law is upheld. Nobody is supposed to be above the law. The rule of law is supposed to apply to spy agencies such as the CIA every bit as much as it does to me. In reality, as the events that I have described have demonstrated, much reform will be needed if the West's once-justifiable self-esteem is to regain any real credibility.

Often, all that is left to defend the liberty and the lawful rights of ordinary people is the journalist. He tends to be despised and distrusted by all, but just try thinking of a world without him. Ask somebody from the recently freed Soviet empire what it was like to live in a state where there was no free press and bad men controlled the newspapers. From the collapse of Communism in 1991 in Russia they had corrupt, democratically elected politicians and venal lawyers driving top-of-the-range Mercedes, many in the pocket of the new post-Communist mafia. But, for a time, they also had a free press. It didn't make the Russian mafia go away or the politicians and lawyers less corrupt or venal. But what Russia's new free press did do was report the truth.

Then an ex-KGB boss, President Vladimir Putin, decided to crush Russia's new free press. One by one, independent-minded newspapers and television stations were closed or bought out by the state until there were none left. In parallel with this, Putin deconstructed democracy. Political opponents were locked up in jail, the governors of the various component parts of the federal state, who had been democratically elected from 1991 on, became by a law passed by a puppet central parliament answerable to Putin, who now appoints them himself.

Opinion polls show that Putin is hugely popular in Russia. He has recently stepped down as President to be replaced by a long-time acolyte and become Prime Minister. He has relinquished office but not power. He is likely to run Russia as completely from his new post as he did for eight years in his old one. It has all gone smoothly. Unlike the suffering Iraqi people, who demonstrably want democracy as well as political order, the Russian people do not want democracy. They prefer a traditional Tsar as leader.

Just about the only people fighting for democracy in Russia today are the dwindling band of journalists committed to a free press and to publishing the truth. One such was Anna Politskov-skaya. In 2006 she was shot dead outside her home. The culprit has never been found. She was a fierce critic of Putin and all his doings. She was neither the first nor the last prominent journalistic critic of the regime to be assassinated. Assassination has become a regular tool of politics and business in the new Russia.

Ms Politskovskaya was one of the last journalists who adhered to the principle of telling the truth at all times in all circumstances. And she is dead because of it. Whether Putin himself ordered her death we don't know and are never likely to know. What we do know is that the policy he has been progressively imposing in the eight years of his presidency has led to the end of Russia's free press and created a climate where journalists who seek to tell the truth can be shot dead.

For all its faults, the Western press has over many decades built up a justifiable reputation as free and reliable. It is because of this that when a journalist in the West chooses to prostitute his honourable profession and sell out to a spy agency the crime that journalist commits is a terrible one. He betrays the fundamental principle of his profession: that truth comes first.

One of my predecessors on the Master of Science in Foreign Service course at Georgetown University's School of Foreign Service in the era of the Shah in the 1970s was an Iranian student called Sadeq Gotsadeq. He was recruited as an agent by the CIA and sent to Paris, where, under explicit CIA orders, he infiltrated the circle around the exiled opposition leader to the Shah, the Shiite religious leader, the Ayatollah Ruhollah Khomeini.

Gotsadeq did well. He became the Ayatollah's personal secretary. At the fall of the Shah in 1979, Gotsadeq became the Foreign Minister of Iran's first revolutionary government. A fluent English-speaker, he became an articulate, high-profile spokesman for the new regime, appearing daily on CNN, parroting the regime's line that the USA is 'the Great Satan' and glibly (and cynically) justifying the daily execution by firing squad of senior figures in the old regime as the just retribution for traitors whoring for 'the Great Satan'.

When more than 50 US nationals were taken hostage and held in degrading conditions in the US Embassy in Teheran by radical Iranian students, backed to the hilt by the new regime, which did nothing to free the hostages or dislodge the students, Gotsadeq, with his suave good looks, expensive, hand-made Paris suits and daily anti-American invective, quickly became the most hated man in America. Except to his real bosses at CIA headquarters at Langley, Virginia.

However, at some point the new regime learned who Gotsadeq was really working for. In 1980, he was arrested and was tortured and interrogated. Before he met his inevitable end, up against the wall, Gotsadeq was obliged to submit to what must have been a humiliating, live, public confession on Iranian television. He said the CIA had recruited him in the time of the fallen Shah at Georgetown University's School of Foreign Service, while he was a postgraduate foreign student on the Master of Science in Foreign Service course. He was executed by firing-squad, just as thousands of the deposed Shah's followers had been executed previously. As Revolutionary Iran's Foreign Minister, he had glibly and cynically justified those killings on CNN only a few months earlier.

I tell the story because, in 1983, I heard the CIA officer Allan E. Goodman tell jokes about Gotsadeq and his fate. Perhaps he tells similar jokes about me. Perhaps he shouldn't.

Every time the state resorts to an argument like the one that was used to justify what was done to me, it is wrong. Any and every time a journalist, whatever the threats, blackmail or inducements, chooses to work for a spy agency under the cover of his career as a journalist, that journalist is wrong, too, and his is the greater crime.

If mine has been the 'unpitied sacrifice' of an 'unperson', it has been a willing sacrifice. It will be for you, my kind readers, to do whatever is in your power to make my sacrifice worthwhile by making sure that never again are the uncaring, unsupervised institutions of today's police state allowed to do to any of you what they did – for so long – to me.

Today, at the end of this book, I say of the duty of a journalist to defend and protect the existence of a free press in a free society, proudly and defiantly, what Chateaubriand said in his essay *On Liberty* – 'If I were the last to defend it, I should never cease to proclaim its rights.'